Confessions of a

Kitchen Diva

by
claudine
destino

Author Claudine Destino

P. O. Box 769122
Roswell, GA 30076

KitchenDiva2003@yahoo.com

Copyright © 2003

By Happicook, Inc.

ISBN: 0-9728462-0-4

1st printing   October 2003   5,000 copies

WIMMER
COOKBOOKS

ConsolidatedGraphics

1-800-548-2537

Acknowledgements

A big fat thank you goes to my friends and family who supported me throughout this whole process: writing a book is like giving birth without drugs!

—To my friends Cindy Martin, Tonya Dale, Patricia Fabian, Tina Harwood and Kim Anderson who cajoled me, appeased me, and gave me the confidence to pursue my dream (as well as typed, edited, proofread and opined on the artwork).

—To all my family and friends who have shared recipes, techniques and tips with me over the years. All my knowledge and love of cooking came from you. You teach me something new every day.

—To my mother, Hazel Stowe, and my mother-in-law, Rose Destino, who taught me by example that I can be the best of both worlds: thoroughly modern yet deeply old fashioned and who proved that the best food is simply served up from the heart and to my Father-in-law, Carm Destino, the only Father I've ever known who has always treated me like a daughter.

—To Tiffany Steffes whose awesome writing talents beautifully summed up the contents of the book on the back cover and to Suzanne Cavin whose brilliant photography somehow made me look younger. (Back photograph is taken in Doug and Suzanne's kitchen).

—To my design group at Infinitee, Inc.: Barbara McGraw, David Kelker, and Brian Shively who captured the essence of my ideas with the amazing cover design. (Visit their website at Infinitee.com)

—And finally to my loving husband, Jim, and my children Alex, Chris and Lindsey, thank you for your unending support, love and understanding even when I make you crazy! I love you guys!

Introduction

I confess: I love to cook. I love to spend time in my kitchen with family and friends. My kitchen is my playroom filled with "toys".

My first recollection of cooking is playing with my tea set in the sandbox, "cooking" up some concoction of grass, sand and water. I remember standing in a chair at the stove in my mother's kitchen stirring scrambled eggs when I was 5 years old. A few years passed and my dad tragically died, leaving my Mom to raise four kids. I became the family cook while my mom worked. Upon entering college, I entertained my dorm mates at the University of Georgia with the likes of barbecue chicken and mashed potatoes. And then I impressed my husband-to-be (30 years together and still counting) by tackling a recipe for Shrimp Creole when we were dating. The fact is, I cannot remember a time in my life not associated with cooking. My family has always appreciated my endeavors that provided comfort, nourishment and memories from the kitchen. By learning from my mistakes, I developed enough confidence in the kitchen to join the ranks of Kitchen Diva.

Also, I have been collecting and recording family recipes over the years to preserve the family legacy that has been shared with me. This book is my gift to my two sons, Alex and Chris, and my daughter, Lindsey, with hopes that they too will continue to enjoy cooking.

"Confessions of a Kitchen Diva" is filled with original recipes, tips, and a splash of humor. As you read through, I ask you to adhere to my southern credo: "take my recipes, take out what you don't like, add what you do like and call it your own." None of the recipes listed here are difficult as each recipe is explained in detail. I also share my entertaining and "tablescaping" ideas, as well as party planning and organizational tips.

Follow my simple recipes and tips, learn from any mistakes and you too will gain enough confidence to create your own signature dishes and become a Kitchen Diva.

As you wander through this book, you will be taking a trip into my kitchen. Welcome! Sit down, relax, and have a bite.

Claudine
KitchenDiva2003@yahoo.com

Table of Contents

Once upon a time I planned to be

An artist of celebrity.

A song I thought to write one day,

And all the world would homage pay.

I longed to write a noted book,

But what I did was—learn to cook.

For life with simple tasks is filled,

And I have done, not what I willed,

Yet when I see boys' hungry eyes

I'm glad I make good apple pies!

Reprinted from

Apples of Gold

with permission from

C.R. Gibson, Inc.

Diva's Tips

- **Anchovy paste** is found in a tube next to the anchovies in a can in specialty shops and grocery stores.

- One of the best gadgets in my kitchen is an **apple corer/slicer**. In one swift action it removes the core and cuts the apple into 8 equal slices. It is great for reducing the time for making pies, desserts or apple salads or makes a quick snack for the kids.

- **Asparagus** is plentiful during its peak season February through June. Choose fresh, firm stalks, ½-inch in diameter with tightly closed caps. To remove tough ends, bend each spear until it snaps. For thicker stalks, peel the outer layer to the tender middle. To store: put ½-inch water in a tall, narrow jar or glass. Cut off ½-inch from the butt end of the asparagus and place in the jar. Make a tent with plastic wrap or plastic bag and refrigerate. Will keep fresh up to 1 week if the water is changed daily.

- Buy **avocados** that are firm but yield to gentle pressure. If avocados are bright green, store on the countertop until they turn a brownish/black color. When ripe, store in the refrigerator up to 1 week. To peel, cut through the skin down to the pit from top to bottom. Twist the halves apart and remove pit by tapping it sharply with the blade of the knife. Twist the knife to release pit. Cut the flesh into a dice or slices while still in the skin with the tip of a knife. Scoop out the flesh with a spoon and gently separate with your fingers. The flesh of avocados can be stored in the freezer by mashing with 2 tablespoons lemon juice.

- For easy removal of **bacon** slices, roll the whole package into a cylinder beginning with the short end; unroll and pieces will "peel" off each other better. If you only use bacon occasionally, separate into individual slices, wrap each piece in plastic wrap, and place wrapped pieces in a zip top freezer bag. Store in the freezer up to 3 months. When a recipe calls for a few slices of bacon, remove only as many as needed.

- To cook **bacon**: remove desired number of slices from package in one piece. Chop or cut all slices into small pieces with kitchen scissors or a knife. Fry over medium-high heat, separating pieces as they cook. Cook until crisp and golden brown.

- To prevent burns, it is safer to add boiling water to the second pan after the pans have been put in the oven. Pull out the oven rack slightly and place the pans on it. Pour the water into the second pan and the carefully slide the rack back into the oven and proceed with baking. Baking puddings or custards in a **bain-marie** (water bath) promotes even cooking.

- **Baking bags** can be found in the grocery aisle with aluminum foil and plastic wrap.

- **Baking powder** still active? To test, drop ½ teaspoon into a glass of warm water; if it fizzes it is o.k. to use. Always measure and level off the measuring spoon. Never put a wet spoon into the container; it will deactivate the whole can.

- To test **baking soda** for freshness, mix ¼ teaspoon baking soda into ¼ cup vinegar; if it bubbles like crazy, it is fresh. Never cook with baking soda after it has been used as a refrigerator freshener.

- **Balsamic vinegar** is a dark-aged Italian vinegar, fermented 10-15 years, and has a slightly sweet taste. Buy the best you can afford (the best is from Modena, Italy). Most balsamic vinegars sold in grocery stores are just caramel-colored vinegars.

- Cut around the stem of **bell peppers**, remove the seeds, and white membrane inside before slicing.

- **Boursin cheese** is a mixture of cream cheese and butter, flavored with herbs and garlic. Look for it in the specialty cheese section.

- Save all your dried, leftover bread-baguettes, sandwich bread, bagels, crackers, rolls, etc.-and put into the bowl of your food processor or blender and pulse until you have fine crumbs. Or rub dried bread on a grater, catching the crumbs in a bowl. Store crumbs in a zip top plastic bag in the freezer and use as your recipe directs. Homemade **breadcrumbs** tastes superior to store prepackaged.

- 2 slices of bread = 1 cup **fresh breadcrumbs**. Put bread in the bowl of an electric blender or food processor and pulse until finely grated.

- The perfect place for **bread to rise** is in a cold oven over a pan of hot water placed on the bottom rack.

- Fresh **broccoli** will have firm stalks with tightly bunched heads. The florets should be a blue-green color. If broccoli shows signs of the buds beginning to turn yellow, it is past its prime. Refrigerate broccoli in a plastic bag up to 4 days. If broccoli becomes limp, trim the bottom off the stem and stand in a container of cool water. Refrigerate overnight.

- To store **brown sugar**: place opened bag of sugar in another plastic bag. Remove as much air as possible and tightly close. If sugar has hardened, soften by placing in a microwave-safe dish, covering tightly and microwave on high power for about 30 seconds. Generally, light-brown or dark-brown sugar can be interchanged for each other. When measuring, always lightly pack sugar in measuring cup.

- No **buttermilk**? To make a good substitute, stir 1-tablespoon vinegar or lemon juice into enough milk to measure 1 cup and let sit 5 minutes.

- A ripe **cantaloupe** should have a sweet, melon aroma. Choose a melon with a soft stem end and raised netting with a yellow/tan undertone. Avoid shriveled, green or rock-hard melons.

- **Capers** can be found in the pickle aisle of your local grocery store.

- **Cheesecakes** need to cool slowly after baking to prevent cracking.

- **Chèvre cheese** is a deliciously tart cheese, ranging in textures from moist and creamy to dry and firm and can be found with the specialty cheeses. Wrap any leftover Chèvre in plastic and store in the refrigerator up to 2 weeks.

- To cook chicken for use in any recipe requiring cooked chicken: sprinkle lemon pepper (or season with salt and pepper) on chicken breasts (boneless or rib-in) and place inside a baking bag (smaller version of the kind used to bake turkeys at Thanksgiving) or tightly seal in aluminum foil. Put on a baking sheet in a 350° oven about 1 hour. Remove from oven and cool in the bag. Remove and chop chicken as recipe directs. Reserve any accumulated juices in the cooking bag by pouring into a container and storing in the refrigerator up to 2 days or 3 months in the freezer. These juices are "liquid gold". Use in any recipe that requires chicken broth or bouillon.

- Boneless, skinless **chicken** breasts should be even thickness to prevent some parts from drying out before the whole breast is cooked through. Pound breast between 2 sheets of plastic wrap until ½-inch even thickness.

- Remove the **white tendon in the chicken** tenders: grasp the end of the tendon with a paper towel. Pull the tendon towards you while holding the chicken with the edge of a knife.

- Remove **chicken or meat** from refrigerator 1 hour before cooking or grilling to allow it to come to room temperature so that it will cook more evenly.

- **Chicken or meat** slice easier and thinner when partially frozen. Slice chicken the length of the breast and all meat across the grain.

- **Chives** are a member of the onion family but have a much milder flavor. Snip fresh chives with kitchen scissors to desired length. Store rinsed and dried fresh chives in a plastic bag in the refrigerator up to 1 week.

- To melt **chocolate**: chop chocolate bars into small pieces. 1) Place uncovered in a microwave-safe dish and microwave on high power (100%); stir every 20 seconds. Chocolate can be removed from oven while still lumpy; the heat of the dish and the chocolate will continue to melt lumps. Be careful not to overheat; chocolate burns at a low temperature; Or 2) Put chocolate pieces into the top of a double boiler and place over hot water. Stir occasionally until chocolate is melted. (Do not let any water droplets or steam mix with chocolate or it will become a hardened, grainy mass. If this happens, stir in a small amount of melted vegetable shortening, 1 teaspoon at a time, until chocolate returns to a liquid state.

- To **grate or shave chocolate**: rub chocolate bar over a coarse grater or shave with a vegetable peeler.

- To make **chocolate dessert cups**: melt chocolate chips. Coat the bottom and 3-inches up the insides of a small paper cup with the melted chocolate. Cool until set. Repeat. Refrigerate until completely hardened. Carefully peel away the paper from the chocolate. Trim the top if edges are ragged.

- To **toast coconut**: place on a large cookie sheet. Bake at 350° until lightly toasted, about 12 minutes, stirring frequently.

- **Coconut milk and red curry paste** can be found in the Oriental section of most grocery stores.

- To make **cookie crumbs**: 1) Place cookies in a plastic bag (don't close all the way). Smash with a meat pounder or rolling pin, Or 2) place cookies in a food processor or blender and process until fine crumbs.

- **Heavy cream**, bowl and beaters should be very cold before whipping. If you over whip cream (it separates into solids and liquids), gently fold in a few tablespoons of milk or more cream. To stabilize whipped cream (to keep it in soft peaks longer), add 2 tablespoons nonfat dry milk or 1 teaspoon cornstarch to every cup of heavy cream before you whip it.

- Buy **cream sherry or dry sherry** in the wine section of the grocery store or specialty shop.

- To make **crème fraîche**, mix ¼ cup buttermilk into 1 cup cream in a jar or container. Lightly cover jar and set in a warm place for about 24-36 hours, until mixture is thickened. Cover and chill (it will thicken more as it gets cold like soft yogurt). Whipped crème fraîche will keep whipped in the refrigerator up to a week or several hours at room temperature. Or it can be located in some grocery stores in the dairy section.

- **Crème fraîche** substitute: mix 1 cup whipping cream with ½ cup sour cream. Whip until soft peaks form

- To make **croutons**: slice slightly stale, hearty French bread into slices. Brush slices with extra virgin olive oil or vegetable oil (for garlic croutons add 1 clove crushed garlic to the oil). Stack a few slices on top of each other and cut into cubes with a serrated knife. Put in a single layer on a baking sheet and bake in a 350° oven 10-15 minutes or until crunchy, stirring midway of the baking time.

- To make **cracker crumbs**: place crackers in a plastic bag and finely crush with a rolling pin, wine bottle, meat pounder or with hands. Or put crackers in the bowl of a food processor or blender and pulse until crackers are crushed.

- **Dale's steak seasoning** is a soy sauce based sauce and is found in most grocery stores next to other steak sauces.

- To **debone chicken breast**: slip a thin knife or fingers under the breastbones and pull away from the flesh. Slit the flesh around the larger bones with a knife and carefully lift out bone avoiding taking too much flesh with the bone.

- If you do not have a **double boiler,** you can easily make one by nestling a smaller saucepan in a larger one or use any heat-proof bowl that will sit securely on top of a saucepan without touching the boiling water. The heat of the steam, generated by the boiling water, cooks the food.

- Fresh **eggplant** has a smooth, glossy, dark purple skin. Buy eggplant that feels heavy, has a green stem, and unblemished skin. Store in the refrigerator up to 2 days.

- To cook **hard-boiled eggs**: place eggs in a boiler in a single layer and cover with cold water to come 1 inch above eggs. Bring to a boil, immediately cover, remove from heat and let sit for 15 minutes. Remove from hot water and immerse in cold water to cool fast. Tap eggs all around to crack the shell and peel under cold running water.

- **Eggs** separate easier when cold. Break egg into a funnel or into your fingers over first bowl. The white will easily slip into the bowl and the yolk will remain in the funnel or your fingers (as long as it is not broken). Transfer white to a separate bowl and yolk to a third bowl. This keeps an accidentally broken yolk from contaminating the whites already separated. Whites with even a small amount of yolk will not beat up to soft peaks. Repeat with remaining eggs over the first bowl. Freeze leftover egg whites individually in an ice cube tray. When frozen remove from tray and place in a plastic bag. Thaw whites in the refrigerator when a recipe calls for egg whites.

- Add a dash of salt to left over **egg yolks** and store in the freezer (1 month) or refrigerator (1 day). Use in custards or add to scrambled eggs.

- All ingredients for baking should be room temperature: to warm **eggs**, put unbroken eggs in their shells into hot tap water and let sit for a few minutes while assembling other ingredients. Dry the shells and proceed with recipe.

- Buy **fish** that is odor-free. Filets should lay flat and look moist. Fish is highly perishable and should be cooked the day of purchase. Store in a plastic bag surrounded by ice packs in the refrigerator to keep fish at its maximum freshness. Serve a 6-8 ounce filet or 8-ounce fish steak per person.

- Instead of sifting, stir **flour** with a spoon in the storage container until light and separated. Spoon into a graduated, dry-ingredient measuring cup (nesting cups) and level off with a knife or straight edge (never pack down).

- For the best results in baking cakes or pie crusts, I use **cake flour** or White Lily®, but you may use your favorite national brand.

- To make **self-rising flour**, add 1 teaspoon baking powder and ¼ teaspoon salt to every cup of flour; mixing thoroughly.

- To **fold** ingredients together: insert large rubber spatula in the center of the mix; drag it across the bottom and then up the sides, rotating spatula and bringing some of the bottom of the mix to the top. Keep repeating this movement while turning the bowl to mix from all sides.

- **Fontina** is a buttery-tasting Italian cheese (there are also American and Danish varieties), like a cross between a Swiss cheese and Brie.

- To crush **garlic**: peel off papery skin by whacking clove with the side of a knife; paper should slip right off. Place the clove between two sheets of plastic wrap and smash with a meat pounder or the bottom of a heavy pan until pulverized. Scrape garlic off plastic wrap and use in recipe as directed.

- Fresh **gingerroot**: 1 ounce = 3 tablespoons minced ginger; 1-inch x 1-inch piece = 1 tablespoon minced or grated. Store extra ginger peeled or unpeeled in the freezer in 1-inch slices. While still frozen, grate or cut into small cubes and push through a garlic press. Or cover fresh, peeled ginger with vodka and store in the refrigerator.

- **Gorgonzola cheese** is a semi-soft, bleu veined cheese with a distinctively sharp flavor yet creamy textured. Best substitute: English Stilton.

- Fresh **grapes** will cling to their stems if shaken gently. Grapes should be plump and firm and stems should be green and moist-looking. Grapes are covered by a thin layer of dust, dirt and pesticides. To clean: fill a large bowl with cold water and dissolve 1 teaspoon baking soda and 1 teaspoon Fruit Fresh (citric acid). Let grapes sit in this water for a few minutes and then swish around. Rinse thoroughly. Drain on paper towels and allow to air dry. Clean, dry grapes will keep fresh for several days stored in an airtight container in the coldest part of the refrigerator.

- To **grease and flour baking pans**: cover fingers with plastic wrap or a plastic sandwich bag and spread about ½ tablespoon butter or vegetable shortening over the inside baking surface of the pan. Spoon in 1 tablespoon flour, shaking pan to evenly distribute flour. Turn pan up side down and remove excess flour by tapping edge of pan on the counter.

- To substitute **dried herbs** for fresh: a good rule of thumb is to use one-third the amount of dried as fresh (1 teaspoon dried = 1 tablespoon fresh). Always crush dried herbs between your fingers before adding them to your recipe for optimum flavor.

- To **chop fresh herbs**: roll herbs into a tight bundle and finely chop crosswise with a sharp knife. Or snip with kitchen scissors. To prevent fresh basil and tarragon from darkening while cutting, sprinkle with a few drops of vegetable oil.

- To **store fresh herbs** (parsley or cilantro): wash herbs in plenty of cold water; drain on paper towels. Roll clean, damp herbs in dry paper towels and place in a tightly covered plastic container. Store 1-2 weeks in the coldest part of your refrigerator. Basil can be kept fresh for 3-4 days with the stems submerged in cool water in a container at room temperature. Refresh water every day.

- **Prepared horseradish** can be found in the dairy case of most grocery stores next to the kosher items. (Don't confuse with horseradish sauce next to the mayonnaise.) Or you can finely grate your own fresh, peeled horseradish root.

- To create an **ice block** for serving and keeping shrimp cold: fill a large, deep rectangular pan one-half full with water. Place on a level surface in the freezer and freeze completely (24 hours). Dampen the top of the block of ice, and decorate the edges with fresh herbs or anything edible. Fill with additional water to secure the decoration. When ready to serve, carefully remove ice block from pan. Place ice block on a larger serving tray or on a rack over a pan to catch the melting ice; arrange shrimp over the top of the ice.

- To squeeze the maximum amount of **juice** from fresh **citrus fruits** (lemons, limes and oranges): heat fruit in the microwave, 20 seconds for 1 fruit, 30 seconds for two and 50 seconds for three or more. (Or let fruit sit in very hot water for a few minutes. Dry fruit thoroughly before squeezing.) Rub fruit between your palms or roll on the counter with gentle pressure. Cut fruit in half. Stick a fork in the middle: rotate fork in one direction and fruit in the opposite direction, while gently squeezing. Catch juice in a bowl or measuring cup. Buy fruits that feel heavy for their size with firm, fresh rind. Citrus fruits will keep refrigerated 3-4 weeks.

- If **lid** does not fit snuggly on the pan, cover the pan tightly with aluminum foil and then place the lid over the foil.

- Small bottles (airline serving size—about 3 tablespoons) of **liqueurs** can be purchased at most liquor stores.

- **Lobster base** can be found next to the bouillon in some grocery or specialty stores.

- Ripe **mangoes** should be mostly red and yield to a gentle squeeze. To ripen: place in a paper bag at room temperature. Once ripe, store in a plastic bag in the refrigerator for several days.

- To slice **mangoes**: Without peeling, stand the mango on its end, with the stem end pointing up. With a sharp knife, cut straight down on one "flat" side, just grazing the pit. Repeat on the other "flat" side. Trim off the remaining flesh from the pit. Carefully score the cut side of the mango halves in a crisscross pattern through the flesh, just down to the peel. Bend the peel back, turning the halves inside out; cubes of fruit will pop out allowing them to be cut off the peel.

- **Marshmallows** will keep fresh longer if stored in a tightly sealed plastic bag in the freezer.

- **Marinate poultry**, meat, fish or vegetables in zip top plastic bags, squeezing out as much air as possible and sealing the bag. Place bag in a glass dish or bowl and refrigerate, turning bag several times for even marinating. Remove bag from the refrigerator 1 hour before cook time to bring meat to room temperature. Discard marinade.

- **Madeira** is a sweet, fortified white wine that leaves a rich taste after the alcohol has been cooked off. It blends deliciously with most meats without being too sweet.

- Allow **cooked meat**, no matter what cut or kind, to "rest" 10-15 minutes before slicing or carving to allow the juices to settle back into the meat and prevent them from "flooding" out when meat is cut.

- Tough cuts of meat (**chuck and shoulder roasts and brisket**) need to cook by braising - cooking in a small amount of liquid at a low temperature for a long time to tenderize.

- To keep **meringue** from shrinking and weeping, spread over hot filling bringing meringue all the way to the edges making sure it touches the crust all around.

- Fresh **mozzarella cheese** is a creamy white ball, sometimes called Buffalo mozzarella, and can be found stored in a brine mixture in some grocery stores or specialty shops.

- To keep **muffins** warm without getting soggy bottoms, tip each muffin on its side in the muffin cups.

- Choose **mushrooms** with the caps closed around the stems, with smooth tops and without blemishes. Exposed black gills are signs of old age. Never immerse mushrooms in water; they will absorb liquid like a sponge. The best way to clean mushrooms is to wipe with a damp paper towel. Store mushrooms in a paper bag in the refrigerator.

- Freshly grated **nutmeg** has a superior flavor over ground nutmeg found in a can or jar. Whole nutmegs can be located in most spice sections in your local grocery store. Use a very fine grater or a small nutmeg grater for best results. Whole nutmegs can be kept indefinitely in a jar in a cool, dark place.

- **Toasting nuts** adds crispness and intensifies the flavor. Spread in a single layer on a baking sheet or pan. Preheat oven to 350°; place pan in oven and bake 5-10 minutes, or until nuts release their aroma, being careful not to burn. A smaller portion of nuts will toast much quicker than a larger amount. Toast a larger amount than needed and store in the freezer up to 1 year in a tightly sealed container. Four ounces nuts equals about 1 cup.

- To **chop nuts**: place ½ to 1 cup nuts in a plastic bag and smash with a meat pounder on a hard surface. Turn bag over and repeat on the other side. Smashing takes a fraction of the time chopping or slicing does.

- **Sesame oil** and **chili oil** can be found in the Oriental food section of the grocery store or in specialty shops and should be stored in the refrigerator to slow oil from becoming rancid.

- Small bottles of **almond** or **walnut oil** can be found in the grocery store with the vegetable oils. Nut oils become rancid very quickly; store in the refrigerator up to 6 months.

- **Old Bay seasoning** can be found in the spice aisle of the grocery store.

- Avoid canned **olives** if at all possible. Brine-cured olives that are packed in oil have a superior taste. Some grocery stores or specialty shops offer olives from the deli counter.

- To **chop an onion**: slice off top and just the outer end of the root. Peel outer layer of skin off the onion. Cut the onion in half, down through the root. Cut onion in a crisscross pattern almost down to the root. Turn the onion on its flat side and slice thin or thick, starting at the end opposite the root. By leaving the root end intact, the onion will not fall apart as you slice and you will have perfectly diced onion pieces. Discard root piece.

- To **slice an onion**: cut off top and just the outer end of the root. Peel outer layer of skin off the onion. Cut onion in half through the root. Turn the onion pieces on their flat side and slice thin or thick, starting at the end opposite the root. By leaving the root end intact, the onion will not fall apart as you slice. Discard root piece.

- To **section an orange** or **grapefruit**: slice off the top and bottom. Stand the fruit on one of the cut ends; following the contour of the fruit, slice off all the peel and white pith in thick strips. After all peel has been removed, cut along each side of the membrane and orange section while holding over a bowl to catch the sections and any juice. When all sections have been removed, squeeze all the remaining juice from the membranes into the bowl. Discard membranes.

- **Parchment paper** can be purchased in some grocery stores (check near the wax paper and foil) or specialty shops.

- **Parchment paper (or wax paper) liners** for baking pans can be made by placing the desired pan on a sheet of paper and tracing around the outside of the pan; trim shape with scissors. Cut multiple layers of paper at the same time and store in a large manila envelope for use later. Lining pans with paper almost always guarantees a recipe does not stick to the bottom of the pan.

- A ripe **peach** will be a deep golden color with a strong perfumy aroma. For the fullest flavor store peaches (and all fruit with a pit) at room temperature.

- To speed ripening of **pears**, wrap individually in paper and store in a paper bag at room temperature until they yield to gentle pressure at the stem end.

- To **chop peanuts** or **almonds**: use a food processor or place ½ to 1 cup nuts in a plastic bag and smash with a meat pounder on a hard surface. Turn bag over and repeat on the other side. Repeat as necessary.

- If possible wear rubber gloves when handling **hot peppers** and refrain from rubbing your eyes. Wash hands thoroughly to remove any juice that can burn your skin.

- **Pico de gallo** is a combination of diced fresh tomatoes, diced onion, chopped jalapeño pepper, and fresh cilantro tossed with a squeeze of lime, a dash of extra virgin olive oil and seasoned with salt and pepper.

- To minimize waste, buy **pineapple juice** in small, individual, 6-pack containers. Or reserve and freeze the juice from unsweetened, canned pineapple and use in recipes calling for pineapple juice.

- **Mini phyllo shells** can be found in the freezer section of the grocery store next to the phyllo dough and frozen puff pastry.

- A good substitute for the **phyllo shells**: separate 8 flaky, refrigerated biscuits into 4 pieces by peeling the layers apart. Press into 1-inch mini muffin tins and bake at 400° for 8 minutes or until golden and set. Proceed as recipe directs.

- The best kitchen tool to thinly slice potatoes is a **mandolin**. If you don't have one, use a food processor or a very sharp knife. If you slice with a knife, for safety, cut off a thin slice of potato to make a flat surface so that the potato will not roll around as you slice.

- There are 6-7 tablespoons of **pudding mix** in each 3.4 or 3.9 ounce box

- **Puree soup** in small batches in the blender until smooth. (Caution! Hot soup will explode out of the blender if the container is more than ⅓ full and the lid is put on too tight.)

- Choose **raspberries** that have no visible decay or mold. Store in an airtight container in the refrigerator up to 3 days. Carefully rinse, just before serving. Storing damp berries hastens decay.

- To make 2 cups **cooked rice**: bring 1⅓ cups water to a boil; add ⅔ cup long grain rice. Lower heat, tightly cover and simmer 14-18 minutes until all liquid has been absorbed. (1 cup dry rice plus 2 cups liquid will make 3 cups cooked rice.)

- **Basmati rice** has a distinctive, perfumy, nutty flavor and aroma. It is used widely in Indian cuisines and pilafs.

- **Freshly roasted red peppers**: heat grill to high heat. Place washed red bell peppers over high heat. Or place peppers on a foil-lined baking sheet and place under the broiler. As peppers blacken, rotate to cook on all sides. Remove from heat and place in a tightly covered bowl 30 minutes. Peel away blackened skin; remove seeds and membranes inside by gently scraping. Use as directed in recipe.

- To **perk up bottled salad dressings**, stir in 2 tablespoons freshly squeezed lemon juice and 1 clove crushed garlic.

- **Jam** or **jelly** is a natural thickener in salad dressings that are slightly sweet, allowing for less oil. Substitute any seedless jam or jelly as desired.

- To wash and store **salad greens**: cut off the stem end from romaine, red leaf, green leaf or iceberg lettuce. Separate leaves and rinse thoroughly with cold water. Shake or spin dry to remove excess water. In a 2-gallon zip top plastic bag, alternate single layers of salad leaves and paper towels. Repeat layers until paper towels surround all the leaves. Remove as much air as possible, close bag and place in the coldest part of the refrigerator (bottom). Salad will stay crisp and ready to eat for up to 1 week.

- Serve 1-2 oz. (1-2 cups) of **salad greens** per person.

- **Baby salad greens** or **mesclun** is a mix of baby greens usually in a wide range of colors, textures, and tastes. Handle carefully: like all babies they are very delicate. Because they are very perishable, purchase and store no more than one day ahead of serving.

- To **toast sesame seeds**: place in a preheated, dry skillet in a single layer. Shake pan or stir seeds over medium-high heat until seeds turn a golden color about 4-5 minutes, being careful not to burn. Toasting intensifies the flavor.

- **Sesame seeds** and **poppy seeds** tend to go rancid very quickly. Store them in the refrigerator 6 months or freeze up to 1 year.

- **Shallots** look like a cross between garlic and yellow onions. Buy shallots that are tight, with papery-looking skins and no green sprouts. They are mild and are used to season foods in which onions would be too strong. Substitute an equal amount of scallions. Store in a cool, dry place for weeks.

- To **peel shrimp**: pull tail off. Grasp legs and peel shell up the side removing entire hard, outer covering.

- To **devein shrimp**: slice the back curve of the shrimp with a small paring knife. Pull out the gritty-looking black vein with the knife or your fingers; rinse under cold water. Or before peeling, grasp the end of the black vein at the head end of shrimp with the tip of a small paring knife and gently but firmly pull it out.

- **Shrimp** is very perishable and must be eaten within 24 hours of purchasing. When buying shrimp, it should have no odor. Keep shrimp in a plastic bag surrounded by ice packs in the refrigerator or it may be kept frozen up to 2 months. The best method for freezing is to completely submerge shrimp in water and freeze. Thaw in the refrigerator or under cold running water.

- To **soften cream cheese**: unwrap and place on a microwave-safe dish. Microwave 30 seconds.

- To **soften butter** or **margarine**: place in a microwave-safe dish and microwave on 20% power 1 minute.

- Draining off any accumulated liquid in **sour cream** carton makes the sour cream thicker and creamier.

- Triple washed **spinach** in bags is a great convenience food. Use it directly from the bag removing any stems or large ribs from the leaves. To store spinach, leaves should be very dry and should be kept in a tightly sealed bag or plastic container with as much air removed as possible.

- Buy **strawberries** that are shiny and deep red with no visible decay or moldy spots. Green cap (leaves) should be flat. To store: leave in original container and enclose tightly in a plastic bag, removing as much air as possible. Place in the coldest part of your refrigerator (back, bottom shelf). If bought fresh, will keep for several days to a week. Wash strawberries before removing the cap under cold running water. Never submerge berries in water: they absorb water like a sponge. Wash right before using: storing damp berries hastens decaying.

- **Superfine sugar** has very fine crystals and dissolves quickly. Do not confuse it with powdered sugar.

- Canned **sweet potatoes** can be substituted for fresh. Three medium sweet potatoes are generally equivalent to one 16-ounce can or 2 cups mashed.

- **Thyme** and **rosemary** are woody herbs. Strip and chop the green leaves off the woody stems.

- **Tomatillos** look like small green tomatoes wrapped in a papery skin. They have a tart, lemony, herbal flavor. Most grocery stores carry them in the fresh produce department.

- Buy **tomatoes** which are firm, but yield to gentle pressure and are deep red. A ripe tomato should smell like a garden. Tomatoes should be stored on your counter and not in the refrigerator. Cold temperature robs tomatoes of some of their flavor. Tomatoes should last 3-5 days at room temperature.

- Small quantities of **tomato paste** can be purchased in tubes in the tomato paste aisle of the grocery store. Or freeze remaining tomato paste from the can in 1 tablespoon increments on a flat sheet; transfer to a zip top plastic bag and store in the freezer up to 3 months.

- For **vinaigrette**: whisk together vinegar and spices or sugar until dissolved. Salt, sugar and spices will become suspended in the oil if not dissolved in vinegar first. Slowly whisk oil in a fine stream to incorporate thoroughly (or use a blender).

- Cook with an inexpensive **wine** that you would drink. Cooking wine found in the vinegar section of the grocery store is poor quality and high in sodium.

- To extend the shelf life of **dry yeast** up to 6 months past the expiration date, store unopened packages in the freezer.

- To **zest** lemon, lime or orange: wash fruit well in hot water. Before cutting or juicing, remove zest (the very outermost layer of the fruit-the thin, colored part, avoiding the white pith which is bitter) with the finest part of a grater, or by peeling with a vegetable peeler and finely chopping with a knife or remove zest with a special tool called a zester.

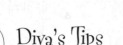

Appetizers

Appetizers

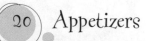

Candied Bacon Knots

This is decadence's middle name!

50-60 pieces

1 cup brown sugar
1 pound thinly sliced bacon[1]

1. Preheat oven to 350°.

2. Line a broiler pan with foil. Place broiler rack over foil and coat with a nonstick cooking spray.

3. Put brown sugar in a shallow dish.

4. Cut bacon pieces in half. Cross one end of the bacon over the other to form a "V".

5. Press one side of the bacon into the brown sugar, coating well.

6. Arrange knots in a single layer, sugar side up, on the prepared broiler rack.

7. Bake 15-20 minutes or until bacon is crisp and sugar is bubbly.

8. Drain and cool on cooling racks, sugar side up. Can be made up to 3 hours ahead and held at room temperature.

Diva Tips

[1]If you only use **bacon** occasionally, separate into individual slices, wrap each piece in plastic wrap, and place wrapped pieces in a zip top freezer bag. When a recipe calls for a few slices of bacon, remove only as many as needed.

Every Kitchen Diva should have:

—one good knife

—a wooden spoon

—and a black lace bra

Kahlúa Pecan Brie

18-20 servings

¼ cup Kahlúa (or any coffee-flavored liqueur[1])

¾ cup **pecans, toasted**[2] and chopped

3 tablespoons brown sugar

1 (14-16 ounces) mini Brie round crackers or mini toasts

1. Mix Kahlúa, pecans, and brown sugar in a small bowl.
2. Lightly scrape the white coating off the rind of the Brie.
3. Place Brie on an oven-safe dish and spoon the Kahlúa topping over the top.
4. Bake in a preheated 350° oven 10-15 minutes just until soft and Brie begins to ooze.
5. Serve with crackers or toasts.

Diva Tips

[1]Small bottles (airline serving size- about 3 tablespoons) of **liqueurs** can be purchased at most liquor stores.

[2]**Toasting nuts** adds crispness and intensifies the flavor. Spread in a single layer on a baking sheet or pan. Preheat oven to 350°; place pan in oven and bake 5-10 minutes, or until nuts release their aroma, being careful not to burn. A smaller portion of nuts will toast much quicker than a larger amount. Toast a larger amount than needed and freeze extras up to 1 year in a tightly sealed container. Four ounces of nuts equals about 1 cup.

Lemon Italian Sausage

Jim and I first tasted this sausage at an Italian restaurant in Dallas in 1982. We have been making it ever since.

About 48 pieces

1 pound mild, sweet Italian sausage links

2 lemons cut into wedges

1. Preheat grill to medium heat.
2. Cook sausage 20-25 minutes until cooked through (or cook under the broiler of the oven).
3. Remove from the heat and cut each link into ½-inch rounds.
4. While still hot, squeeze the juice of 1 lemon over all the sausage pieces. Scatter the remaining lemon wedges over the sausage.
5. Serve with toothpicks or pretzel sticks.

Roquefort Grapes

This appetizer is always a surprise favorite among my guests.

40-50 pieces

I	**package (8-ounces) cream cheese, softened**
⅛	**pound (¼ cup) bleu cheese, room temperature**
2	**tablespoons heavy cream**
1	**pound seedless grapes[1], washed and thoroughly dried**
1½	**cups nuts, toasted[2] and finely chopped**

1. Combine cheeses and cream, beating until smooth.

2. Drop a few grapes at a time into cheese and stir gently by hand to coat.

3. Roll cheese-coated grapes in chopped nuts.

4. Chill until ready to serve.

5. May be prepared up to one day ahead, tightly covered and refrigerated.

Diva Tips

[1]Fresh **grapes** will cling to their stems if shaken gently. Grapes should be plump and firm and stems should be green and moist-looking. Grapes are covered by a thin layer of dust, dirt and pesticides. To clean, fill a large bowl with cold water and dissolve 1 teaspoon baking soda and 1 teaspoon Fruit Fresh (citric acid). Let grapes sit in this water for a few minutes and then swish around. Rinse thoroughly. Drain on paper towels and allow to air dry. Clean, dry grapes will keep fresh for several days stored in an airtight container in the coldest part of the refrigerator.

[2]**Toasting nuts** adds crispness and intensifies the flavor. Spread in a single layer on a baking sheet or pan. Preheat oven to 350°; place pan in oven and bake 5-10 minutes, or until nuts release their aroma, being careful not to burn. A smaller portion of nuts will toast much quicker than a larger amount. Toast a larger amount than needed and freeze extras up to 1 year in a tightly sealed container. Four ounces of nuts equals about 1 cup.

English Crab Canapés

A great hors d'oeuvre to have on hand in the freezer for unexpected guests. One of my friends, Sue Farrell, bakes the English muffins whole and serves them to her family as an accompaniment to soup for a quick and easy meal.

48 pieces

1 **package (6 count) English muffins**
1 **jar (4-ounces) Old English cheese**[1]
½ **cup (1 stick) butter or margarine, softened**
½ **teaspoon season salt**
¼ **teaspoon garlic powder**
1 **can (6-ounces) white crabmeat, drained**

1. Split each muffin into 2 halves; set aside.

2. Mix cheese and butter together. Stir in season salt and garlic powder until thoroughly mixed. Gently fold in crab.

3. Divide mixture evenly between 12 English muffin halves, spreading to cover.

4. Cut muffins into ¼'s. Place on a foil-lined cookie sheet and freeze.

5. When ready to serve, preheat oven to 400° and bake frozen muffins, cheese side up, 10 minutes or until hot and bubbly.

6. Will keep frozen 3 months.

Diva Tips

[1]**Old English cheese** can usually be found in small juice-size jars near the Velveeta cheese in the grocery store.

Spiced Pecans

These pecans are delicious served with a cheese tray and Champagne.

6 cups

½ **cup sugar**
1 **tablespoon cinnamon**
½ **teaspoon salt**
1 **egg white**[1]
1 **pound whole pecan halves**

1. Preheat oven to 300°.

2. In a small bowl, combine sugar and cinnamon; set aside.

3. In a medium mixing bowl, beat egg white with salt until frothy. Add pecans and stir until coated. Sprinkle cinnamon/sugar mixture over pecans and stir to mix well.

4. Spread in a single layer on a baking sheet. Bake 20 minutes.

5. Remove nuts from pan while warm and cool on waxed paper. Store in an airtight container.

Diva Tips

[1]**Eggs separate** easier when cold. Break egg into a funnel or into your fingers over a bowl. The white will easily slip into the bowl and the yolk will remain in the funnel or your fingers (as long as it is not broken). Whites with even a small amount of yolk will not beat up to soft peaks. Add a dash of salt to left over egg yolks and store in the freezer (1 month) or refrigerator (1 day). Use in custards or add to scrambled eggs.

Party Antipasto

16 servings

1 **pound small, white mushrooms[1]**
1 **can (14-ounces) artichoke hearts, drained**
½ **cup water**
½ **cup vegetable oil (preferably extra virgin olive oil)**
1 **clove garlic, crushed (½ teaspoon)**
¼ **teaspoon black peppercorns**
¾ **teaspoon fresh thyme (remove leaves from woody stems)**
¼ **cup cider vinegar**
¼ **cup fresh lemon juice (1 lemon)**
2 **teaspoons salt**
½ **teaspoon sugar**
1 **large bay leaf**
1 **tablespoon chopped fresh basil[2]**
1 **tablespoon chopped fresh oregano**
1 **pint cherry tomatoes, rinsed**
½ **cup black olives[3]**
1 **pound pepperoni, cut into slices**
1 **pound imported sharp provolone cheese, cut into cubes (may substitute Swiss cheese)**

1. If mushrooms are large, cut in half through stems.

2. Quarter artichoke hearts.

3. In a large bowl, combine mushrooms and artichoke hearts.

4. Combine the next 10 ingredients in a small saucepan and heat over low heat until hot but not boiling. Pour over mushroom mixture and refrigerate overnight, up to two days.

5. Remove peppercorns and bay leaf and discard. Stir in fresh basil and oregano; toss with remaining ingredients.

6. Line a shallow bowl with romaine leaves. Spoon in mixture; serve with toothpicks.

Diva Tips

[1]Never immerse **mushrooms** in water; they will absorb liquid like a sponge. The best way to clean mushrooms is to wipe with a damp paper towel. Store mushrooms in a paper bag in the refrigerator.

[2]**Basil** can be kept fresh for 3-4 days with the stems submerged in cool water in a container and kept on the counter. Refresh water every day.

[3]Avoid canned **olives** if at all possible. Brine-cured olives that are packed in oil have superior taste. Some specialty stores offer olives from the deli counter.

Shrimp Tartlets

30 pieces

- ⅓ **cup shredded Swiss cheese**
- ⅓ **cup Parmesan cheese**
- ¾ **cup mayonnaise**
- ¼ **teaspoon Worcestershire sauce**
- ⅛ **teaspoon hot sauce**
- 1 **can (4-ounces) tiny shrimp, drained**
- 2 **packages (15 count each) frozen mini phyllo dough shells[1]**
- 30 **small frozen, cooked shrimp, thawed (for garnish)**

1. Preheat oven to 400°.
2. Combine cheeses, mayonnaise, and sauces.
3. Fold in shrimp.
4. Divide mixture evenly in mini shells.
5. Bake 8-10 minutes.
6. Top each tartlet with a small shrimp and serve immediately.

Diva Tips

[1]**Mini phyllo shells** can be found in the freezer section of most grocery stores or specialty shops next to the phyllo dough and puff pastry. A good substitute for the phyllo shells: separate 8 flaky, refrigerated biscuits into 4 pieces by peeling the layers apart. Press into (1-inch) mini muffin tins and bake at 400° 8 minutes or until golden and set. Proceed as recipe directs.

Tuscany Bruschetta

Bruschetta is offered on almost every menu in Italy and is made with the freshest ingredients. This tasty recipe is my version and the same applies here: fresh ingredients are a must.

24 pieces

1   (14x2-inch) crispy baguette, sliced into ½-inch rounds
1   pint cherry **tomatoes**[1], quartered
1   clove garlic, crushed (½ teaspoon)
2   tablespoons chopped fresh **basil**[2] (do not substitute dried)
2   tablespoons finely chopped, oil-packed sun dried tomatoes, drained
1   tablespoon red wine vinegar
1   tablespoon extra virgin olive oil
½   teaspoon salt (or to taste)
    freshly ground pepper

1. Heat grill or griddle to medium-high heat. Toast baguette slices until golden on both sides. (Grill will impart a delicious, smoky flavor.) Remove from grill and set aside.

2. Stir remaining ingredients together. Taste and adjust salt and pepper if necessary.

3. Pile mixture on toasted baguette slices and serve immediately.

Diva Tips

[1]**Tomatoes** should be stored on your counter and not in the refrigerator. Cold temperature robs tomatoes of some of their flavor. Tomatoes will last for 3-5 days at room temperature.

[2]**Basil** can be kept fresh 3-4 days with the stems submerged in cool water in a container and kept on the counter. Refresh water every day.

Nutty Mushrooms

Mushrooms: you either love 'em or hate 'em. I bet you're gonna love these! Serve these mushrooms as an appetizer or as an elegant first course sitting atop a tossed salad.

24 pieces

24 medium **mushrooms**[1]

1 package (3-ounces) cream cheese, softened

2 ounces (¼ cup) finely grated Gruyère cheese (or Swiss)

4 slices bacon, cooked crisp and crumbled

1 tablespoon Parmesan cheese

2 tablespoons finely chopped, toasted pecans

1 tablespoon dry breadcrumbs

1 tablespoon finely minced green onion (1 onion)

1 tablespoon white wine or dry **sherry**[2]

4 tablespoons melted butter or olive oil

1. Twist stems to separate from mushrooms caps or scoop out stem with a spoon or melon baller to create a cavity. Reserve stems for another use or discard.

2. In a medium mixing bowl, combine the next 8 ingredients until well blended.

3. Brush caps with melted butter; divide mix evenly between the caps. Mushrooms may be prepared up to this point, covered and refrigerated up to one day.

4. When ready to serve broil stuffed mushrooms 3-5 minutes (add an additional 2-3 minutes for refrigerated mushrooms) until they begin to brown and filling is bubbly.

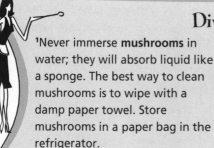

Diva Tips

[1]Never immerse **mushrooms** in water; they will absorb liquid like a sponge. The best way to clean mushrooms is to wipe with a damp paper towel. Store mushrooms in a paper bag in the refrigerator.

[2]Cook with an inexpensive wine or **sherry** that you would drink. Cooking wine found in the vinegar section of the grocery store is poor quality and high in sodium.

Crab-Stuffed Mushrooms

about 18 pieces

1 pound medium **mushrooms**[1]
2 tablespoons butter or margarine
1 medium shallot (1-2 tablespoons), finely chopped
1 clove garlic, crushed (½ teaspoon)
2 tablespoons all-purpose flour
1 cup bottled clam juice (or substitute chicken broth)
1 tablespoon dry sherry
½ teaspoon white wine Worcestershire sauce (Worcestershire for chicken)
½ teaspoon salt
⅛ teaspoon cayenne pepper
½ pound crabmeat (may substitute baby shrimp)
2 tablespoons Parmesan cheese (freshly grated is best)
2 tablespoons chopped fresh **parsley**[2]
2 tablespoons **fresh breadcrumbs**[3] (if needed)
2 tablespoons melted butter
18 (1½-inch) rounds of buttered toast

1. Twist stems of mushrooms to separate from caps or scoop out stem with a spoon or melon baller to create a cavity. Chop stems and set aside. Wipe mushrooms clean.

2. Melt butter in a large, heavy skillet over medium heat; add shallots and garlic. Sauté until shallots have turned clear and mixture is fragrant. Stir in mushroom stems and cook until soft and liquid is absorbed.

3. Add flour to pan; stirring constantly, cook over medium heat until mixture has thickened and has slightly changed color, about 2-3 minutes.

4. Add clam juice or broth and continue cooking until thick and bubbly.

5. Stir in sherry, Worcestershire sauce, salt and pepper. Cook an additional 2 minutes. Remove from heat.

6. Add crabmeat, cheese and parsley. Add breadcrumbs only if mixture seems too thin.

7. Brush mushroom caps with melted butter. Place mushrooms, hollowed side up, on the baking sheet lined with aluminum foil. Spoon crab mixture in the mushrooms; place under the broiler and cook about 5 minutes.

8. Serve mushrooms and any leftover crab mixture on buttered rounds of toast.

Diva Tips

[1]Never immerse **mushrooms** in water; they will absorb liquid like a sponge. The best way to clean mushrooms is to wipe with a damp paper towel. Store mushrooms in a paper bag in the refrigerator.

[2]To store fresh herbs (**parsley** or cilantro), wash herbs in plenty of cold water; drain on paper towels.

Roll clean, damp herbs in dry paper towels and place in a tightly covered plastic container. Store 1-2 weeks in the coldest part of your refrigerator.

[3]2 slices of bread = 1 cup **fresh breadcrumbs**. Put bread in the bowl of an electric blender or food processor and pulse until finely chopped.

Appetizers

Party Quiche Bites

This recipe makes a ton, is easy to prepare, and can be made ahead and frozen. That's everything you can ask of a recipe.

75 pieces

2 tablespoons butter or margarine

1 cup dry **breadcrumbs**[1], divided

½ cup (1 stick) butter or margarine

1 cup (1 medium) chopped onion

2 cloves garlic, crushed (1 teaspoon)

4 slices white sandwich bread

⅔ cup milk (for soaking)

1 package (20-ounces) of frozen, chopped broccoli, thawed

1 package (8-ounces) cream cheese, softened

1 package (3-ounce) cream cheese, softened

4 large eggs

dash hot sauce

1 teaspoon salt

¼ teaspoon pepper

2 cups (8-ounces) grated sharp Cheddar cheese

Diva Tips

[1]Save all your dried, leftover bread-baguettes, sandwich bread, bagels, crackers, rolls, etc.-to make your own breadcrumbs. Put into the bowl of your food processor or blender and pulse until you have fine crumbs. Or rub dried bread on a grater, catching the crumbs in a bowl. Store crumbs in a zip top plastic bag in the freezer and use as your recipe directs. Homemade **breadcrumbs** tastes superior to store prepackaged.

1. Preheat the oven to 350°.

2. Prepare a (15x10x1-inch) baking pan (jelly roll pan) by greasing with 2 tablespoons butter and dusting with ½ cup breadcrumbs. Set aside.

3. Melt the stick of butter in a large skillet; add onion and garlic and cook until soft. Remove from pan and set aside.

4. Soak the bread in milk (milk should cover bread; if needed, add more milk, 1 tablespoon at a time); set aside.

5. Place broccoli in the skillet used to cook onions and cook over low heat, just long enough to completely dry broccoli, being careful not to scorch. Remove from pan and finely chop.

6. In a large mixing bowl, beat the cream cheese until smooth and light. Add the eggs, one at a time, mixing well. Add the onions and garlic with their butter, the soaked bread (with liquid), dry broccoli and a dash of hot sauce. Mix thoroughly and season with salt and pepper; taste and adjust seasonings if necessary.

7. Pour into prepared pan. Sprinkle evenly with the Cheddar cheese, and remaining ½ cup breadcrumbs.

8. Bake 20-30 minutes or until set and puffed in the middle. Remove from oven and allow to cool completely until firm.

9. Can be stored in the refrigerator up to 3 days or frozen up to 6 weeks. To serve from freezer: thaw in the refrigerator, then bake at 350° about 5 minutes to reduce any collected moisture. Cool to room temperature before cutting into (1x2-inch) pieces. Serve room temperature. This recipe can easily be multiplied for large batches.

Mini Goat Cheese Tartlets

Even if you are not a fan of goat cheese, these are so tasty and easy to prepare, you should try them at least once.

30 tartlets

1	package (5-ounces) chèvre mild goat cheese
1	tablespoon butter or margarine
1	large egg, slightly beaten
1½	tablespoons heavy cream
¼	teaspoon pepper
⅛	teaspoon cayenne (or to taste)
1½	tablespoons minced green onion
2	packages (15 count each) mini **phyllo shells**[1]
2	tablespoons apricot or peach preserves
1	teaspoon Grand Marnier **liqueur**[2] (or orange juice)
½	cup walnuts, toasted
2	tablespoons sugar

1. Preheat oven to 375°.

2. In a food processor or small mixing bowl, combine chèvre and butter. Add the egg and cream and mix until well blended. Season with pepper and cayenne. Process or mix until completely smooth. Stir in green onions. (Can be prepared up to this point and refrigerated 1 day).

3. Divide filling evenly among phyllo shells that have been placed on a cookie sheet; bake 15-20 minutes or until custard is set.

4. Remove from oven and cool slightly.

5. Meanwhile, mix the preserves with Grand Marnier; set aside.

6. Melt 2 tablespoons of sugar in a heavy, small skillet over medium-high heat. When sugar has melted (caution! sugar will burn quickly), toss in walnuts, coating with the melted sugar. Immediately remove walnuts from skillet and cool on a piece of aluminum foil that has been lightly buttered or sprayed with a nonstick cooking spray. When cool, break into small pieces.

7. Spoon ½ teaspoon preserves mixture over the cooked tartlets and top with a piece of candied walnut.

Diva Tips

[1]Mini **phyllo shells** can be found in the freezer section of the grocery store next to the phyllo dough and frozen puff pastry.

[2]Small bottles (airline serving size-about 3 tablespoons) of **liqueurs** can be purchased at most liquor stores.

Georgia Brie Appetizers

30 pieces

1 package (3-ounces) cream cheese, softened

4 ounces Brie, room temperature

1 large egg

½ teaspoon almond extract

⅛ teaspoon salt

⅛ teaspoon pepper

2 packages (15 count each) mini **phyllo dough shells**[1]

⅔ cup peach preserves

1 tablespoon amaretto **liqueur**[2]
    (or ½ teaspoon almond extract plus 1 tablespoon orange juice)

½ cup sliced almonds, toasted

1. Preheat oven to 350°.

2. Thoroughly mix together cream cheese, Brie, egg, almond extract, salt and pepper. Mixture may be lumpy. (Can be made to this point and kept refrigerated one day.)

3. Divide filling evenly among phyllo shells that have been placed on a cookie sheet; bake 10-12 minutes or until custard is set.

4. Meanwhile mix peach preserves with amaretto.

5. Remove shells from oven; top with 1 teaspoon peach mixture and sprinkle with almond slices.

Diva Tips

[1]Mini **phyllo shells** can be found in the freezer section of the grocery store next to the phyllo dough and frozen puff pastry.

[2]Small bottles (airline serving size-about 3 tablespoons) of **liqueurs** can be purchased at most liquor stores.

Cheese Times Four

This recipe makes a delicious, savory cheesecake served with fresh fruit slices: a different presentation from other appetizers. The apple and pear slices offer a healthy alternative to crackers. My friend, Tina Harwood, suggests soaking the fruit slices in Sprite or 7-Up to prevent them from browning.

12-16 servings

3   packages (8-ounces each) cream cheese, softened and divided

2   tablespoons sour cream

2   cups finely chopped **pecans, toasted**[1] and divided

4   ounces Camembert cheese, room temperature

4   ounces Gruyère (or Swiss cheese), finely shredded to make 1 cup

4   ounces bleu cheese, room temperature

2   **Cortland**[2] **apples** (or any red apple), sliced into wedges

2   **Ginger Gold**[3] **apples** (or Golden Delicious apples), sliced into wedges

2   **Asian**[4] **pears** (or any pears), sliced into wedges

2   teaspoons fresh lemon juice

2   cups water

1. Line the inside of a (9-inch) quiche dish or cake pan with plastic wrap (will aid in the removal of the cake).

2. In a small bowl, combine 1 package cream cheese with sour cream and mix well. Spread evenly over the bottom of the quiche pan. Top with 1 cup chopped pecans.

3. In a medium bowl, combine Camembert, Gruyère, bleu cheese and remaining 2 packages of cream cheese. Mix until well blended. Spread over pecans.

4. Cover with plastic wrap and press to the surface; refrigerate at least 4 hours or up to 3 days.

5. Remove top layer of plastic wrap and invert onto a serving plate. Peel off bottom layer of plastic wrap and top with remaining chopped pecans.

6. When ready to serve, mix lemon juice with water and dip apple and pear slices. Drain and arrange around cheesecake. (Or use Tina's trick and soak fruit slices in a lemon-lime carbonated beverage.)

7. Guests enjoy the cheesecake spread on the fruit slices.

Diva Tips

[1]**Toasting nuts** adds crispness and intensifies the flavor. Spread in a single layer on a baking sheet or pan. Preheat oven to 350°; place pan in oven and bake 5-10 minutes, or until nuts release their aroma, being careful not to burn. A smaller portion of nuts will toast much quicker than a larger amount. Toast a larger amount than needed and freeze extras up to 1 year in a tightly sealed container. Four ounces of nuts equals about 1 cup.

[2-4]**Cortland, Ginger Gold apple** and **Asian pear** varieties are slower to brown.

Fiesta Cheesecake

A beautiful, delicious, easy, savory cheesecake. Is that too many adjectives to describe one appetizer? Not this one!

12-16 servings

¾ cup crushed corn tortilla chips

2 tablespoons butter, melted

2 packages (8-ounces each) cream cheese, softened

1 package (3-ounces) cream cheese, softened

2 large eggs

2½ cups (10-ounces) shredded Monterey Jack cheese

1 can (4-ounces) chopped green chilies

¼ teaspoon ground cumin

¼ teaspoon cayenne pepper (optional)

1 cup (8-ounces) sour cream

1 envelope (1.25-ounces) taco seasoning mix

½ cup chopped green pepper

½ cup chopped yellow pepper

½ cup chopped sweet red pepper

½ cup chopped green onions, (1 bunch)

¼ cup sliced black **olives**[1]

2 tablespoons chopped fresh **cilantro**[2] (optional)

Diva Tips

[1]Avoid canned **olives** if at all possible. Brine-cured olives packed in oil have superior taste. Some specialty stores offer olives from the deli counter.

[2]To store fresh herbs (parsley or **cilantro**), wash in plenty of cold water; drain on paper towels. Roll clean, damp herbs in dry paper towels and place in a tightly covered plastic container. Store 1-2 weeks in the coldest part of your refrigerator.

1. Preheat oven to 350°.

2. Combine tortilla chips and butter; press into the bottom of a lightly greased (9-inch) springform pan (or to substitute a 9-inch cake pan: line pan with aluminum foil; lightly grease). Bake 12-15 minutes until lightly browned. Remove from oven and cool on a wire rack.

3. Beat cream cheese at medium speed with an electric mixer until light and fluffy, about 2 minutes. Add eggs, one at a time, beating after each addition. Stir in shredded cheese, chilies, cumin and cayenne.

4. Pour into prepared pan. Bake 30-40 minutes or until center is just set (cheesecake is done when edges are firm but center still jiggles a little when pan is shaken).

5. Remove from oven and cool completely on a wire rack. Gently run a knife around the edge of the pan to release sides of the springform pan; carefully remove sides or foil. (If using cake pan, lift cake with the aluminum foil out of pan when cake is thoroughly cooled.)

6. Mix sour cream and taco seasoning; spread evenly over the top of cheesecake. Cover and chill thoroughly. (Can be made up to this point and refrigerated up to 2 days).

7. Sprinkle top with peppers, onions, black olives and cilantro. Serve with tortilla chips or crackers.

Fish in the Red Sea

Shape this spread like a fish. If you can't imagine a fish, look at goldfish crackers or in a child's book. Don't worry how it turns out; mine usually looks like a whale. When this happens, shred the top of a green onion, shove it in the top of the whale's head and pretend it is spouting water!

10-12 servings

1 package (8-ounces) cream cheese, softened

½ teaspoon lemon pepper

1 teaspoon Worcestershire sauce for chicken (white wine Worcestershire)

1 tablespoon freshly squeezed lemon juice

1 can (6-ounces) fancy white crabmeat, drained

1 slice of a stuffed green olive (for garnish)

½ cup sliced almonds (for garnish)

1 green onion (for garnish)

¾ cup catsup

1 tablespoon freshly squeezed lemon juice

2 tablespoons **prepared horseradish**[1], or to taste

2 teaspoons Worcestershire sauce

buttery crackers

1. Blend cream cheese, lemon pepper, Worcestershire sauce, and lemon juice.

2. Gently stir in drained crabmeat.

3. On a serving dish with a lip, shape the spread like a fish. Use 1 slice of a green olive for the eye, sliced almonds for the scales and fins, and a green onion spray for the spouting water.

4. Thoroughly mix the remaining ingredients for the seafood sauce. Pour around the fish for a "red sea".

5. Can be made up to 1 day ahead and refrigerated.

6. Serve with buttery crackers.

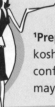

Diva Tips

[1]**Prepared horseradish** can be found in the dairy section next to the kosher items. Or finely grate fresh, peeled horseradish root. Don't confuse prepared horseradish with the horseradish sauce in the mayonnaise aisle.

Mushroom Toasts

If you are running short on time, mound this mouth-watering mushroom spread in the middle of a serving dish with the crispy baguettes around, and let your guests help themselves.

32 toasts

2   tablespoons butter or margarine
1   small onion, finely chopped (½ cup)
2   cloves garlic, crushed (1 teaspoon)
1   package (8-ounces) white mushrooms[1], coarsely chopped
½   teaspoon lemon pepper
1   tablespoon dry sherry (or substitute dry white wine)
1   package (3-ounces) cream cheese, softened
¼   cup dry breadcrumbs
½   tablespoon Worcestershire for chicken (white wine Worcestershire)
1   tablespoon chopped fresh **basil**[2]
2   tablespoons chopped fresh **parsley**[3] (do not use dried)
¼   cup Parmesan cheese
1   cup (4-ounces) grated sharp Cheddar cheese
1   (2½-inch) thin French baguette
8   cherry tomatoes, quartered
    chives, cut into 1-inch pieces

1. Melt butter in a large skillet over medium heat. Add chopped onions and cook until clear, about 5 minutes, stirring occasionally. Stir in crushed garlic and cook an additional minute.

2. Turn up the heat to medium-high and add mushrooms to the pan. Cook until all the liquid released from the mushrooms is absorbed. Stir in the lemon pepper and sherry; bring to a boil stirring constantly. Remove from heat.

3. Add the softened cream cheese and mix in completely. Add the breadcrumbs, Worcestershire, basil, parsley, Parmesan and Cheddar. (Can be made up to this point and refrigerated 1 day).

4. Lightly grease a (1-quart) baking dish (or coat with a nonstick cooking spray).

5. Spoon in the mushroom mixture and bake at 350° 20 minutes or until the middle is bubbly.

6. To make the baguette toasts: slice the baguette into ½-inch slices. Place on a cookie sheet and bake in a 350° oven until toasts are crispy and barely colored, about 10 minutes. Remove from oven and cool on cooling racks. (One 18-inch baguette will make about 32-36 toasts).

7. Spread 2 teaspoons of mushroom mixture on the toasts. Garnish with ¼ of a cherry tomato and a chive, if desired.

Diva Tips

[1]Never immerse **mushrooms** in water; they will absorb liquid like a sponge. The best way to clean mushrooms is to wipe with a damp paper towel. Store mushrooms in a paper bag in the refrigerator.

[2-3]To store fresh herbs (**parsley** or cilantro), wash in plenty of cold water; drain on paper towels. Roll clean, damp herbs in dry paper towels and place in a tightly covered plastic container. Store 1-2 weeks in the coldest part of your refrigerator. **Basil** can be kept fresh for 3-4 days with the stems submerged in cool water in a container on the counter. Refresh water every day.

Quiche Antipasto

My friend, Kathy Hocevar, gave me this recipe in 1994 and that is about how many times I have made it since. Thank you Kathy for such a great appetizer!

20 servings

2	packages (8-count each) **refrigerated crescent rolls**
¼	**pound provolone cheese slices (about 6-8)**
¼	**pound Swiss cheese slices (about 6-8)**
¼	**pound baked ham slices (about 6-8)**
¼	**pound hard salami slices (about 12-14)**
1	jar (24-ounces) **roasted red peppers**[1], **thoroughly drained** (or 3-4 roasted large red peppers)
3	**large eggs**
¼	**cup Parmesan cheese**
⅛	**teaspoon black pepper**

1. Preheat oven to 350°.

2. Lightly grease a (9x13-inch) baking pan (or coat with a nonstick cooking spray).

3. Unroll 1 package of rolls and cover the bottom of prepared pan, firmly pressing perforations to seal, stretching to fit as necessary.

4. Layer one layer of cheese, covering all of dough.

5. Layer second cheese covering the first layer.

6. Next lay ham over cheese; cover ham with salami.

7. Pat peppers dry with a paper towel. Lay out flat over salami (if peppers were left whole, split open to lay flat).

8. Mix eggs, Parmesan and pepper together. Pour ¾'s of egg mixture over the peppers.

9. Unroll remaining can of rolls over the top of the peppers and egg mixture (press perforations together to seal), stretching dough to cover roasted peppers.

10. Brush the top of the dough with remaining egg mixture.

11. Cover the pan with foil and bake 30 minutes. Remove foil and bake an additional 10-15 minutes or until top is golden brown. Remove from oven and let cool slightly before cutting. (For smaller servings, cut each piece into a triangle.)

12. Can be made a day ahead, refrigerated and served at room temperature.

Diva Tips

[1]To make freshly **roasted red peppers**, heat grill to high heat. Place washed red bell peppers over high heat. Or place peppers on a foil-lined baking sheet and under the broiler in your oven. As peppers blacken, rotate to cook on all sides. Remove peppers and place in a tightly covered bowl for 30 minutes. Peel away blackened skin; remove seeds and membranes inside. Use as directed in recipe.

Almond Chicken Bites

Everyone always asks for this recipe when I serve it at a party. I love that it can be made way ahead and refrigerated or frozen: the perfect party food!

40 bites

1   **package (8-ounces) cream cheese, softened**

2   **tablespoons orange marmalade**

1   **teaspoon curry powder**

1   **teaspoon lemon pepper**

½   **teaspoon salt**

¼   **teaspoon pepper**

2   **cups cooked chicken[1] breast, finely chopped**

¼   **cup finely chopped dried apricots**

¼   **cup finely chopped celery**

2   **tablespoons finely chopped green onions**

1   **cup finely chopped almonds, toasted**

1. In a large mixing bowl, beat cream cheese, marmalade, curry, lemon pepper, salt and pepper together until smooth.

2. Stir in chicken, apricots, celery and onions.

3. Shape into (1-inch) balls and roll in almonds.

4. Chill at least 1 hour before serving.

5. Can be made up to 2 days ahead and refrigerated or frozen up to 1 month. If frozen, omit rolling in almonds. Before serving, remove from freezer, thaw slightly and roll in toasted almonds.

Diva Tips

[1]To **cook chicken** for use in any recipe requiring cooked chicken, sprinkle lemon pepper (or season with salt and pepper) on chicken breasts (boneless or rib-in) and place inside a baking bag (smaller version of the kind used to bake turkeys at Thanksgiving) or tightly seal in aluminum foil. Put on a baking sheet in a 350° oven about 1 hour. Remove from oven and cool in the bag. Remove and chop chicken as recipe directs. Reserve any accumulated juices in the cooking bag by pouring into a container and storing in the refrigerator up to 2 days or 3 months in the freezer. These juices are "liquid gold". Use in any recipe that requires chicken broth or bouillon.

Mini Crab Cakes

This Kitchen Diva loves these small bites of heaven. I cheat and make them as a main dish sometimes. The ingredient list looks long and intimidating, but no recipe could be easier.

12 pieces

1 can (6-ounces) fancy white crabmeat, completely drained

1 egg white[1], beaten until frothy

¼ cup dry breadcrumbs

3 tablespoons finely chopped red bell pepper

2 tablespoons finely chopped fresh parsley

1 tablespoon mayonnaise

2 tablespoons finely chopped green onion (about 2 onions)

dash salt

½ teaspoon Old Bay seasoning

½ teaspoon Worcestershire for chicken (white wine Worcestershire)

⅛ teaspoon dry mustard

¼ teaspoon cayenne pepper (optional)

1 tablespoon freshly squeezed lemon juice

¼ teaspoon baking powder

½ cup dry breadcrumbs

2 tablespoons vegetable oil

2 tablespoons butter or margarine

Remmy Sauce

1. Drain crabmeat and set aside.

2. Combine the next 12 ingredients in a medium bowl. Gently stir in crabmeat.

3. Scoop out (1 tablespoon) crab mixture and shape into mini patties.

4. Coat each patty with breadcrumbs.

5. Melt the butter and oil in a skillet over medium-high heat. When oil is hot, cook the patties until golden on both sides, being careful when turning to keep patties from breaking apart.

6. Remove from pan and drain on paper towels.

7. Serve hot with Remmy Sauce.

Every Kitchen Diva should know that she can't change:

—the length of her legs

—the width of her hips

—or the recipe her mother-in-law passed along to her.

Remmy Sauce

This is my version of Rémoulade sauce. It may just take the place of tartar sauce at your table.

1 cup

2 **hard-boiled egg yolks[2]**
   (reserve whites for another use)

2 **tablespoons catsup**

1 **cup mayonnaise**

1 **tablespoon chopped fresh parsley**

1 **clove garlic, crushed, (½ teaspoon)**

2 **teaspoons dried chervil**

2 **teaspoons sweet paprika**

1 **tablespoon Creole mustard**

4 **teaspoons freshly squeezed lemon**
   juice

2 **teaspoons Worcestershire sauce**

¼ **teaspoon onion salt**
   dash cayenne pepper (optional)

1. Finely mash the egg yolks. Stir in remaining ingredients. Refrigerate 1-2 hours before serving to allow flavors to meld together. Can be made up to 2 days ahead and refrigerated.

Diva Tips

[1]Add a dash of salt to left over **egg** yolks and store in the freezer (1 month) or refrigerator (1 day). Use in custards or add to scrambled eggs.

[2]To cook **hard-boiled eggs**, place eggs in a pan in a single layer and cover with cold water to come 1-inch above eggs. Bring to a boil; immediately cover, remove from heat and let sit for 15 minutes. Remove from hot water and immerse in cold water to cool fast. Tap eggs all around to crack the shell and peel under cold running water.

Florentine Con Queso

Who said you can't enjoy restaurant appetizers at home? When the restaurant refused to share its recipe for Spinach Artichoke Dip with me, I marched home and figured it out for myself. Now, I think of them every time I make it and smile-their secret is safe with me!

3 cups

1   package (10-ounces) frozen chopped spinach
2   tablespoons butter or margarine
¼   cup finely **chopped onion**[1]
1   clove **garlic, crushed**[2] (½ teaspoon)
½   cup sour cream
⅓   cup mayonnaise
½   cup Parmesan cheese
½   teaspoon pepper
1   can (14-ounces) artichoke hearts, drained and roughly chopped
1   cup shredded mozzarella or Jack cheese
    tortilla chips
    sour cream
    salsa

1. Cook spinach according to package directions; drain thoroughly. When cool enough to handle squeeze as much liquid out as possible. Set aside.

2. Melt butter in a large skillet. Sauté onions until soft, about 2 minutes. Add garlic and cook an additional minute.

3. Remove from heat and add remaining ingredients up to mozzarella cheese.

4. Pour into a lightly greased (1-quart) baking dish (or coat with a nonstick cooking spray).

5. Bake in a preheated 350° oven 25-30 minutes or until bubbly in the middle.

6. Remove from oven and top with mozzarella. Return to oven and bake an additional 5 minutes just until cheese is melted.

7. Serve with tortilla chips, additional sour cream and salsa.

Diva Tips

[1]To **chop an onion**, slice off top and the outer end of the root. Peel outer layer of skin off the onion. Cut the onion in half, down through the root. Cut onion in a crisscross pattern almost down to the root. Turn the onion on its flat side and slice thin or thick, starting at the end opposite the root. By leaving the root end intact, the onion will not fall apart as you slice and you will have perfectly diced onion pieces. Discard root piece.

[2]To **crush garlic**, peel off papery skin by whacking clove with the side of a knife; paper should slip right off. Place the clove between two sheets of plastic wrap and smash with a meat pounder or the bottom of a heavy pan until pulverized. Scrape garlic off plastic wrap and use in recipe as directed.

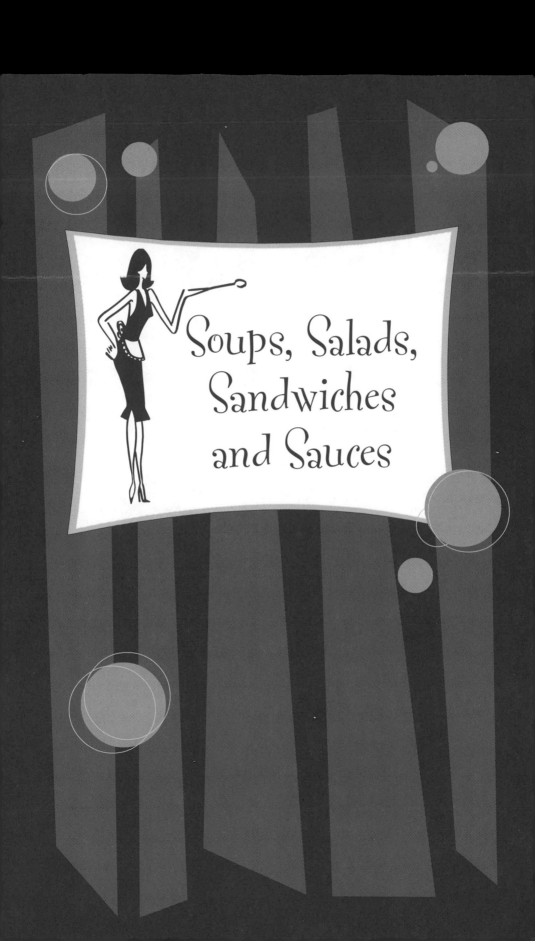

Soups, Salads,
Sandwiches
and Sauces

Soups, Salads, Sandwiches and Sauces

Soups

Salads

Sandwiches

Sauces

Taco Soup

Nothing tastes better on a cool autumn night than this super easy soup. If you can operate a can opener, you can make this soup. Dress it up as you would tacos with chopped tomatoes, sour cream, grated cheese, sliced olives or any garnish you might dare dream up.

8-10 servings

1 **pound extra lean ground sirloin** (or ground round)

1 large **onion, chopped**[1] (1 cup)

2 **cloves garlic, crushed** (1 teaspoon)

1 **package (1.25-ounces) dry taco seasoning mix**

1 **can (10-ounces) Rotel tomatoes, undrained**

1 **can (14-ounces) stewed tomatoes, undrained**

1 **can (4.5 ounces) chopped green chilies**

1 **can (6-ounces) tomato paste**

1 **package (1-ounce) dry ranch salad dressing mix**

1 **can (8-ounces) cream style corn**

1 **can (15-ounces) whole corn**

1 **can (14-ounces) chicken broth**

2 **cans (15-ounces each) Ranch Style Texas beans, undrained**

1 **cup (8-ounces) sour cream (for garnish)**

1 **cup (4-ounces) shredded sharp Cheddar cheese (for garnish)**

1. Heat a soup pot over medium-high heat and brown the meat until it sizzles, breaking apart with a fork as it cooks.

2. Add the onions and garlic and cook until onions soften, about 5-8 minutes, stirring occasionally. Add taco seasoning.

3. In a mixing bowl, stir together Rotel tomatoes (for milder soup substitute mild Rotel tomatoes), stewed tomatoes, chilies, tomato paste, and ranch dressing, breaking the tomatoes into smaller pieces with a fork.

4. Stir tomato mixture into the meat until thoroughly mixed. Add the corns, chicken broth and beans. Mix together and heat through over medium-high heat.

5. Serve hot; garnish with 1-tablespoon sour cream and cheese, if desired. Soup will keep refrigerated up to 6 days or freeze up to 3 months.

Diva Tips

[1]To **chop an onion**, slice off top and only the outer end of the root. Peel outer layer of skin off the onion. Cut the onion in half, down through the root. Cut onion in a crisscross pattern almost down to the root. Turn the onion on its flat side and slice thin or thick, starting at the end opposite the root. By leaving the root end intact, the onion will not fall apart as you slice and you will have perfectly diced onion pieces. Discard root piece.

Spicy Chicken Tortilla Soup with Crispy Tortillas

Open your own restaurant and feature this soup. It is that good! Although this soup may be a little too spicy for small children or finicky adults, you can make it with less heat just by adding mild Rotel® tomatoes.

8-10 servings

Soup

3　tablespoons vegetable oil

1　large onion, finely chopped (1 cup)

4　cloves garlic, crushed (2 teaspoons)

2　teaspoons ground cumin

2　teaspoons chili powder

1　quart chicken broth or 3 (14-ounce) cans

1　can (14-ounces) stewed tomatoes, undrained and finely chopped

1　can (10-ounces) Rotel® tomatoes, undrained

3　cans (10.5-ounces each) cream of chicken soup

2　cups cooked, chopped chicken

1　teaspoon salt (or to taste)

⅛　teaspoon cayenne pepper (optional)

¼　cup chopped fresh cilantro

1　cup (8-ounces) sour cream (for garnish)

1　teaspoon ground cumin (for garnish)

1　cup (4-ounces) shredded cheese (sharp Cheddar or Monterey Jack) (for garnish)

　Crispy Tortilla Strips (for garnish)

1. Heat oil in a large stockpot or Dutch oven.

2. Sauté the onion over medium heat until soft, stirring occasionally. Add garlic and cook just until it releases its aroma about 1 minute, stirring constantly. Stir in the cumin and chili powder and cook for an additional minute to release flavor from the spices.

3. Add chicken broth, stewed tomatoes, Rotel tomatoes, cream of chicken soup, cooked chicken, and salt. Bring to a boil, reduce heat and simmer 30 minutes.

4. Taste and adjust seasonings if necessary, adding cayenne (to kick up the heat) and the chopped cilantro if desired.

5. Stir together sour cream and 1 teaspoon ground cumin.

6. Ladle soup into bowls, garnish with 1-tablespoon sour cream mixture, crispy tortilla strips, and shredded cheese. Serve at once.

Crispy Tortilla Strips

12　(6-inch) corn tortillas

¼　cup vegetable oil

1. Preheat oven to 375°.

2. Brush both sides of tortillas with oil (or for a low-fat version, spray each side of the tortillas with a nonstick cooking spray).

3. Cut into ¼-inch strips with a sharp knife or kitchen scissors.

4. Bake in a single layer on a cookie sheet 5 minutes. Stir and bake an additional 5 minutes or until crisp and golden brown.

Potato and Corn Chowder

Could you ever imagine that preparing soup could be this easy and still taste like it was made in a 5-Star restaurant? Shhhh! It contains a surprise ingredient: crumbled Tater Tots!

8 servings

2	tablespoons butter or margarine
¼	cup finely chopped onions
1	clove garlic, crushed (½ teaspoon)
1	can (10.5 ounces) cream of potato soup
1	can (10.5 ounces) cream of chicken soup
1	can (10.5 ounces) Cheddar cheese soup
3	soup cans milk
1	can (14-ounces) low-sodium chicken broth
1	can (10-ounces) whole corn kernels
1	package (8-ounces) cream cheese, cut into 1-inch cubes and softened
1	pound Tater Tots®, thawed and crumbled
½	cup sour cream (optional garnish)
8	slices bacon[1-2], cooked and crumbled (optional garnish)
¼	cup chopped green onions (optional garnish)

1. Melt butter in a (4-quart) saucepan. Add onions and cook over medium heat until clear and limp, about 4 minutes, stirring occasionally. Add garlic and cook an additional minute.

2. Add soups, milk, chicken broth and corn, stirring to mix thoroughly.

3. When soup is heated through, add cream cheese, stirring until cheese is melted into the soup.

4. Add crumbled Tater Tots®. Heat soup until hot, but do not let it come to a boil, stirring occasionally, being careful not to let the soup burn on the bottom. If soup seems too thick, add additional chicken broth to desired consistency.

5. Spoon into bowls and garnish as desired with sour cream, bacon, and green onions.

6. Refrigerate leftovers up to 4 days.

Diva Tips

[1]To cook **bacon**, remove desired number of slices from package in one piece. Chop or cut through all slices into small pieces with kitchen scissors or a knife. Fry over medium-high heat, separating pieces as they cook. Cook until crisp and golden brown.

[2]For easy removal of **bacon** slices, roll the whole package into a cylinder beginning with the short end; unroll and pieces will "peel" off each other better. If you only use bacon occasionally, separate into individual slices, wrap each piece in plastic wrap, and place wrapped pieces in a zip top freezer bag and freeze up to 3 months. When a recipe calls for a few slices of bacon remove only as many as needed.

Chili Sketti

Everyone has his or her favorite chili recipe. Jim and I love to serve our chili over cooked spaghetti.

6 servings

1   pound ground sirloin or ground round
1   medium onion, chopped (1 cup)
1   cup chopped celery (about 3 stalks)
½   cup chopped green bell pepper
2   cloves garlic, crushed (1 teaspoon)
1   tablespoon chili powder
1   teaspoon ground cumin
½   teaspoon dried oregano
1   can (14.5-ounces) stewed tomatoes, undrained
1   can (8-ounces) tomato sauce
½   cup dry red **wine**[1] or beer
1   teaspoon sugar
1   can (15-ounces) pinto beans, drained and rinsed
    salt and pepper to taste
    cooked spaghetti
    Parmesan cheese (for garnish)

1. Heat a stockpot over medium-high heat and brown the meat until it sizzles, breaking apart with a fork as it cooks.

2. Add onion, celery and green pepper; cook until tender, about 5-7 minutes. Add garlic, chili powder, cumin, and oregano and cook an additional minute, stirring constantly.

3. Stir in tomatoes, tomato sauce, wine (or beer) and sugar. Bring to a boil, reduce heat and simmer 30 minutes.

4. Add pinto beans. Taste and adjust seasonings with salt and pepper. Heat through and serve over spaghetti. Top with grated Parmesan cheese, if desired.

Diva Tips

[1]Cook with an inexpensive **wine** that you would drink. Cooking wine found in the vinegar section of the grocery store is poor quality and high in sodium.

Zuppa de Ceci's

Ceci beans are Italian for garbanzos or chickpeas. They are very nourishing: loaded with protein and fiber. In this recipe the beans are pureed so no one will know they are eating healthy.

3	tablespoons butter or margarine
1	large onion, chopped (1½ cups)
4	cloves garlic, crushed (2 teaspoons)
1½	cups chopped celery (about 4 stalks)
2	cans (14-ounces each) low-sodium chicken broth or stock
2	cans (14-ounces each) garbanzo beans (chickpeas)
1	pint (2 cups) heavy cream
½	teaspoon dried marjoram
½	teaspoon dried thyme
½	cup shredded Swiss cheese (2 ounces)
	salt and pepper to taste
2	tablespoons dry **sherry**[1]
2	tablespoons chopped fresh parsley
2	tablespoons **Parmesan cheese**
	croutons[2]

1. Melt the butter in a large soup pot over low heat. Add onions, garlic and celery; cook over low heat for 15-20 minutes until onions and celery are tender and lightly colored.

2. Add chicken broth and garbanzo beans with their liquid to the onion mixture. Bring to a boil, reduce heat and simmer 10 minutes to let flavors meld.

3. Puree soup in small batches in the blender until smooth. (Caution! Hot soup will explode out of the blender if the container is more than ⅓ full and the lid is put on too tight.)

4. Return soup to the pot; add cream, marjoram and thyme and heat through.

5. Stir in Swiss cheese just until melted. Taste and adjust seasonings with salt and pepper if desired.

6. Just before serving, stir in sherry, parsley and Parmesan cheese. Garnish with croutons if desired.

Diva Tips

[1]Purchase dry **sherry** in the wine section of the grocery store or specialty shop.

[2]To make **croutons**: slice slightly stale, hearty French bread into slices. Brush slices with extra virgin olive oil or vegetable oil (for garlic croutons add 1 clove crushed garlic to the oil). Stack a few slices on top of each other and cut into cubes with a serrated knife. Place bread cubes in a single layer on a baking sheet and bake in a 350° oven 10-15 minutes or until crunchy, stirring midway of the baking time.

Pasta E Fagioli

Pronounced pasta fazool, this soup is simply pasta with beans. It is thick, hearty and luscious. It is usually made with dried white beans that are soaked overnight, but I have streamlined it so that it can be made in about 30 minutes.

6 servings

2   tablespoons vegetable oil (preferably extra virgin olive oil)
1   medium onion, finely chopped (1 cup)
2   cloves garlic, crushed (1 teaspoon)
1   stalk celery, finely chopped
1   quart chicken stock or broth
1   teaspoon dried basil
½   teaspoon dried oregano
    salt and pepper to taste
2   cans (14-ounces each) white beans
2   cups cooked ditalini pasta (or any small pasta)
2   tablespoons pesto[1] (optional)
6   tablespoons Parmesan cheese

1. Heat the oil in a large stockpot. Add the onions, garlic, and celery and cook over medium heat until soft but not brown, 4-6 minutes.

2. Add chicken stock and seasonings. Simmer 20 minutes to allow flavors to meld.

3. Add 1 can of beans with liquid. Mash the remaining can of beans with a fork and stir into soup.

4. Stir in cooked pasta and heat through. Spoon into bowls and garnish with 1 teaspoon pesto and 1 tablespoon cheese.

Diva Tips

[1]**Pesto** is a sauce made with 2 cups fresh basil leaves (packed), ¼ cup pine nuts (or walnuts), 2 cloves garlic, 1 teaspoon salt. Process in food processor (or by finely crushing ingredients with a mortar and pestle). Add ¼ cup extra virgin olive oil. Stir in ⅓ cup Parmesan cheese. Can be refrigerated several days or frozen in 1 tablespoon portions.

Italian Wedding Soup

I'm not sure how this soup got its name (also called Stracciatella), but I would guess that it was made to serve the hordes of people invited to an Italian wedding. If you have never been privileged to attend one of these extraordinary events, find an Italian family, make friends and then be sure you are included at the next nuptial celebration!

8 servings

1	**tablespoon vegetable oil (preferably extra virgin olive oil)**
½	**cup finely chopped celery**
1	**cup finely chopped carrots**
8	**cups chicken stock or broth**
3	**cups chopped cooked chicken**
1	**pound ground sirloin or round**
1	**can (14-ounces) small green peas, drained**
	salt and pepper to taste
2	**large eggs, lightly beaten**
	Parmesan cheese, for garnish

1. Heat oil in a large stockpot and cook celery and carrots over medium heat until just beginning to soften, but not browned, about 5 minutes.

2. Add chicken stock and bring to a boil. Add chopped chicken.

3. Meanwhile, pinch off enough ground meat and roll into mini ½-inch meatballs. Repeat until all ground meat is used. Drop meatballs into the boiling chicken stock. Reduce heat and cook until meatballs are cooked, about 5 minutes, skimming off any brown foam as it accumulates.

4. Add the peas.

5. Taste and adjust seasonings with salt and pepper, if desired.

6. Just before serving, heat soup to a boil and pour in beaten eggs in a thin stream. Serve immediately, garnishing with Parmesan cheese if desired.

Do illiterate people get the full effect of alphabet soup?

Acorn Squash Soup

This soup always reminds me of formal holiday dinners. For a great presentation, serve it in hollowed out small pumpkins.

6 servings

2	(medium-size) acorn squash, scrubbed, cut in half and seeds removed
2	apples (any kind), cut in half and cored
4	tablespoons butter
1	medium onion, chopped (1 cup)
1	medium **shallot**[1], chopped
½	teaspoon curry powder
½	teaspoon ground cumin
½	teaspoon coriander
6	cups low-sodium chicken stock or broth
1	cup white **wine**[2]
1	cup cream or half-and-half
	salt and pepper to taste
½	cup sour cream (for garnish)
1	Granny Smith apple, unpeeled, cored and finely chopped (for garnish)

1. Place squash and apples, cut side down, in a glass baking pan. Add boiling water to the depth of ½-inch. Bake at 375° for 45 minutes or until tender, replacing water as necessary.

2. Remove squash and apples from pan to cool slightly.

3. Meanwhile, melt butter in a large soup pot over low heat. Add onions, shallots, curry powder, cumin and coriander and cook until onions are tender, about 10-15 minutes.

4. When squash and apples are cool enough to handle, scrape flesh from peels into the soup pot with onions, discarding peels. Add chicken stock, and wine. When soup comes to a boil, reduce heat and simmer 10-15 minutes for flavors to develop.

5. Puree soup in batches in the blender until smooth. (Caution! Hot soup will explode out of the blender if the container is more than ⅓ full and the lid is put on too tight).

6. Return soup to the pot, add cream and heat through. Taste and adjust seasonings with salt and pepper if desired. When ready to serve, ladle soup into bowls, spoon 1 tablespoon sour cream in the center and garnish with chopped apple, if desired. (Soup can be made 2 days ahead of time; reheat until hot and steaming but do not let it boil).

Diva Tips

[1]**Shallots** look like a cross between garlic and yellow onions. Buy shallots that are tight, with papery-looking skins and no green sprouts. They are mild and are used to season foods in which onions would be too strong. If you can't find shallots, substitute an equal amount of scallions. Store in a cool, dry place for weeks.

[2]Cook with an inexpensive **wine** that you would drink. Cooking wine found in the vinegar section of the grocery store is poor quality and high in sodium.

Wild Mushroom Bisque

Thick, creamy and woodsy. This soup is elegant enough to serve at a formal setting.

8 servings

8 tablespoons (1 stick) butter or margarine, divided
1 medium onion, chopped (about ¾ cup)
1 clove garlic, crushed (½ teaspoon)
1½ pounds assorted fresh **mushrooms**[1] (cremini, porcini, white button or morels)
4 cups low-sodium chicken stock or broth
1 pint (2 cups) heavy cream or half-and-half
   salt and pepper to taste
2 tablespoons dry **sherry**[2]
2 tablespoons chopped fresh parsley

1. Melt 7 tablespoons butter in a large soup pot over low heat. Add onions and garlic; cook over low heat for 15-20 minutes until onions are tender and lightly colored.

2. Remove stems from 8 mushrooms. Slice caps and reserve for garnish.

3. Chop mushroom stems and remaining mushrooms. Add to onions and cook just until mushrooms begin to loose their liquid.

4. Stir in chicken broth; heat to simmer and continue cooking over low heat 15 minutes until mushrooms are cooked.

5. Puree soup in small batches in the blender until smooth. (Caution! Hot soup will explode out of the blender if the container is more than ⅓ full and the lid is put on too tight.)

6. Return soup to the pot; add cream and heat through. Taste and adjust seasonings with salt and pepper if desired.

7. Just before serving, sauté reserved sliced mushroom caps in remaining 1 tablespoon butter. Heat soup to serving temperature and stir in sherry. Ladle soup into bowls and garnish with sautéed mushrooms and parsley.

Diva Tips

[1] Never immerse **mushrooms** in water; they will absorb liquid like a sponge. The best way to clean mushrooms is to wipe with a damp paper towel. Store mushrooms in a paper bag in the refrigerator.

[2] Buy dry **sherry** in the wine section of the grocery store or specialty shop.

Lobster Bisque

This soup is a little fussy, but the taste is worth the effort.

4-6 servings

- 2 tablespoons butter or margarine
- 2 shallots, finely chopped
- 2 tablespoons **tomato paste**[1]
- 4 mini lobster tails (about 1 pound)
- ½ pound shrimp, deveined and peeled (reserve shells)
- 1 quart chicken stock, divided
- 2 tablespoons butter or margarine
- 2 cups dry **white wine**[2]
- ½ cup uncooked rice
- 2 cups half-and-half
- 2 tablespoons **lobster base**[3] or bouillon
- ¼ teaspoon paprika
  salt and pepper to taste
- 2 tablespoons sour cream, optional (for garnish)
- 4-6 thin slices buttered and toasted French bread (for garnish)

Diva Tips

[1]For small amounts, buy tomato paste in a tube (near the **tomato paste** in cans in the grocery store) or buy a small can and freeze remainder in 1 tablespoon portions; store portions in a zip top freezer bag and use as needed.

[2]Cook with an inexpensive **wine** that you would drink. Cooking wine found in the vinegar section of the grocery store is poor quality and high in sodium.

[3]**Lobster base** can be found next to the bouillon in some grocery or specialty stores.

1. Heat 2 tablespoons butter in a small sauté pan and cook shallots over medium heat just until soft; add tomato paste and cook for 1 minute stirring constantly. Remove from heat and set aside.

2. Cover lobster tails and shrimp with chicken stock and cook just until seafood turns pink. Remove from stock, chop into small pieces and set aside reserving stock. (Refrigerate chopped seafood if preparing ahead of time.)

3. In a stockpot, melt additional 2 tablespoons butter and sauté lobster shells and shrimp shells until they turn pink. Add white wine and reduce to 1 cup. Strain out solids and discard. Return reduced wine to the pot. Add reserved chicken stock used to cook lobster and any remaining chicken stock not used. Stir in shallot mixture. Bring to a boil; stir in rice, cover and cook 15 minutes.

4. Puree soup in a blender. (Caution! Hot soup will explode out of the blender if the container is more than ⅓ full and the lid is put on too tight). Return to soup pot.

5. Add half-and-half. Stir in lobster base and paprika. Taste and adjust the seasonings with salt and pepper if necessary. Can be prepared to this point and refrigerated. When ready to serve, heat soup to serving temperature. Add reserved lobster and shrimp. Ladle into bowls. Garnish with 1 teaspoon sour cream and a slice of toasted bread. Serve immediately.

Chicken Stock

Chicken stock is so easy to make, but it takes a little time to simmer. Chicken legs, thighs and necks make a richer stock. Homemade stock is also a good way to use limp vegetables from your produce drawer in the refrigerator.

2 quarts

1 tablespoon butter or margarine

3-4 pounds chicken legs, thighs, necks or a combination

2 medium onions, peeled and quartered

2 celery ribs with leaves[1], halved

2 carrots, peeled and quartered

2 cloves garlic, whole

2 quarts water

2 sprigs fresh thyme (optional)

1 bay leaf

12 whole black peppercorns

4-5 sprigs fresh parsley (do not use dried)

1. Melt butter in a large stockpot. Add chicken, onions, celery, carrots and garlic. Cook over medium-high heat stirring occasionally about 5 minutes, until chicken starts to brown.

2. Add water, thyme, bay leaf, peppercorns and parsley. Bring to a boil, reduce heat and skim off any foam that accumulates.

3. Simmer 1½ hours, continually skimming off any foam.

4. Remove chicken pieces and take meat from the bones; reserve meat and discard bones.

5. Strain stock through a fine mesh strainer into a bowl, pressing on the solids to remove all liquid (discard solids).

6. If not using the stock within the hour, **chill**[2] it as quickly as possible. When cooled, pour into individual containers and refrigerate. When thoroughly chilled, remove any hardened fat that has risen to the surface and cover. Freeze up to 3 months in 1-quart portions. Use as directed for soups or freeze in smaller portions and use instead of water to cook vegetables (gives them a richer flavor).

Diva Tips

[1]**Celery leaves** have a more intense celery flavor.

[2]To **chill** hot stock quickly, fill sink partially with ice water. Place hot stockpot in the ice bath stirring occasionally until thoroughly cooled.

Fish Stock

Freshly made fish stock is superior in quality and well worth the effort when making fish soups or chowders. Seafood and fish are very expensive, so to get the most bang for your buck, make your own stock and store it in the freezer.

1 quart

1   **large onion, quartered**

2   **celery stalks, with leaves, coarsely chopped**

1   **medium carrot, peeled and quartered**

2   **tablespoons butter or margarine**

2   **pounds fish bones and tails[1] (rinsed clean of any traces of blood) from any white, non-oily fish such as cod, sole, flounder or halibut, cut into smaller pieces (also add shrimp shells and lobster shells if available)**

2   **tablespoons freshly squeezed lemon juice**

1   **cup dry white wine**

1   **quart water**

3-4 **sprigs fresh Italian parsley (do not use dried)**

3-4 **sprigs fresh thyme**

1   **tablespoon black peppercorns**

1   **bay leaf**

1. In a large stockpot, cook onion, celery and carrot in the butter until softened. Add fish bones, lemon juice and wine. Bring to a boil and cook until wine is reduced by half, about 5 minutes.

2. Add water and remaining ingredients (adding more water if solids not completely covered by liquid); simmer 1 hour, skimming off any white foam as it accumulates.

3. Strain through a fine mesh strainer into a bowl, pressing on solids to remove all liquids (discard solids). If not using the stock within the hour, **chill**[2] it as quickly as possible. Cover after it has completely cooled and keep refrigerated up to 3 days or freeze up to 2 months.

Diva Tips

[1]Ask your local fish market to save some **bones** and **tails** for you as they filet the fish.

[2]To **chill** stock quickly, fill sink partially with ice water. Place hot stockpot in the ice bath, stirring occasionally until thoroughly cooled.

Veal Stock

This stock takes the most effort, but the results are well worth it. Keep this stock in your freezer and use in place of bouillon cubes. Your guests and family will swear that you are a master chef! (And indeed you are if you keep veal stock in your freezer.)

2 quarts stock; 2 pints demi-glace

1 tablespoon vegetable oil

3 pounds veal or beef bones, in 2-inch pieces (ask butcher to save bones)

2 pounds stew beef, cut in 1½-inch cubes

2 medium onions, quartered

2 carrots, peeled and quartered

2 tablespoons **tomato paste**[1]

4 quarts water

2 celery stalks, with leaves, cut in half

4 cloves garlic, whole

4-5 fresh parsley sprigs (do not use dried)

2-3 sprigs fresh thyme

1 bay leaf

1. Preheat the oven to 400°.

2. Brush the bottom and sides of a roasting pan with the vegetable oil. Spread the bones and meat in the pan and place in the hot oven. Roast 25 minutes.

3. Add the onions and carrots, and roast the mixture, stirring once or twice, 30 minutes or more until it is well browned.

4. Spread the tomato paste on the meat and bones and roast an additional 10 minutes.

5. Transfer bones, meat and vegetables to a large stockpot. Pour off any fat in the roasting pan, add 2 cups of water and deglaze the pan over high heat, scraping up the browned bits on the bottom of the pan. Add the liquid to the stockpot with remaining water. Bring to a boil, skimming off any foam.

6. Reduce heat, add remaining ingredients and simmer the mixture 4 hours, skimming any foam that accumulates. Strain the stock through a fine mesh sieve into a bowl. If a more concentrated flavor is desired (to make demi-glace, the flavoring professional chefs use) return liquid to the pot and continue simmering 2-3 hours.

7. Remove from heat and cool to warm. Refrigerate uncovered until thoroughly **chilled**[2]. Remove any solidified fat; cover and keep refrigerated 2 days or frozen up to 3 months. Freeze in smaller portions and add to gravies or any dish that requires bouillon cubes.

Diva Tips

[1]Small portions of **tomato paste** can be found in tubes or freeze any leftover canned tomato paste in 1 tablespoon portions.

[2]To **chill** stock quickly, fill sink partially with ice water. Place hot stockpot in the ice bath, stirring occasionally until thoroughly cooled.

Casual Tomato and Cucumber Salad

This is one of my favorite summertime salads prepared in a flash. Use the freshest tomatoes available.

4 servings

- 1 **cup Italian salad dressing**
  juice from ½ lemon
- 1 **clove garlic, crushed**
- 2 **medium cucumbers, peeled and sliced into rounds**
- ½ **head iceberg lettuce, shredded**
- 2 **medium tomatoes[1], cut into wedges**
- 1 **medium Vidalia onion, sliced and divided into rings**
  salt and pepper, to taste

1. Mix dressing with lemon juice and garlic. Toss with cucumbers.

2. Divide lettuce on 4 serving plates. Top with cucumbers, tomatoes, and onion rings.

3. Drizzle with salad dressing and season to taste with salt and pepper.

Diva Tips

[1]Buy **tomatoes** which are firm, but yield to gentle pressure and are deep red. A ripe tomato should smell like a garden. Tomatoes should be stored on your counter and not in the refrigerator. Cold temperature robs tomatoes of some of their flavor. Tomatoes will last for 3-5 days at room temperature.

Caprese Tomato Salad

Transport your taste buds to Tuscany with this classic Italian Salad.

6 servings

Tomato Salad

4   medium, firm, ripe **tomatoes**[1], sliced
½   pound **fresh** (soft) **mozzarella cheese**[2], sliced
    whole fresh basil leaves

Balsamic Basil Vinaigrette

¼   cup balsamic vinegar
1   clove garlic, crushed (½ teaspoon)
    salt and pepper to taste
¼   cup extra virgin olive oil

1. Alternate tomatoes and cheese on a serving dish tucking a basil leaf in between.

2. Whisk vinegar, garlic, salt and pepper together. Add oil in a fine stream, stirring briskly until incorporated. Refrigerate.

3. When ready to serve, drizzle vinaigrette over tomatoes and cheese. Or omit vinaigrette and drizzle tomatoes and cheese with extra virgin olive oil and season with salt and pepper.

Diva Tips

[1]Buy **tomatoes** which are firm, but yield to gentle pressure and are deep red. A ripe tomato should smell like a garden. Tomatoes should be stored on your counter and not in the refrigerator. Cold temperature robs tomatoes of some of their flavor. Tomatoes will last for 3-5 days at room temperature.

[2]Fresh **mozzarella** is a creamy white ball, sometimes called Buffalo mozzarella, and can be found in a brine mixture in some grocery stores or specialty shops.

Continental Salad

The beauty of most salads is that you can add ingredients you love and leave out the ingredients that you dislike. Create your own salad and give it any exotic name it deserves.

8 servings

1   pound **salad greens**[1], any kind
2   cups cherry tomatoes, sliced in half
1   large cucumber, sliced
1   cup niçoise olives
1   cup Kalamata (Greek) **olives**[2]
1   small red onion, sliced
    shaved Parmesan cheese
    Italian salad dressing

1. Divide salad greens between serving plates.

2. Dress each plate with tomatoes, cucumbers, olives, onions and shaved Parmesan cheese.

3. Drizzle with your favorite Italian dressing.

Diva Tips

[1]To wash and store **salad greens**, cut off the stem end from romaine, red leaf, green leaf or iceberg lettuce. Separate leaves and rinse thoroughly with cold water. Shake or spin dry to remove excess water. Alternate single layers of salad leaves and paper towels in a 2-gallon zip top plastic bag. Repeat layers until paper towels surround all the leaves. Remove as much air as possible, close bag and place in the coldest part of the refrigerator (bottom). Salad will stay crisp and ready to eat for up to 1 week. Serve 1-2 ounces (1-2 cups) of salad greens per person.

[2]Avoid canned **olives** if at all possible. Brine-cured olives packed in oil have superior taste. Some specialty or grocery stores offer olives from the deli counter.

Provençal Bleu Cheese Salad

Like that little black dress that we all own (or dream about), this salad is simple, elegant and yet stunning.

½ pound organic **baby salad mix**[1] (or mesclun)

3 tablespoons white wine vinegar (Champagne vinegar if available)

½ cup (4-ounces) Gorgonzola cheese, divided (or any bleu cheese)

pinch dried oregano

1 tablespoon finely chopped fresh basil (or substitute 1 teaspoon dried)

¼ cup extra virgin olive oil or vegetable oil

salt and pepper to taste

2 shallots, finely sliced

½ cup **walnuts**[2], **toasted**

1. Carefully rinse salad; spin dry or drain on paper towels being careful not to bruise delicate leaves.

2. Combine vinegar and ¼ cup (2 ounces) Gorgonzola, mashing cheese to incorporate into vinegar. Mix in oregano and basil. Stir in olive oil. If dressing seems too thick, add a little more vinegar; if too thin, add more cheese. Taste and adjust seasonings with salt and pepper if desired.

3. Carefully toss salad with shallots and enough dressing to coat.

4. Divide salad among serving dishes and top with toasted walnuts and remaining cheese. Serve immediately.

Diva Tips

[1]**Baby salad greens** or mesclun is a mix of baby greens usually in a wide range of colors, textures, and tastes. Handle carefully: like all babies they are very delicate. Because they are very perishable, purchase and store no more than one day ahead of serving.

[2]**Toasting nuts** adds crispness and intensifies the flavor. Spread in a single layer on a baking sheet or pan. Preheat oven to 350°; place pan in oven and bake 5-10 minutes, or until nuts release their aroma, being careful not to burn. A smaller portion of nuts will toast much quicker than a larger amount. Toast a larger amount than needed and freeze extras up to 1 year in a tightly sealed container. Four ounces of nuts equals about 1 cup.

Insalata Italiano

This salad is quick, easy and delicious with pizza. Make the salad; order the pizza. Better yet, let someone else do the honors. All divas deserve at least one night off.

8 servings

Italian Lemon Vinaigrette

½ **cup white wine vinegar**
4 **tablespoons freshly squeezed lemon juice (1 lemon)**
1 **clove garlic, crushed (½ teaspoon)**
1 **envelope (.75-ounces) Good Seasons Italian Salad Dressing**
1 **cup extra virgin olive oil or vegetable oil**

Salad

1 **pound assorted salad greens[1]**
1 **cup cherry tomatoes**
  Italian black olives[2] (optional)
  pepperoncini peppers, sliced into rings
1 **small red onion, sliced**
1 **small red bell pepper, sliced**
  shaved Parmesan cheese

1. Shake vinegar, lemon juice, garlic and Italian salad dressing mix together in a jar. Add oil and shake until all mixed together.

2. Toss salad greens with enough dressing to coat.

3. Arrange salad on individual plates and garnish with tomatoes, olives, pepperoncini peppers, red onion and red bell pepper.

4. Garnish with shaved Parmesan cheese. Better yet, let them do it. It's your night off.

Diva Tips

[1]To wash and store **salad greens**, cut off the stem end from romaine, red leaf, green leaf or iceberg lettuce. Separate leaves and rinse thoroughly with cold water. Shake or spin dry to remove excess water. In a 2-gallon zip top plastic bag, alternate single layers of salad leaves and paper towels. Repeat layers until paper towels surround all the leaves. Remove as much air as possible, close bag and place in the coldest part of the refrigerator (bottom). Salad will stay crisp and ready to eat for up to 1 week. Serve 1-2 ounces (1-2 cups) of salad greens per person.

[2]Avoid canned **olives** if at all possible. Brine-cured olives packed in oil have superior taste. Some specialty or grocery stores offer olives from the deli counter.

Greek Salad

Opa!

8 servings

Greek Vinaigrette

- 3 tablespoons freshly squeezed lemon juice
- ¼ cup red wine vinegar
- 1 teaspoon salt
- ¼ teaspoon pepper
- 2 cloves garlic, crushed (1 teaspoon)
- ½ teaspoon dried oregano
- 2 tablespoons **apple jelly**[1] (or substitute 2 teaspoons sugar)
- ¾ cup vegetable oil (preferably extra virgin olive oil)

Salad

- 1 head Romaine **lettuce**[2], washed and torn into pieces
- 2 cups iceberg **lettuce**[3], washed and torn into pieces
- 1 small red onion, sliced
- 1 cucumber, peeled and sliced
- 2 tomatoes, quartered
- 1 cup Kalamata olives (or any Greek olive)
- ½ cup pepperoncini pepper slices
- 1 green bell pepper, sliced
- ½ cup feta cheese crumbles

1. For the vinaigrette: whisk together lemon juice, vinegar, salt, pepper, garlic, and oregano. Melt the apple jelly (In the microwave or stovetop) and stir into the vinegar mixture. Add oil in a fine stream, stirring briskly until incorporated (or use a blender). Refrigerate.

2. Mix the lettuces with the onion and toss with enough dressing to coat.

3. Divide salad among individual serving plates and top with cucumbers, tomatoes, olives, peppers and feta cheese.

4. Drizzle with additional dressing. Serve immediately.

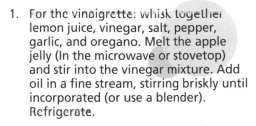

Diva Tips

[1]**Jam or jelly** is a natural thickener in salad dressings that are slightly sweet, allowing for less oil. Substitute any seedless jam or jelly as desired.

[2-3]To wash and store **salad greens**, cut off the stem end from romaine, red leaf, green leaf or iceberg lettuce. Separate leaves and rinse thoroughly with cold water. Shake or spin dry to remove excess water.

In a 2-gallon zip top plastic bag, alternate single layers of salad leaves and paper towels. Repeat layers until paper towels surround all the leaves. Remove as much air as possible, close bag and place in the coldest part of the refrigerator (bottom). Salad will stay crisp and ready to eat for up to 1 week. Serve 1-2 ounces (1-2 cups) of salad greens per person.

Balsamic Caesar Salad

My version of the classic.

6-8 servings

Caesar Dressing

¼ **cup balsamic vinegar**
1   **clove garlic, crushed (½ teaspoon)**
1   **teaspoon anchovy paste[1]**
     (optional, but worth it)
1   **teaspoon sugar**
1   **tablespoon Dijon mustard**
2   **tablespoons grated Parmesan cheese**
½ **cup extra virgin olive oil**

Salad

1   **pound Romaine lettuce, torn into**
     pieces
1   **cup (4-ounces) shaved, aged Parmesan**
     cheese
2   **cups croutons[2]**
     freshly ground pepper (optional)

1. Whisk vinegar, garlic, anchovy paste, sugar, mustard and cheese together. Slowly whisk or briskly stir oil in a fine stream to incorporate thoroughly.

2. Toss romaine with just enough dressing to coat.

3. Put into individual salad bowls or plates. Top with Parmesan cheese, croutons and pepper. Serve immediately.

Diva Tips

[1]**Anchovy paste** is found in tubes next to the anchovies in tins in specialty shops and grocery stores.

[2]To make **croutons**, slice slightly stale, hearty French bread or pumpernickel bread into slices. Brush slices with extra virgin olive oil or vegetable oil (for garlic croutons add 1 crushed clove garlic to the oil). Stack a few slices on top of each other and cut into cubes with a serrated knife. Put in a single layer on a baking sheet and bake in a 350° oven 10-15 minutes or until crunchy, stirring midway of the baking time. If desired, Parmesan cheese can be sprinkled over hot croutons.

Classic Caesar Salad

By heating the anchovies in the oil, the fishy taste becomes nutty and salty. Use freshly grated Parmesan cheese in the salad for superior flavor. This recipe also uses pasteurized eggs which are safer than regular eggs.

8 servings

½ **cup extra virgin olive oil**

1 **tin (2-ounces) flat filet of anchovies in oil, drained**

1 **small clove garlic, crushed (½ teaspoon)**

1 **teaspoon Worcestershire sauce**

½ **teaspoon dry mustard**

2 **tablespoons freshly squeezed lemon juice, (½ lemon)**

¼ **cup pasteurized egg product (found in the dairy aisle)**

   freshly ground pepper

½ **cup freshly grated Parmesan cheese, divided**

2 **heads romaine lettuce[1], coarsely chopped**

   croutons

1. Heat olive oil and anchovies in a small saucepan over low heat. Cook 2-3 minutes, stirring until anchovies have "melted" into the oil. Remove from heat and cool.

2. Rub crushed garlic in the bottom of salad bowl. Pour oil mixture over garlic. Whisk or briskly stir in Worcestershire sauce, mustard, lemon juice, and egg. Season with pepper and ¼ cup Parmesan cheese.

3. Add lettuce, croutons and remaining cheese. Toss and serve immediately.

4. To make croutons, slice slightly stale, hearty French bread or pumpernickel bread into slices. Brush slices with extra virgin olive oil or vegetable oil (for garlic croutons add 1 crushed clove garlic to the oil). Stack a few slices on top of each other and cut into cubes with a serrated knife. Put in a single layer on a baking sheet and bake in a 350° oven 10-15 minutes or until crunchy, stirring midway of the baking time. If desired, Parmesan cheese can be sprinkled over hot croutons.

Diva Tips

[1]To wash and store **salad greens**, cut off the stem end from romaine, red leaf, green leaf or iceberg lettuce. Separate leaves and rinse thoroughly with cold water. Shake or spin dry to remove excess water. In a 2-gallon zip top plastic bag, alternate single layers of salad leaves and paper towels. Repeat layers until paper towels surround all the leaves. Remove as much air as possible, close bag and place in the coldest part of the refrigerator (bottom). Salad will stay crisp and ready to eat for up to 1 week. Serve 1-2 ounces (1-2 cups) of salad greens per person.

Salad Lyonnaisse

This is an elegant salad with an easy bleu cheese dressing. Once you make this dressing, you will never buy bottled bleu cheese again.

6 servings

Salad

2   **cups fresh baby spinach**
1   **small head curly endive[1] (or chicory), torn into pieces**
1   **head butter lettuce[2], torn into bite-size pieces**
½   **bunch fresh parsley, stems removed**
1   **pint cherry tomatoes, cut in half**
1   **cup shredded Swiss cheese**
2   **hard-boiled eggs[3], finely chopped**

Easy Bleu Cheese Dressing

½   **cup bottled Italian dressing**
½   **cup crumbled bleu cheese**

1. Mix greens and parsley together with tomatoes.

2. Heat a nonstick skillet over medium-high heat. Spoon 1 tablespoon shredded Swiss in piles into the skillet. When the cheese turns a light golden color at the edges, about 1 minute and can be moved with a spatula, turn over and cook an additional 15 seconds. Remove from the skillet and set on a plate to cool. Reserve.

3. Mash bleu cheese into a small amount of Italian dressing. Stir bleu cheese mix into remaining dressing.

4. Toss dressing with salad greens and divide between salad plates. Top with chopped egg and cheese crisps. Serve immediately.

Diva Tips

[1-2] To wash and store **salad greens**, cut off the stem end of lettuce. Separate leaves and rinse thoroughly with cold water. Shake or spin dry to remove excess water. In a 2-gallon zip top plastic bag, alternate single layers of salad leaves and paper towels. Repeat layers until paper towels surround all the leaves. Remove as much air as possible, close bag and place in the coldest part of the refrigerator (bottom). Salad will stay crisp and ready to eat for up to 1 week. Serve 1-2 ounces (1-2 cups) of salad greens per person.

[3] To cook **hard-boiled eggs**, place eggs in a saucepan in a single layer and cover with cold water to come 1-inch above eggs. Bring to a boil, immediately cover; remove from heat and let sit 15 minutes. Remove from hot water and immerse in cold water to cool fast. Tap eggs all around to crack the shell; peel under cold running water. Eggs that are not too fresh, peel easier when cooked.

California Salad

A super-easy, basic salad that will please everyone!

6-8 servings

Salad

¼ pound **romaine lettuce**[1]
¼ pound **iceberg lettuce**[2]
½ pound **baby organic field greens**[3]
(or mesclun)
1 pint strawberries, sliced
1 cup sunflower seeds
2-3 green onions, sliced on the diagonal

Red Wine Vinaigrette

¼ cup red wine vinegar
½ teaspoon dry mustard
¼ cup sugar (or to taste)
salt and pepper to taste
¾ cup vegetable oil

1. Tear romaine and iceberg into bite-size pieces and place in a large salad bowl.

2. Toss with organic field greens being careful not to bruise tender baby lettuces.

3. Place strawberries, sunflower seeds, and onions in the center. Refrigerate until ready to serve.

4. Whisk together red wine vinegar, dry mustard, sugar, salt and pepper until sugar has dissolved. Slowly whisk oil in a fine stream to incorporate thoroughly (or use a blender).

5. When ready to serve, toss salad with enough of the vinaigrette to coat. Serve immediately.

Diva Tips

[1,2]To wash and store **salad greens**, cut off the stem end from romaine, red leaf, green leaf or iceberg lettuce. Separate leaves and rinse thoroughly with cold water. Shake or spin dry to remove excess water. Alternate single layers of salad leaves and paper towels in a 2-gallon zip top plastic bag. Repeat layers until paper towels surround all the leaves. Remove as much air as possible, close bag and place in the coldest part of the refrigerator (bottom). Salad will stay crisp and ready to eat for up to 1 week. Serve 1-2 ounces (1-2 cups) of salad greens per person.

[3]Baby **salad greens** or mesclun is a mix of baby greens usually in a wide range of colors, textures, and tastes. Handle carefully: like all babies they are very delicate. Because they are very perishable, purchase and store no more than one day ahead of serving.

Excessive Raspberry Salad

Excessive use of raspberries in this salad could lead to a penalty. It's overflowing with raspberries: from the raspberry jam to the raspberry vinegar to the fresh raspberries tossed in at the last minute.

6-8 servings

Raspberry Vinaigrette

¼ **cup seedless raspberry jam**[1]

¼ **cup raspberry vinegar**

¼ **cup sugar**

½ **teaspoon dry mustard powder**
   salt and pepper to taste

½ **cup vegetable oil**

Salad

1 **pound mixed salad greens**[2] **(any kind)**

1 **small red onion, sliced**

½ **pint fresh raspberries**[3]

1 **cup pistachio nuts**

1. Combine jam, vinegar, sugar and mustard powder in a blender, mixing thoroughly. Slowly add oil in a fine stream with motor running to incorporate thoroughly. (If you don't have a blender, melt the jam in the microwave or over low heat and whisk or briskly stir all ingredients together.) Taste and adjust seasonings with salt and pepper if desired.

2. Toss salad greens with a small amount of dressing.

3. Arrange greens on individual serving plates; add a few raspberries and onions.

4. Drizzle with vinaigrette; top with pistachios. Serve immediately.

Diva Tips

[1]**Jam or jelly** is a natural thickener in salad dressings that are slightly sweet, allowing for less oil. Substitute any seedless jam or jelly as desired.

[2]To wash and store **salad greens**, cut off the stem end from romaine, red leaf, green leaf or iceberg lettuce. Separate leaves and rinse thoroughly with cold water. Shake or spin dry to remove excess water. In a 2-gallon zip top plastic bag, alternate single layers of salad leaves and paper towels. Repeat layers until paper towels surround all the leaves. Remove as much air as possible, close bag and place in the coldest part of the refrigerator (bottom). Salad will stay crisp and ready to eat for up to 1 week. Serve 1-2 ounces (1-2 cups) of salad greens per person.

[3]Choose **raspberries** that have no visible decay or mold. Store in an airtight container in the refrigerator up to 3 days. Carefully rinse, just before serving.

Fresno Mandarin Salad

If you are afraid of the caramelized nuts in this recipe, omit the sugar and toss salad with just the toasted nuts, but you should expand your horizons and try this method one time. Caramelized nuts add such a delicious dimension to your salads. Come on! Be adventuresome. Where would this country be without explorers or risk-takers?

6-8 servings

Spicy Vinaigrette

⅓ cup white wine vinegar (or raspberry vinegar)

¼ cup sugar

½ teaspoon salt

¼ teaspoon freshly ground pepper

½ tablespoon dry parsley flakes

dash Tabasco sauce

½ cup vegetable oil

Salad

½ cup slivered almonds, toasted

3 tablespoons sugar

1 small head **romaine lettuce**[1] (½ pound), washed and torn into pieces

½ head iceberg **lettuce**[2] (½ pound), washed and torn into pieces

2 cans (11-ounces each) Mandarin oranges, drained

4 ribs celery, chopped

4 green onions, sliced

1. Stir first 6 ingredients of dressing together until sugar has dissolved (or use a blender). Add oil in a fine stream, stirring briskly until incorporated. Refrigerate until ready to use.

2. Place 3 tablespoons sugar in the bottom of a small, heavy skillet and heat over medium-high until sugar completely melts. As soon as sugar melts, remove from heat (caution: sugar burns easily) and stir almonds in to coat. Remove from the pan and pour on a lightly buttered piece of aluminum foil (or coat with nonstick cooking spray) to cool. When cool, break into small pieces.

3. Combine the remaining salad ingredients together and toss with just enough dressing to coat.

4. Divide among individual salad plates and top with almonds. Serve immediately.

Diva Tips

[1,2]To wash and store **salad greens**, cut off the stem end from romaine, red leaf, green leaf or iceberg lettuce. Separate leaves and rinse thoroughly with cold water. Shake or spin dry to remove excess water. In a 2-gallon zip top plastic bag, alternate single layers of salad leaves and paper towels. Repeat layers until paper towels surround all the leaves. Remove as much air as possible, close bag and place in the coldest part of the refrigerator (bottom). Salad will stay crisp and ready to eat for up to 1 week. Serve 1-2 ounces (1-2 cups) of salad greens per person.

Pear, Endive and Gorgonzola Salad

Pears, blue cheese and walnuts were made for each other.

6-8 servings

Pear Vinaigrette

2 **pears[1], soft-ripe (Bartlett or Bosc)**
1 **cup white wine vinegar**
¼ **cup honey**
½ **teaspoon Dijon mustard**
1 **teaspoon salt**
¼ **teaspoon pepper**
¼ **cup walnut oil[2]**

1. Peel, core and slice pears.

2. In a heavy saucepan, simmer pears with vinegar until liquid is reduced by half, about 15 minutes.

3. Transfer pear mixture to a blender and mix with honey, mustard, salt and pepper until smooth. With motor running, add oil in a very thin stream until mixture is emulsified. (Can be made up to 1 week ahead and stored in the refrigerator.)

Salad

¾ **pound romaine lettuce (medium bunch)**
4 **Belgian endive, sliced**
2 **pears, firm-ripe (red Comice, if available), peeled, cored and sliced**
½ **cup Gorgonzola or other good quality bleu cheese, crumbled**
1 **cup red seedless grapes[3], cut in half**
1 **cup walnuts, toasted and coarsely chopped**

1. Tear romaine into bite-size pieces.

2. Thoroughly rinse Belgian endive and drain; thinly slice crosswise and mix with romaine.

3. Toss salad with just enough vinaigrette to coat; divide between individual salad plates.

4. Arrange the pear slices on top; sprinkle with cheese, grapes and walnuts. Serve immediately.

Diva Tips

[1]To speed ripening of **pears**, wrap individually in paper and store in a paper bag at room temperature until they yield to gentle pressure at the stem end.

[2]Almond and **walnut flavored oils** should be stored in the refrigerator to slow oil from becoming rancid.

[3]Fresh **grapes** will cling to their stems if shaken gently. Grapes should be plump and firm and stems should be green and moist-looking. Grapes are covered by a thin layer of dust, dirt and pesticides. To clean, fill a large bowl with cold water and dissolve 1 teaspoon baking soda and 1 teaspoon Fruit Fresh (citrus acid). Let grapes sit in this water for a few minutes and then swish around. Rinse thoroughly. Drain on paper towels and allow to air dry. Clean, dry grapes will keep fresh for several days stored in an airtight container in the coldest part of the refrigerator.

Cloissoné Salad

A salad as delicious for the eyes as the palate: a beautiful arrangement of colors and flavors. This salad is slightly fussy because of the oranges and almonds. If you must, substitute canned, drained Mandarin oranges and omit the sugar to caramelize the almonds.

8 servings

Salad Dressing

¼ cup white wine vinegar
    (preferably Champagne vinegar)
¼ cup sugar
1 teaspoon dried parsley flakes
½ teaspoon salt
¼ teaspoon pepper
1 dash Tabasco sauce
½ cup vegetable oil
    reserved orange juice (from oranges
    below)

Salad

1 bag (10-ounces) fresh spinach
    (about 6 cups)
1 small head Romaine lettuce,
    thoroughly washed and torn into
    pieces
2 **oranges, sectioned[1]** (reserve juice)
1 pint strawberries, sliced
1 apple (Gala or Cortland), julienned
3 tablespoons sugar
½ cup slivered almonds, toasted
1 small red onion, thinly sliced
4 ounces **chèvre cheese[2]** (mild goat
    cheese), crumbled (optional)

1. Stir first 6 ingredients of salad dressing together in a small bowl (or mix in a blender). Add oil in a fine stream, stirring briskly until incorporated. Add reserved orange juice. Refrigerate dressing until serving time.

2. Mix greens together; top with orange sections and sliced strawberries. Toss apples with a little dressing to prevent browning; set aside.

3. Place sugar in the bottom of a small, heavy skillet and heat over medium-high until sugar completely melts. As soon as sugar melts, remove from heat (caution: sugar burns easily) and stir almonds in to coat. Remove from the pan and pour on a lightly buttered piece of aluminum foil (or coat with nonstick cooking spray) to cool. When cool, break into small pieces.

4. Toss salad with onions, apples and enough dressing to coat. Divide among individual serving plates. Top with cheese and almonds and serve immediately.

Diva Tips

[1]To **section an orange**, slice off the top and bottom. Stand the fruit on one of the cut ends. Following the contour of the fruit, slice off all the peel and white pith in thick strips. After all peel has been removed, cut along each side of the membrane and orange section while holding the orange over a bowl to catch the sections and any juice. When all sections have been removed, squeeze all the remaining juice from the membranes into the bowl. Discard membranes.

[2]**Chèvre cheese** is a deliciously tart cheese, ranging in textures from moist and creamy to dry and firm and can be located with the specialty cheeses. Wrap any leftover chèvre in plastic and store in the refrigerator up to 2 weeks.

Unorthodox Spinach Salad

A healthy salad filled with orange sections, avocados, and bacon and dressed with an extraordinary orange-cumin salad dressing.

6-8 servings

Salad

1 package (10-ounces) fresh spinach, torn into pieces
1 small head romaine lettuce, rinsed and torn into pieces
4 **oranges, sectioned**[1] (reserve juice) (or substitute canned Mandarin oranges)
1 small red onion, sliced
1 ripe Haas **avocado**[2], sliced
4 slices bacon, cooked crisp and crumbled

Orange-Cumin Dressing

reserved juice from oranges (4-5 tablespoons)
1 tablespoon freshly squeezed lemon juice
2 tablespoons white wine vinegar
¼ teaspoon ground cumin
¼ cup sugar
   salt and pepper to taste
½ cup vegetable oil

1. Toss greens together in a large salad bowl.

2. Top with oranges, onions, avocados, and bacon.

3. To make the dressing: stir orange and lemon juices, vinegar, cumin, sugar, salt and pepper together until sugar has dissolved. Add oil in a fine stream, stirring briskly until incorporated.

4. Toss salad with just enough dressing to coat. Serve immediately.

Diva Tips

[1]To **section an orange**, slice off the top and bottom. Stand the fruit on one of the cut ends; following the contour of the fruit, slice off all the peel and white pith in thick strips. After all peel has been removed, cut along each side of the membrane and orange section while holding the orange over a bowl to catch the sections and any juice. When all sections have been removed, squeeze all the remaining juice from the membranes into the bowl. Discard membranes.

[2]Buy **avocados** that are firm but yield to gentle pressure. If avocados are bright green, store on the countertop until they turn a brownish/black color. When ripe, store in the refrigerator up to 1 week. To peel, cut through the skin down to the pit from top to bottom. Twist the halves apart and remove pit by tapping it sharply with the blade of the knife. Twist the knife to release pit. Cut the flesh into a dice or slices while still in the skin with the tip of a knife. Scoop out the flesh with a spoon and gently separate with your fingers. The flesh of avocados can be stored in the freezer by mashing with 2 tablespoons lemon juice.

Warm Bacon Spinach Salad

I love spinach salads because they are healthy and delicious.

8 servings

Salad

½ **pound fresh spinach leaves**

½ **pound head red leaf lettuce**[1]

1 **package (8-ounces) mushrooms, sliced**

1 **small red onion, sliced**

4 **slices bacon, cooked and crumbled (reserving 1 tablespoon bacon drippings)**

½ **cup pecans, toasted**[2] **and chopped**

Warm Dressing

¼ **cup red wine vinegar**

2 **teaspoons freshly squeezed lemon juice**

1 **teaspoon Dijon mustard**

1 **tablespoon sugar**

¼ **teaspoon garlic powder**

salt and pepper to taste

¼ **cup extra virgin olive oil**

1 **tablespoon reserved bacon drippings**

1. Toss spinach, lettuce, mushrooms, onion and bacon together. Refrigerate until ready to serve.

2. Combine the first 6 dressing ingredients together, whisking until sugar has dissolved. Slowly whisk in oil.

3. When ready to serve, heat bacon drippings over medium heat. Slowly add dressing and heat through, stirring constantly.

4. Toss salad with just enough warm dressing to evenly coat.

5. Top with toasted pecans and serve immediately.

Diva Tips

[1]To wash and store **salad greens**, cut off the stem end from romaine, red leaf, green leaf or iceberg lettuce. Separate leaves and rinse thoroughly with cold water. Shake or spin dry to remove excess water. Alternate single layers of salad leaves and paper towels in a 2-gallon zip top plastic bag. Repeat layers until paper towels surround all the leaves. Remove as much air as possible, close bag and place in the coldest part of the refrigerator (bottom). Salad will stay crisp and ready to eat for up to 1 week.

Serve 1-2 ounces (1-2 cups) of salad greens per person.

[2]**Toasting nuts** adds crispness and intensifies the flavor. Spread in a single layer on a baking sheet or pan. Preheat oven to 350°; place pan in oven and bake 5-10 minutes, or until nuts release their aroma, being careful not to burn. A smaller portion of nuts will toast much quicker than a larger amount. Toast a larger amount than needed and freeze extras up to 1 year in a tightly sealed container. Four ounces of nuts equals about 1 cup.

Strawberry Spinach Salad with Caramelized Pecans

Have extra copies of this recipe available when you serve it to guests. Everyone loves this salad! Don't be afraid to make this salad because of the caramelized pecans. Just omit the 3 tablespoons sugar and top salad with plain toasted pecans.

4-6 servings

Poppyseed Dressing

⅓ **cup white wine vinegar**
⅓ **cup sugar**
1 **teaspoon dry mustard**
½ **teaspoon salt**
¾ **cup vegetable oil**
1 **tablespoon dry minced onions**
1 **tablespoon poppyseeds**[1]

Spinach Salad

1 **package (10-ounces) fresh spinach**
1 **pint fresh strawberries, sliced**
3 **tablespoons sugar**
1 **cup pecans, toasted**[2] **and coarsely chopped**

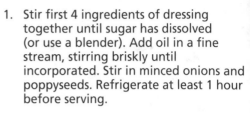

1. Stir first 4 ingredients of dressing together until sugar has dissolved (or use a blender). Add oil in a fine stream, stirring briskly until incorporated. Stir in minced onions and poppyseeds. Refrigerate at least 1 hour before serving.

2. In a large salad bowl, toss spinach with strawberries. Set aside.

3. Place 3 tablespoons sugar in the bottom of a small, heavy skillet and heat over medium-high until sugar completely melts. As soon as sugar melts, remove from heat (caution: sugar burns easily) and stir pecans in to coat. Remove from the pan and pour on a lightly buttered piece of aluminum foil (or coated with nonstick cooking spray) to cool. When cool, break into small pieces.

4. Toss spinach with enough salad dressing to coat.

5. Divide among individual serving plates and top with caramelized pecans.

Diva Tips

[1]**Poppyseeds** tend to go rancid very quickly. Store them in the refrigerator 6 months or freezer up to 1 year.

[2]**Toasting nuts** adds crispness and intensifies the flavor. Spread in a single layer on a baking sheet or pan. Preheat oven to 350°; place pan in oven and bake 5-10 minutes, or until nuts release their aroma, being careful not to burn. A smaller portion of nuts will toast much quicker than a larger amount. Toast a larger amount than needed and freeze extras up to 1 year in a tightly sealed container. Four ounces of nuts equals about 1 cup.

Mimosa Fruit Parfait

Serve this fruit salad in those martini glasses or wine flutes for a beautiful presentation. This alcohol version is for adults only, please. A non-alcoholic, kid-friendly version is included at the end of the recipe.

8 servings

- **2** cups **cantaloupe**[1] cubes
- **1** cup fresh pineapple chunks
- **1** cup red or black **grapes**[2], cut in half
- **2** kiwi, peeled and cubed
- **1** can (6-ounces) frozen orange juice concentrate, thawed
- **½** cup Grand Marnier (or other orange liquor)
- **8** fresh strawberries
- **½** pint fresh raspberries
- **1** small bottle (called a split or about 12 ounces) Champagne, chilled
- **8** sprigs of mint (optional)

1. Layer first 4 fruits in order given in martini glasses or wine flutes.

2. Mix orange juice concentrate and Grand Marnier. Drizzle over fruit.

3. Refrigerate until ready to serve.

4. When ready to serve, add 1 whole strawberry per glass and raspberries to fruit cups.

5. Fill glass with chilled Champagne. Garnish with mint sprigs if desired.

   (Note: For kid-friendly version, omit Grand Marnier and substitute Champagne with sparkling white grape juice (found in the juice aisle of the grocery store) or with chilled ginger ale.)

Diva Tips

[1]A ripe **cantaloupe** should have a sweet, melon aroma. Choose a melon with a soft stem end and raised netting with a yellow undertone. Avoid shriveled, green or rock-hard melons.

[2]Fresh **grapes** will cling to their stems if shaken gently. Grapes should be plump and firm and stems should be green/brown and moist-looking. Grapes are covered by a thin layer of dust, dirt and pesticides. To clean: fill a large bowl with cold water and dissolve 1 teaspoon baking soda and 1 teaspoon Fruit Fresh (citrus acid). Let grapes sit in this water for a few minutes and then swish around. Rinse thoroughly. Drain on paper towels and allow to air dry. Clean, dry grapes will keep fresh for several days stored in an airtight container in the coldest part of the refrigerator.

Heavenly Fruit Hash

Get your kids in the kitchen and give them the gift of learning how to cook. Any 6-year old can easily make this salad.

6 servings

1	can (20-ounces) pineapple chunks, drained
1	can (11-ounces) Mandarin oranges, drained
1	cup flaked coconut
1	cup mini **marshmallows**[1]
1	cup **sour cream**[2]
¼	cup maraschino cherry halves, drained

1. Mix all ingredients together and chill at least 1 hour (or overnight).

Diva Tips

[1]**Marshmallows** will keep fresh longer if stored in a tightly sealed plastic bag in the freezer.

[2]Draining off any accumulated liquid in **sour cream** makes the sour cream thicker and creamier.

New Waldorf Salad

This recipe is a new rendition of an old favorite using whipped cream instead of mayonnaise.

4 servings

½	cup heavy cream
¼	cup sugar
1	tablespoon Champagne vinegar (or white wine vinegar)
1	Gala apple, unpeeled, cored and diced
1	cup sliced celery
½	cup red grapes, cut in half
½	cup walnuts or pecans, toasted and roughly chopped

1. Mix cream, sugar and vinegar; whip until soft peaks form. Set aside.

2. Mix remaining ingredients together.

3. Toss with whipped cream. Chill and serve within 2 hours.

Ramen Crunch Slaw

I calculated that I have made this recipe about 120 times. Keep extra copies of the recipe handy because everyone will want one.

8-10 servings

Dressing

⅓ **cup white vinegar**

⅓ **cup sugar**

2 **packages (3-ounces each) beef-flavored ramen noodle packets (reserve noodles for slaw)**

1 **cup vegetable oil**

Slaw

½ **pound green cabbage, shredded**

½ **pound red cabbage, shredded**

2 **carrots, peeled and shredded**

1 **bunch green onions, chopped**

2 **packages (3-ounces each) reserved ramen noodles**

1 **cup sunflower seeds**

1 **cup slivered almonds, toasted[1]**

1. Dressing should be prepared ahead: stir vinegar, sugar, and contents of seasoning packets together until sugar is dissolved (or use a blender). Add oil in a fine stream, stirring briskly until incorporated. Allow to set in the refrigerator for a couple hours or overnight.

2. Mix cabbages, carrots and onions together.

3. Break up ramen noodles and add to slaw with sunflower seeds and almonds.

4. Toss with dressing.

5. For a beautiful presentation, line a clear salad bowl with the large outer-most leaves of the red cabbage (washed and dried). Spoon in slaw and serve.

Diva Tips

[1]**Toasting nuts** adds crispness and intensifies the flavor. Spread in a single layer on a baking sheet or pan. Preheat oven to 350°; place pan in oven and bake 5-10 minutes, or until nuts release their aroma, being careful not to burn. A smaller portion of nuts will toast much quicker than a larger amount. Toast a larger amount than needed and freeze extras up to 1 year in a tightly sealed container. Four ounces of nuts equals about 1 cup.

Cheese Tortellini Salad

6-8 servings

Salad

1 **package (8-ounces) frozen cheese tortellini**

1 **cup raisins or dried cranberries, steeped in boiling water 5 minutes and drained**

1 **cup chopped celery**

⅓ **cup diced red onion**

1 **Granny Smith apple, cored and diced**

½ **cup slivered almonds, toasted[1]**

Dressing

¼ **cup white wine vinegar**

1 **teaspoon Dijon mustard**

1 **clove garlic, crushed (½ teaspoon)**

¼ **teaspoon salt**

¼ **teaspoon sugar**

¼ **teaspoon pepper**

3 **tablespoons extra virgin olive oil**

2 **tablespoons vegetable oil**

½ **cup bleu cheese, crumbled**

1. Cook tortellini according to package directions.

2. Drain; mix with remaining salad ingredients.

3. Whisk together all dressing ingredients, mashing bleu cheese into dressing.

4. Toss with tortellini mixture. Refrigerate leftovers.

Diva Tips

[1]**Toasting nuts** adds crispness and intensifies the flavor. Spread in a single layer on a baking sheet or pan. Preheat oven to 350°; place pan in oven and bake 5-10 minutes, or until nuts release their aroma, being careful not to burn. A smaller portion of nuts will toast much quicker than a larger amount. Toast a larger amount than needed and freeze extras up to 1 year in a tightly sealed container. Four ounces of nuts equals about 1 cup.

Red Wine Vinaigrette

A basic salad dressing to use with any salad.

1 cup

¼ cup red wine vinegar
½ teaspoon dry mustard
¼ cup sugar (or to taste)
    salt and pepper to taste
¾ cup vegetable oil (preferably extra virgin olive oil)

1 Whisk together red wine vinegar, dry mustard, sugar, salt and pepper until sugar has dissolved. Whisk oil in a fine stream to incorporate (or you may use a blender).

2. When ready to serve, toss salad with enough of the vinaigrette to coat.

3. Store in the refrigerator up to 1 week.

House Dressing

This recipe is a good, basic vinaigrette to keep in the refrigerator at all times.

1½ cups

½ cup white or red wine vinegar
1 teaspoon salt (or to taste)
2 tablespoons **apple jelly**[1], melted over low heat
½ tablespoon sugar
½ teaspoon black pepper
1 tablespoon Dijon mustard
1 clove garlic, crushed (½ teaspoon)
1 cup vegetable oil

1. Whisk together the first 7 ingredients until sugar has dissolved. Add oil in a fine stream, stirring briskly until incorporated (or use a blender).

2. Store in the refrigerator up to 1 week.

Diva Tips

[1]**Jam or jelly** is a natural thickener in salad dressings that are slightly sweet, allowing for less oil. Substitute any seedless jam or jelly as desired.

Over-Stuffed Chicken Croissants

My famous chicken salad is loaded with crunch and great taste. Yum!

6-8 sandwiches

6-8 petite croissants
3 cups **cooked** diced **chicken**[1] breast
   (about 3 breasts)
1 cup chopped celery
1 cup mayonnaise
2 tablespoons sweet pickle relish
1 teaspoon lemon pepper
½ teaspoon salt (or to taste)
½ teaspoon black pepper
1 cup diced apple (1 medium apple)
1 cup **pecans, toasted**[2] and coarsely
   chopped

1. Split croissants in half lengthwise. Place on a baking sheet and toast in a 350° oven for 6-8 minutes. Remove from pan and cool on a wire rack.

2. Mix together the next 7 ingredients. (If mixture seems to dry add a more mayonnaise.)

3. When ready to serve, stir in apple and pecans.

4. Divide evenly among the croissants. Sandwiches can be refrigerated up to 2 hours.

Diva Tips

[1]To **cook chicken** for use in any recipe requiring cooked chicken, sprinkle lemon pepper (or season with salt and pepper) on chicken breasts (boneless or rib-in) and place inside a baking bag (smaller version of the kind used to bake turkeys at Thanksgiving) or tightly seal in aluminum foil. Put on a baking sheet in a 350° oven about 1 hour. Remove from oven and cool in the bag. Remove and chop chicken as recipe directs. Reserve any accumulated juices in the cooking bag by pouring into a container and storing in the refrigerator up to 2 days or 3 months in the freezer. These juices are "liquid gold". Use in any recipe that requires chicken broth or bouillon.

[2]**Toasting nuts** adds crispness and intensifies the flavor. Spread in a single layer on a baking sheet or pan. Preheat oven to 350°; place pan in oven and bake 5-10 minutes, or until nuts release their aroma, being careful not to burn. A smaller portion of nuts will toast much quicker than a larger amount. Toast a larger amount than needed and freeze extras up to 1 year in a tightly sealed container. Four ounces of nuts equals about 1 cup.

Roasted Chicken Pitas

A deliciously different kind of sandwich.

6 sandwiches

2 cups cooked, diced chicken breast (about 2 breasts)

1 medium **tomato**[1], diced

1 jar (2-ounces) chopped pimentos, drained

¼ cup finely chopped onion

¼ cup **sour cream**[2]

¼ cup mayonnaise

½ teaspoon lemon pepper

½ teaspoon salt (or to taste)

¼ teaspoon black pepper

½ tablespoon dry minced onion

1 cup shredded iceberg lettuce

6 red leaf lettuce leaves

3 pita breads, cut in half

1. Combine the first 10 ingredients together. (Can be made to this point and stored in the refrigerator for 1 day.)

2. When ready to serve, gently stir shredded lettuce into chicken salad mixture.

3. Place 1 red leaf lettuce in each pita pocket.

4. Stuff with chicken salad and serve immediately.

Diva Tips

[1]**Tomatoes** should be stored on your counter and not in the refrigerator. Cold temperature robs tomatoes of some of their flavor. Tomatoes will last for 3-5 days at room temperature.

[2]Draining off any accumulated liquid in **sour cream** carton makes the sour cream thicker and creamier.

Every Kitchen Diva should have:

—a youth she's content to leave behind

—and a past juicy enough that she's looking forward to retelling it in her old age.

Fruited Chicken Salad

Fruit meets chicken salad and they lived happily ever after.

Makes a ton or 12 cups

4 cups cooked, diced chicken breast
2 cups chopped celery
½ cup mayonnaise
½ cup sour cream
1 teaspoon lemon pepper
1 teaspoon salt (or to taste)
½ teaspoon black pepper
2 tablespoons freshly squeezed lemon juice
2 cups red **grapes**[1], sliced in half
1 can (10-ounces) pineapple tidbits, drained
1 cup finely chopped apple (1 apple)
1 cup grated carrot
1 cup slivered **almonds, toasted**[2]
shredded lettuce (optional)
bagel halves (optional)

1. Combine the first 8 ingredients together. (Can be made to this point and stored in the refrigerator for 1 day.)

2. When ready to serve, gently stir in remaining ingredients.

3. Serve on a bed of lettuce or on a toasted bagel half.

Diva Tips

[1]**Fresh grapes** will cling to their stems if shaken gently. Grapes should be plump and firm and stems should be green and moist-looking. Grapes are covered by a thin layer of dust, dirt and pesticides. To clean: fill a large bowl with cold water and dissolve 1 teaspoon baking soda and 1 teaspoon Fruit Fresh (citrus acid). Let grapes sit in this water for a few minutes and then swish around. Rinse thoroughly. Drain on paper towels and allow to air dry. Clean, dry grapes will keep fresh for several days stored in an airtight container in the coldest part of the refrigerator.

[2]**Toasting nuts** adds crispness and intensifies the flavor. Spread in a single layer on a baking sheet or pan. Preheat oven to 350°; place pan in oven and bake 5-10 minutes, or until nuts release their aroma, being careful not to burn. A smaller portion of nuts will toast much quicker than a larger amount. Toast a larger amount than needed and freeze extras up to 1 year in a tightly sealed container. Four ounces of nuts equals about 1 cup.

Grilled Veggie Quesadillas

No need to visit your local Mexican eatery to satisfy your craving for quesadillas any more. This vegetarian recipe makes a quick and easy lunch or supper.

4 servings

1   medium zucchini, sliced longwise, ½-inch thick

1   medium yellow squash, sliced longwise, ½-inch thick

1   red bell pepper, sliced in half

4   **portobella mushrooms**[1], brown gills removed

1   large Vidalia onion, sliced ½-inch thick

1   cup Italian salad dressing

4   tablespoons butter or margarine, divided

8   (8-inch) flour tortillas

2   cups (8-ounces) shredded Cheddar cheese

2   cups (8-ounces) shredded Monterey Jack cheese

prepared guacamole (optional)

pico de gallo[2] (optional)

sour cream (optional)

salsa (optional)

1. Marinate sliced vegetables in Italian salad dressing for at least 1 hour, keeping mushrooms separate.

2. Heat grill to high heat. Put veggies on grill (keep onion slices whole), lower temperature to medium-high and cook about 2-3 minutes per side until golden brown but crisp-tender (peppers may take a little longer). Baste with marinade while cooking if desired. (Or cook in a skillet over medium-high heat). Remove to a dish.

3. Slice mushrooms and peppers ½-inch thick.

4. Heat a (10-inch) nonstick skillet to medium-high temperature. Melt ½ tablespoon of butter in skillet.

5. Place 1 tortilla over butter; top with ½ cup Cheddar cheese, making sure cheese covers the entire tortilla.

6. Add a layer of veggies and top with an additional ½-cup Monterey Jack cheese.

7. Cover with another tortilla.

8. When the bottom tortilla is golden and cheese on the bottom has melted, carefully lift quesadilla out of the pan with a large spatula and melt another ½ tablespoon butter; turn quesadilla over and cook the second side until golden and cheese has melted.

9. Remove from pan and repeat with remaining tortillas and veggies.

10. Cut quesadillas into quarters and serve with your choice of guacamole, sour cream, pico de gallo, and/or salsa.

Diva Tips

[1]To remove brown gills from **portobellas**, scrape with a melon baller, spoon or knife.

[2]**Pico de gallo** is a combination of diced fresh tomatoes, diced onion, chopped jalapeño pepper, and fresh cilantro tossed with a squeeze of lime, a dash of extra virgin olive oil and seasoned with salt and pepper.

Grilled Chicken Focaccia

Purchase focaccia bread in your local supermarket or specialty bread store.

8 sandwiches

4   **boneless, skinless chicken breast halves**
4   **tablespoons butter, melted**
3   **tablespoons freshly squeezed lemon juice**
    dash of Tabasco sauce
4   **roasted red bell peppers[1], cut in half (or substitute canned roasted red peppers, thoroughly drained)**
8   **slices provolone cheese**
1   **loaf focaccia bread, cut into 8 squares**
4   **tablespoons honey mustard**
4   **tablespoons mayonnaise**
8   **leaves red leaf lettuce**
½   **red onion, sliced into 8 thin slices**
2   **large tomatoes[2], thinly sliced**

1. Pound chicken breast very thin and cut in half to make 8 pieces.

2. Mix butter, lemon juice and Tabasco to make a basting sauce.

3. Heat grill (or nonstick pan) to high heat. Baste chicken with sauce and grill or cook over high heat 4 minutes per side or until done.

4. Cover each piece of chicken with a slice of roasted pepper and cheese. Cook an additional minute to allow cheese to melt. Remove to a plate. Do not over cook chicken or it will become too dry.

5. To prepare sandwiches: cut focaccia squares in half lengthwise and grill cut-side down until toasty. Remove.

6. Mix mustard and mayonnaise; spread each focaccia half with ½ tablespoon of the mustard mixture.

7. Place one red leaf lettuce on grilled bread; top with cooked chicken. Top chicken with red onion and tomato slice. Cover with the other focaccia slice. Serve immediately.

Diva Tips

[1]To **roast fresh, red peppers,** heat grill to high. Place washed red bell peppers over high heat. Or place peppers on a foil-lined baking sheet and place under the broiler. As peppers blacken, rotate to cook on all sides. Remove and put in a tightly covered bowl for 30 minutes. Peel away blackened skin; remove seeds and membranes inside. Use as directed in recipe.

[2]Buy **tomatoes** which are firm, but yield to gentle pressure and are deep red. A ripe tomato should smell like a garden. Tomatoes should be stored on your counter and not in the refrigerator. Cold temperature robs tomatoes of some of their flavor. Tomatoes will last for 3-5 days at room temperature.

Stromboli

This sandwich is baked inside its own bread. Use frozen or refrigerated bread dough. I have bought dough at my favorite pizzeria to make these sandwiches. Or if you are adventurous, make you own bread dough.

8 servings

1 loaf (1-pound) frozen bread dough, thawed

1 tablespoon butter or margarine, melted

⅛ teaspoon garlic powder

⅛ teaspoon ground black pepper

¼ teaspoon Italian seasoning

2 tablespoons Parmesan cheese, finely grated

1 cup (4-ounces) coarsely shredded sharp provolone cheese

¼ pound sliced provolone cheese (6 slices)

3 ounces pepperoni, very thinly sliced (30-40 slices)

¼ pound sliced smoked ham (6 slices)

¼ pound hard salami (8 slices)

1 large egg white, lightly beaten

2 tablespoons **sesame seeds**[1]

1. Roll or flatten dough into a (15x10-inch) rectangle. Brush with the melted butter.

2. Sprinkle garlic, pepper, Italian seasoning and Parmesan cheese evenly over the butter. Layer remaining ingredients in order listed.

3. Roll up, beginning at the long end, into a cylinder shape. Pinch seam closed.

4. Place seam-side down on a lightly greased baking sheet. Brush with beaten egg white and sprinkle with sesame seeds. Let rise slightly, about 30 minutes.

5. Preheat oven to 375°. Bake 25-30 minutes or until golden brown. Remove from oven, cool and slice.

Diva Tips

[1]**Sesame seeds** and poppyseeds tend to go rancid very quickly. Store them in the refrigerator 6 months or freeze up to 1 year.

B.L.T. Rollups

Try something different for lunch or cut into smaller pieces for snack or hors d'oeuvres. Substitute any meat or cheese that suits your fancy.

16 half rolls

1 **package (8-ounces) cream cheese, softened**

2 **tablespoons mayonnaise**

2 **teaspoons dry ranch-style dressing mix**

¼ **cup minced green onions**

2 **tablespoons Parmesan cheese**

8 **(8-inch) tortillas**
  fresh spinach leaves

8 **deli smoked turkey slices**

16 **provolone cheese slices**

2 **large tomatoes[1], thinly sliced**

16 **slices bacon[2], crispy cooked**

1. Mix the first 5 ingredients together.

2. Divide cheese mixture evenly among the tortillas spreading over the top all the way to the ends.

3. Top each tortilla with spinach leaves leaving 2 inches at the bottom.

4. Top spinach with 1 turkey slice, 2 cheese slices, and 2 slices tomato. Place 2 strips of bacon, end to end in the center.

5. Roll up, jelly roll fashion. Secure with a toothpick if necessary.

6. Refrigerate up to 1 day ahead until ready to serve. Cut in half.

Diva Tips

[1]Buy **tomatoes** which are firm, but yield to gentle pressure and are deep red. A ripe tomato should smell like a garden. Tomatoes should be stored on your counter and not in the refrigerator. Cold temperature robs tomatoes of some of their flavor. Tomatoes will last for 3-5 days.

[2]If you only use **bacon** occasionally, separate into individual slices, wrap each piece in plastic wrap, and place wrapped pieces in a zip top freezer bag. When a recipe calls for a few slices of bacon, remove only as many as needed.

Caramel Sauce

1 quart

½ cup (1 stick) butter
   (margarine not recommended)
2 cups **brown sugar**[1]
1 cup light corn syrup
2 tablespoons water
1 can (14-ounces) sweetened condensed
   milk
1 teaspoon vanilla

1. Melt butter in a large saucepan over medium heat. Stir in brown sugar, corn syrup and water. Stir until sugar has completely dissolved into the butter mixture.

2. Add condensed milk and bring to a boil. Remove from heat and stir in vanilla. Cool and refrigerate.

3. To serve: heat in the microwave and serve over ice cream, desserts or with wedges of apples. Can be stored in the refrigerator up to 1 month (if it lasts that long!)

Diva Tips

[1]To store **brown sugar**, place opened bag of sugar in another plastic bag. Remove as much air as possible and tightly close. If sugar has hardened, soften by placing in a microwave-safe dish, covering tightly and microwave on high power for about 30 seconds. Generally, light-brown or dark-brown sugar can be interchanged for each other. When measuring, always lightly pack sugar in measuring cup.

Hot Fudge Sauce

I catch myself eating this sauce right out of the jar. Serve warm over ice cream or desserts.

1 quart

1 can (13-ounces) evaporated milk (or
   substitute 1⅔ cups heavy cream)
1 cup sugar
1 teaspoon vanilla
1 tablespoon butter or margarine
1 bag (12-ounces or 2 cups) semi-sweet
   chocolate chips

1. Pour milk into a large saucepan. Bring to a boil. Lower heat and add sugar; simmer until sugar has completed dissolved, stirring constantly.

2. Remove from heat and stir in vanilla and butter. Add chocolate chips, stirring until chocolate has melted.

3. Store in the refrigerator up to 2 months. To reheat: heat in the microwave at 30 second intervals or until heated through.

Butterscotch Fruit Dip

1½ cups

1 cup **sour cream**[1]
½ cup **brown sugar**[2]
½ teaspoon vanilla extract

1. Stir together all ingredients until sugar has dissolved.

2. Can be made up to 2 days ahead and refrigerated.

Diva Tips

[1]Drain off any accumulated liquid in **sour cream**; makes the sour cream thicker and creamier.

[2]To store **brown sugar**, place opened bag of sugar in another plastic bag. Remove as much air as possible and tightly close. If sugar has hardened, soften by placing in a microwave-safe dish, covering tightly and microwave on high power for about 30 seconds. Generally, light-brown or dark-brown sugar can be interchanged for each other. When measuring, always lightly pack sugar in measuring cup.

Piña Colada Fruit Dip

Serve as a fresh fruit dip

2 cups

1 package (8-ounces) **cream cheese**, softened
½ cup **sour cream**[1]
1 small can (8.5-ounces) **cream of coconut**[2]
2 tablespoons lemon juice
1 small package (3.4-ounces) instant vanilla pudding
1 can (8-ounces) crushed pineapple
½ cup flaked coconut

1. Beat cream cheese until light and smooth.

2. Add sour cream, cream of coconut and lemon juice; mix until well blended.

3. Stir in instant pudding until mixed.

4. Add crushed pineapple with its juice and coconut.

5. Can be made up to 2 days ahead and stored in the refrigerator.

Diva Tips

[1]Drain off any accumulated liquid in sour cream; makes the **sour cream** thicker and creamier.

[2]**Cream of coconut** can be found in the drink mixer section of the grocery store (a favorite brand of mine is Coco Lopez).

Raspberry Coulis

This fruit sauce is easy to make. To make other flavor fruit sauces, just substitute your favorite fruit, fruit liqueur and seedless jam.

1½ cups

1 package (10-ounces) frozen raspberries, thawed

¼ cup sugar

2 tablespoons **Framboise**[1] (or orange juice)

¼ cup seedless raspberry jam

1. Mash berries in a food processor, blender or with a fork.

2. Push solids through a sieve or strainer to remove seeds.

3. Add sugar and Framboise to the strained juice and thoroughly mix until sugar dissolves.

4. Melt jam in the microwave and stir into juice.

5. Pool coulis on dessert plates and place dessert in it.

6. Can be stored up to 1 week in the refrigerator.

Diva Tips

[1]**Framboise** is a raspberry liqueur. Small bottles (airline serving size—about 3 tablespoons) of liqueurs can be purchased at most liquor stores.

Bavarian Whipped Cream

This whipped topping can be made up to 1 day ahead. The pudding mix keeps the whipped cream from breaking down.

2 cups

1 cup heavy cream

2 tablespoons vanilla pudding mix

2 tablespoons powdered sugar

½ teaspoon vanilla extract

1. Beat all ingredients together in a mixing bowl until soft peaks are formed.

Lemon Curd

Use this topping, a favorite in the British Isles, on pound cake, gingerbread, scones or to fill tarts.

2 cups

2   large eggs, room temperature
3   large **egg yolks[1]**, room temperature
1   cup sugar
½   cup (1 stick) butter (margarine not recommended), softened
2   teaspoons lemon zest (1 lemon)
½   cup freshly squeezed lemon juice, strained (about 3 lemons)

1. In the top of a **double boiler[2]** combine eggs, egg yolks, and sugar, whisking to blend well.

2. Cook over simmering water, stirring frequently, until mixture thickens about 10 minutes.

3. Stir in butter, 1 tablespoons at a time, until each piece is incorporated into egg mixture.

4. Add zest and lemon juice. Continue cooking and stirring frequently until the mixture again thickens and coats the back of a spoon (do not allow mixture to boil).

5. Remove from heat and cool thoroughly. Mixture thickens as it cools.

6. Store up to 3 weeks in the refrigerator.

Diva Tips

[1]**Eggs separate** easier when cold. Break egg into a funnel or into your fingers over first bowl. The white will easily slip into the bowl and the yolk will remain in the funnel or your fingers (as long as it is not broken). Transfer white to a separate bowl and yolk to a third bowl. This keeps an accidentally broken yolk from contaminating the whites already separated. Whites with even a small amount of yolk will not beat up to soft peaks. Repeat with remaining eggs over the first bowl. Freeze leftover egg whites individually in an ice cube tray. When frozen remove from tray and place in a plastic bag. Thaw whites in the refrigerator when a recipe calls for egg whites.

[2]If you do not have a **double boiler**, you can easily make one by nestling a smaller saucepan in a larger one or use any heatproof bowl that will sit securely on top of a saucepan without touching the boiling water. The steam, generated by the boiling water, is used to cook the food.

Mocha Mousse

Use this mousse as a filling for your favorite chocolate cake. For chocolate mousse omit Kahlúa.

2 cups

1   cup heavy cream
1   teaspoon vanilla
3   tablespoons Kahlúa (or your favorite coffee-flavored liqueur or substitute strong coffee)
2   tablespoons instant chocolate pudding mix
¼   cup unsweetened cocoa powder
¼   cup powdered sugar

1. Mix cream, vanilla and Kahlúa in a mixing bowl.

2. Sift together remaining ingredients and whip into cream mixture until soft peaks form.

Zesty Horseradish Sauce

A traditional sauce for roast beef but also tastes great with seafood, turkey, or potatoes.

2 cups

1   cup sour cream
2   tablespoons Creole mustard
⅓   cup prepared **horseradish sauce**[1] (or to taste)
1   tablespoon freshly squeezed lemon juice
¼   cup heavy cream, whipped[2]

1. Stir sour cream, mustard, horseradish, and lemon juice together. (Can be prepared up to this point and refrigerated up to 3 days.)

2. Whip cream until soft peaks form. Fold whipped cream into horseradish mixture just before serving.

Diva Tips

[1]Prepared **horseradish** can be found in the dairy case of most grocery stores next to the kosher items. (Don't confuse with horseradish sauce next to the mayonnaise.) Or you can finely grate your own fresh, peeled horseradish root.

[2]Cream, bowl and beaters should be very cold before whipping. If you over **whip** cream (it separates into solids and liquids), gently fold in a few tablespoons of milk or more cream.

Guacamole

This is the best guacamole on the planet (well at least in the northern hemisphere). Serve it with chips, fajitas or any other dish that needs a little zing! This guacamole can actually be stored in the refrigerator up to a day without turning brown.

2 cups

3	medium Haas **avocados**[1]
2	large **tomatillos**[2], husked and finely chopped
2	cloves garlic, crushed (1 teaspoon)
¼	cup salsa
2	tablespoons sour cream
¼	cup finely chopped fresh cilantro
1	teaspoon ground cumin
3	green onions, finely chopped
2	tablespoons freshly squeezed lime juice
1	teaspoon salt, or to taste

1. Mash avocados and tomatillos with a fork or finely chop with a knife.

2. Stir in remaining ingredients. Taste and adjust seasonings, if needed.

3. Or mix all ingredients (except avocados) in a blender or food processor with gentle pulsing motions. Stir into mashed avocados. Refrigerate in an airtight container until ready to serve.

Diva Tips

[1]Buy **avocados** that are firm but yield to gentle pressure. If avocados are bright green, store on the countertop until they turn a brownish/black color. When ripe, store in the refrigerator up to 1 week. To peel, cut through the skin down to the pit from top to bottom. Twist the halves apart and remove pit by tapping it sharply with the blade of the knife. Twist the knife to release pit. Cut the flesh into a dice or slices while still in the skin with the tip of a knife. Scoop out the flesh with a spoon and gently separate with your fingers. The flesh of avocados can be stored in the freezer by mashing with 2 tablespoons lemon juice.

[2]**Tomatillos** look like small green tomatoes wrapped in a papery skin with a tart, lemony, herbal flavor. Most grocery stores carry them in the fresh produce department.

Pico de Gallo

This is a fresh salsa made with tomatoes and used to garnish Mexican dishes.

2½ cups

1	pound **tomatoes**[1], finely diced (2 cups)
½	cup finely chopped Vidalia onion
2	tablespoons chopped fresh cilantro
½	tablespoon chopped fresh **jalapeño pepper**[2]
2	teaspoons freshly squeezed lime juice
½	teaspoon salt or to taste
2	tablespoons vegetable oil (optional)

1. Gently stir all ingredients together.

Diva Tips

[1]**Tomatoes** should be stored on your counter and not in the refrigerator. Cold temperature robs tomatoes of some of their flavor.

[2]If possible wear rubber gloves when handling **hot peppers** and refrain from rubbing your eyes. Wash hands thoroughly to remove any juice that can burn your skin.

Cranberry Sauce

Quick and easy because the base of this cranberry recipe is canned cranberry sauce.

2½ cups

2	cups fresh cranberries
2	tablespoons apple cider vinegar
⅓	cup sugar
⅓	cup strawberry preserves
1	can (14-ounces) jellied cranberry sauce

1. Mix cranberries, vinegar and sugar in a large saucepan; cook over medium heat until cranberries "pop" and break down, stirring occasionally.

2. Stir in preserves and cook until heated through.

3. Stir in jellied cranberry sauce and heat until melted and mixed with cooked cranberries.

Peach Salsa

Delicious as a condiment when served with fish dishes or grilled pork. Equal amounts of mangos can be substituted for peaches.

2½ cups

1   **pound ripe fresh peaches, peeled and finely diced (2 cups)**

1   **small red bell pepper, finely diced**

½   **tablespoon chopped fresh jalapeño pepper[1]**

3   **tablespoons chopped fresh cilantro[2]**

1   **small red onion, finely chopped (½ cup)**

2   **tablespoons honey**

2   **tablespoons freshly squeezed lime juice**

½   **teaspoon salt or to taste**

1. Stir all ingredients together.
2. Can be made up to 1 day ahead and refrigerated.

Diva Tips

[1]If possible wear rubber gloves when handling **hot peppers** and refrain from rubbing your eyes. Wash hands thoroughly to remove any juice that can burn your skin.

[2]To store fresh herbs (parsley or **cilantro**), wash in plenty of cold water; drain on paper towels. Roll clean, damp herbs in dry paper towels and place in a tightly covered plastic container. Store 1-2 weeks in the coldest part of your refrigerator.

Dill Sauce for Fish

1¼ cups

1   **cup mayonnaise**

¼   **cup Dijon mustard**

2   **cloves garlic, crushed (1 teaspoon)**

1   **tablespoon minced fresh dill**

1   **tablespoon chopped fresh parsley**

1. Mix all ingredients together.
2. Can be refrigerated up to 2 days.

Hollandaise Sauce

Classic sauce served over Eggs Benedict or steamed vegetables.

1 cup

3 large **egg yolks**[1], room temperature

2 tablespoons water

dash cayenne pepper

½ cup (1 stick) butter (margarine not recommended), softened

1 teaspoon freshly squeezed lemon juice, strained

salt to taste

1. Place the egg yolks, water and pepper in the top of a **double boiler**[2]; whisk or stir briskly until foamy. Heat over simmering water (in a double boiler) while continuing whisking until thick and mixture leaves a trail on the surface when the whisk is lifted (or it coats the back of a spoon).

2. Gradually add the butter in 1-tablespoon pieces, thoroughly incorporating each piece before adding more.

3. Stir in lemon juice. Taste and add salt if needed.

4. Serve immediately or keep warm by leaving the sauce in the insert and covering the surface directly with plastic wrap. Place the insert over warm water. If sauce becomes too cold, it will set. Warm it by placing over hot water. If it becomes too hot, it will separate. To bring back together stir in a chip of ice or a few drops of ice water.

Diva Tips

[1]**Eggs separate** easier when cold. Break egg into a funnel or into your fingers over first bowl. The white will easily slip into the bowl and the yolk will remain in the funnel or your fingers (as long as it is not broken). Transfer white to a separate bowl and yolk to a third bowl. This keeps an accidentally broken yolk from contaminating the whites already separated. Whites with even a small amount of yolk will not beat up to soft peaks. Repeat with remaining eggs over the first bowl. Freeze leftover egg whites individually in an ice cube tray. When frozen remove from tray and place in a plastic bag. Thaw whites in the refrigerator when a recipe calls for egg whites.

[2]If you do not have a **double boiler**, make one by nestling a smaller saucepan in a larger one or use any heatproof bowl that will sit securely on top of a saucepan without touching the boiling water. The steam, generated by the boiling water, cooks the food.

Cheddar Cheese Sauce

Use this sauce on omelets, or as a garnish for steamed fresh vegetables.

¾ cup

1   tablespoon butter or margarine
1   tablespoon all-purpose flour
½   cup milk or half-and-half
1   tablespoon dry sherry
⅛   teaspoon salt
**   dash pepper**
½   cup shredded Cheddar cheese
2   tablespoons Parmesan cheese

1. Melt butter in a saucepan over medium heat. Add flour, mixing with a spoon or whisk until smooth. Cook 1-2 minutes, stirring constantly (don't let it brown).

2. Add milk a little at a time, stirring to keep smooth. Continue until all the milk has been added. Cook over medium heat, stirring, until sauce begins to thicken. Stir in sherry.

3. Taste and adjust seasonings with salt and pepper.

4. Remove from heat and stir in cheeses until melted. Serve hot.

Meat Marinade

My sister-in-law, Diane Zornow, shared this recipe with me years ago. I use it to marinate flank steak or London Broil meat.

¾ cup

¼   cup vegetable oil
¼   cup soy sauce (or Dale's steak seasoning[1])
¼   cup red wine vinegar
2   tablespoons catsup
½   teaspoon onion salt
¼   teaspoon garlic powder
¼   teaspoon pepper

1. Mix all ingredients together and marinate meat 1-2 days in the refrigerator in a zip top plastic bag.

Diva Tips

[1]**Dale's steak seasoning** is found in the grocery aisle with the Worcestershire and barbecue sauces.

Madeira Mushroom Sauce

This sauce is delicious over any grilled or roasted meat.

1½ cups

4   tablespoons butter or margarine
1   pound assorted fresh **mushrooms**[1]
    (white button, cremini, shiitake or
    portobella), thinly sliced
⅓   cup **Madeira**[2]
1   can (10-ounces) condensed beef broth
    (or chicken broth)
1½ cups heavy cream
1   teaspoon Worcestershire sauce
    salt and pepper to taste

1. Melt butter in a heavy saucepan over
   medium-high heat. Add mushrooms
   and cook until softened. Remove
   mushrooms from pan.

2. Stir in Madeira and beef broth in the
   same saucepan; bring to a boil and
   reduce by half.

3. Add cream and continue cooking until
   reduced by half again.

4. Stir in Worcestershire sauce. Add
   mushrooms back to sauce. Taste and
   adjust seasonings with salt and pepper
   if needed.

5. Can be made up to 2 days ahead and
   stored in the refrigerator. Reheat
   without boiling before serving.

Diva Tips

[1]Never immerse **mushrooms** in
water; they will absorb liquid like
a sponge. The best way to clean
mushrooms is to wipe with a
damp paper towel. Store
mushrooms in a paper bag in the
refrigerator.

[2]**Madeira** is a sweet, fortified white
wine that leaves a rich taste after
the alcohol has been cooked off. It
blends deliciously with most meats
without being too sweet.

French Reduction Sauce

Most fine French sauces are simply a reduction of wines and stocks.

1½ cups

1   can (14-ounces) low-sodium chicken or beef broth (or stock)
1   cup dry white **wine**[1] or Champagne (red wine if using beef broth)
¼   cup (4 tablespoons) butter (margarine not recommended), softened

1.   Bring broth to boil over medium heat; reduce by half.

2.   Add white wine and reduce again by half.

3.   Stir in butter, 1 tablespoon at a time until sauce is smooth.

4.   Add any additional flavors as desired: juice of 1 lemon; chopped fresh herbs (basil, thyme, or tarragon).

     (Note: Water loss from excessive evaporation can cause the sauce to separate; stir in 1 tablespoon water to bring back together, if necessary.)

Diva Tips

[1]Cook with an inexpensive **wine** that you would drink. Cooking wine found in the vinegar section of the grocery store is poor quality and high in sodium.

Breads,
Breakfasts
and Beverages

Breads, Breakfasts and Beverages

Breads

Breakfasts

Beverages

Beer Muffins

Who would've guessed that a lowly cold beer could render such an easy, delicious bread? For variety, add 1 cup of any shredded cheese and serve with soup.

24 muffins

4   cups biscuit baking mix
5   tablespoons sugar
1   can (12-ounces) cold beer (any kind)

1. Preheat oven to 350°.

2. Stir baking mix and sugar together.

3. Add cold beer and stir just until mix is moistened.

4. Spoon into greased (2 inch) muffin cups and bake 18-20 minutes or until golden brown.

5. Remove from oven and tip each muffin on its side in the muffin cups to keep warm without getting soggy bottoms

Creamed Cornbread

18 medium muffins

2   cups self-rising cornmeal mix
1   large egg, lightly beaten
1   cup milk
½   cup sour cream
¼   cup (½ stick) butter or margarine, melted
1   can (8-ounces) creamed corn
¼   cup finely chopped green bell pepper
1   can (4-ounces) chopped green chilies
½   cup (2-ounces) shredded Cheddar cheese

1. Preheat oven to 375°.

2. Measure all ingredients into a large mixing bowl; mix together just until moistened.

3. Divide evenly among greased medium (2-inch) muffin cups.

4. Bake 18-22 minutes or until puffed and golden brown. Remove from oven and tip each muffin on its side in the muffin cups to keep warm without getting soggy bottoms.

> Love and live life deeply and passionately: it is the only way to a complete life.

Pizza Bread

My sons, Alex and Chris, have loved this bread since they first tasted it and can consume one whole loaf before it even reaches the table. It is delicious as a snack by itself, or served with spaghetti, soup or a salad.

6 servings

1 (1-pound) frozen **bread dough**[1], thawed according to package directions

1 tablespoon butter, melted

⅛ teaspoon garlic powder

⅛ teaspoon black pepper

¼ teaspoon Italian herb seasoning

2 tablespoons Parmesan cheese

3 ounces pepperoni, sliced paper thin

1 cup (4-ounces) shredded sharp provolone cheese

1. Preheat oven to 350°.

2. Press or roll dough to a (12x8-inch) rectangle.

3. Spread butter over the surface of the dough. Sprinkle with garlic powder, pepper, Italian herb seasoning, and Parmesan cheese.

4. Place pepperoni in a single layer over the crust to cover the entire surface. Spread provolone cheese over pepperoni.

5. Beginning at the narrow end, roll dough into a cylinder. Pinch seam closed.

6. Place on a lightly greased baking sheet and bake 25-30 minutes or until golden.

7. Remove from oven and cool slightly before cutting into 2-inch pieces.

Diva Tips

[1]Sometimes I visit my local pizzeria and buy fresh pizza **dough** to use in this recipe.

Dinner Popovers

Allow plenty of time for this bread to bake: 35-40 minutes. Resist the temptation to open the oven door while they are baking so they will rise properly. Besides being a wow! dinner bread, popovers may be split open and filled with scrambled eggs, chicken salad or dessert puddings.

12 servings

3   large eggs[1]
1½ cups milk
½   teaspoon salt
1½ cups all-purpose flour[2]
     (do not use self-rising)
¼   cup shredded Cheddar cheese
     (optional)

1. Preheat oven to 450°.

2. Generously grease 12 medium muffin cups or popover pans.

3. Beat eggs lightly in a medium bowl; add milk and salt. Stir in flour with a whisk or fork just until smooth (do not over beat). Add cheese if desired.

4. Fill prepared cups ¾'s full.

5. Bake 25 minutes. Decrease oven temperature to 325° and bake an additional 10-15 minutes or until a deep golden brown.

6. Immediately remove from the pan and serve hot.

Diva Tips

[1]All ingredients for baking should be room temperature. To warm **eggs**, put unbroken eggs in their shells into a bowl with hot tap water and let sit for a few minutes while assembling other ingredients. Dry the shells and proceed with recipe.

[2]Instead of sifting, stir **flour** with a spoon in the storage container until light and separated. Spoon into a graduated, dry-ingredient measuring cup (nesting cups) and level off with a knife or straight edge (never pack down).

Hearth Bread

I love versatile breads and this one can be used with Italian foods, soups or as a lunch all by itself. Warning! It is highly addictive.

6-8 servings

1   loaf French bread
½   cup (1 stick) butter or margarine, softened
1   clove **garlic, crushed**[1] (½ teaspoon)
½   cup (2-ounces) grated Cheddar cheese
¼   cup Parmesan cheese
     salt and pepper to taste
⅛   teaspoon cayenne pepper (optional)

1. Preheat oven to 450°.

2. Cut bread lengthwise in half.

3. Combine remaining ingredients and spread on cut sides of bread.

4. Place bread cheese side up on a baking sheet. Broil 5 minutes or until cheese is melted.

Diva Tips

[1] To **crush garlic**, peel off papery skin by whacking clove with the side of a knife; paper should slip right off. Place the clove between two sheets of plastic wrap and smash with a meat pounder or the bottom of a heavy pan until pulverized. Scrape garlic off plastic wrap and use in recipe as directed.

Every Kitchen Diva should have:

—8 matching plates

—wine glasses with stems

—and her own special recipe that will make her guests feel honored.

Granny's Biscuits

My Aunt Kathleen Martin never measures any ingredients to make these biscuits. She can tell by the "feel" of the dough if it is mixed right. Of course, she has only practiced many, many years!

8-10 biscuits

2 cups **self-rising flour**[1]
¼ cup **shortening**
½ cup **heavy cream**
½ cup **buttermilk**[2]
   extra flour for rolling biscuits

1. Preheat oven to 425°.

2. Cut shortening into flour with a pastry blender or rub between your fingers until crumbly.

3. Add cream and buttermilk, stirring just until flour mixture is moistened (dough will be very wet).

4. With a spoon, break off about a (2-inch) piece of dough. With generously floured hands, roll into a ball and place on a lightly greased baking sheet. Flatten with the palm of your hand to about a ¾-inch thickness.

5. Repeat with remaining dough. Bake 10-14 minutes until golden brown.

Diva Tips

[1]To make **self-rising flour**, add 1 teaspoon baking powder and ¼ teaspoon salt to every cup of flour; mixing thoroughly.

[2]No **buttermilk**? To make a good substitute, stir 1½-teaspoons vinegar into enough milk to measure ½ cup and let sit for 5 minutes.

Not-Your-Usual Cheese Rolls

Don't be afraid of working with yeast. This recipe is an easy one for beginners.

12 rolls

1 envelope (2¼ teaspoons) **dry yeast**[1]
2 cups all-purpose flour, divided
1 jar (5-ounces) process cheese spread
   (like Cheez Whiz®)
½ cup water
¼ cup shortening
2 tablespoons sugar
½ teaspoon salt
1 large egg
1 **egg white**[2], beaten until frothy
   (for brushing the tops)
   sesame seeds[3]

1. Combine yeast and 1-cup flour in a medium mixing bowl; set aside.

2. Combine cheese, water, shortening, sugar and salt in a small saucepan.

3. Heat over low heat to 105°-115°, stirring constantly.

4. Add warm cheese mixture and egg to flour and yeast mixture. Beat ½ minute at low speed of an electric mixer, scraping the sides of the bowl. Beat 3 minutes at high speed.

5. Stir in remaining cup of flour.

6. Turn dough onto a lightly floured surface; knead 1-2 minutes.

7. Divide and shape the dough into 12 pieces. Place each ball in well-greased muffin cups.

8. Cover and let rise in a warm place free from drafts for 1-2 hours or until doubled in size.

9. Carefully brush with beaten egg white and sprinkle with sesame seeds. Bake in a preheated oven 15-18 minutes or until golden brown. Remove from oven and tip each muffin on its side in the muffin cups to keep warm without getting soggy bottoms.

Diva Tips

[1]To extend the shelf life of **dry yeast** up to 6 months past the expiration date, store unopened packages in the freezer.

[2]Add a dash of salt to left over **egg** yolks and store in the freezer (1 month) or refrigerator (1 day).

Use in custards or add to scrambled eggs.

[3]**Sesame seeds** tend to go rancid very quickly. Store them in the refrigerator 6 months or freezer up to 1 year.

Irish Soda Bread

My good friend, Mary Ellen Urbanowicz, introduced me to this delicious bread when we were neighbors in Memphis. I miss sitting in her kitchen, sipping hot tea and eating warm bread.

8-10 servings

3	cups all-purpose flour
½	teaspoon baking soda
½	teaspoon salt
1	cup sugar
¼	teaspoon nutmeg
6	tablespoons butter or margarine
½	cup raisins
1	tablespoon **caraway seeds**[1]
1	large egg, beaten
1	cup **buttermilk**[2]
1	tablespoon butter or margarine, melted (for brushing the top)
1	tablespoon sugar (for the top)

1. Preheat oven to 350°.

2. In a large bowl, combine all the dry ingredients, mixing well; stir in the raisins and caraway seeds.

3. Cut the butter into flour mixture with a pastry blender or rub between your fingers until crumbly.

4. Mix egg with buttermilk.

5. Gradually stir into flour mixture just until dry ingredients are moistened.

6. Turn dough out onto a lightly floured surface and bring together into a smooth ball.

7. Pat dough into a greased (9-inch) round cake pan (or coat with a non-stick cooking spray). Score the top of the loaf with a very sharp knife; brush the top with melted butter and sprinkle with sugar.

8. Bake 40-45 minutes until golden brown or until a toothpick inserted in the center comes out clean. Cool in pan for 5 minutes; loosen edges with a knife. Remove from pan and let cool on a wire rack. Cut into wedges.

Diva Tips

[1]All **seeds** tend to go rancid very quickly. Store them in the refrigerator 6 months or freezer up to 1 year.

[2]No **buttermilk**? To make a good substitute, stir 1-tablespoon vinegar into enough milk to measure 1 cup and let sit 5 minutes.

Banana Tea Bread

This tea bread is delicious even though it is low in fat.

1 (9-inch) loaf

2½ cups all-purpose flour
1   cup sugar
3½ teaspoons baking powder
1   teaspoon salt
3   tablespoons vegetable oil
¾   cup milk
1   large egg
1   cup mashed ripe banana (2-3 medium)
1   cup **nuts, toasted¹** and finely chopped

1. Preheat oven to 350°.

2. Measure all ingredients into a large mixing bowl. Mix on medium speed of an electric mixer about ½ minute, scraping sides of pan.

3. Spread mixture into a greased and floured (9-inch) loaf pan (or coat with a nonstick cooking spray).

4. Bake 55-65 minutes until center is puffed and wooden toothpick inserted in the center comes out clean.

5. Let rest in pan 5 minutes. Remove from pan and cool completely before slicing. Store leftovers in the refrigerator.

Diva Tips

¹Toasting nuts adds crispness and intensifies the flavor. Spread in a single layer on a baking sheet or pan. Preheat oven to 350°; place pan in oven and bake 5-10 minutes, or until nuts release their aroma, being careful not to burn. A smaller portion of nuts will toast much quicker than a larger amount. Toast a larger amount than needed and freeze extras up to 1 year in a tightly sealed container. Four ounces of nuts equals about 1 cup.

Pumpkin Bread

When you smell this bread baking, Fall can't be too far away.

1 (9-inch) loaf

1½ cups sugar
1¾ cups all-purpose flour
¼ teaspoon **baking powder**[1]
¾ teaspoon salt
½ teaspoon cloves
½ teaspoon nutmeg
1 teaspoon cinnamon
½ cup vegetable oil
2 large eggs
1 cup canned pumpkin
½ cup water
½ cup raisins
½ cup chopped dates
1 cup **nuts, toasted**[2] and finely chopped

1. Preheat oven to 350°.

2. Measure all ingredients into a large mixing bowl. Mix together until all ingredients are moistened.

3. Pour into a greased and floured (9-inch) loaf pan (or coat with a nonstick cooking spray).

4. Bake 1- 1½ hours or until center is puffed and wooden toothpick inserted in the center comes out clean.

5. Let rest in pan 5 minutes. Remove from pan and cool completely on a wire rack before slicing. Store leftovers in the refrigerator.

Diva Tips

[1]**Baking powder** still active? To test, drop ½ teaspoon into a glass of warm water; if it fizzes it is o.k. to use. Always measure and level off. Never put a wet spoon into the container; it will deactivate the whole can.

[2]**Toasting nuts** adds crispness and intensifies the flavor. Spread in a single layer on a baking sheet or pan. Preheat oven to 350°; place pan in oven and bake 5-10 minutes, or until nuts release their aroma, being careful not to burn. A smaller portion of nuts will toast much quicker than a larger amount. Toast a larger amount than needed and freeze extras up to 1 year in a tightly sealed container. Four ounces of nuts equals about 1 cup.

Carrot Zucchini Bread

This bread is delicious to serve for breakfast when you're on the run or with a relaxing cup of tea in the afternoon.

2 (9-inch) loaves

3	**large eggs**
½	**cup vegetable oil**
½	**cup applesauce**
2	**cups sugar**
1	**tablespoon vanilla extract**
2	**cups grated zucchini (2 medium)**
1	**cup grated carrot (2 medium)**
3¼	cups all-purpose flour
1	teaspoon baking soda
1	tablespoon cinnamon
¼	teaspoon **nutmeg**[1]
1	teaspoon salt
1	cup **walnuts, toasted**[2] and chopped

1. Preheat oven to 350°.

2. Lightly butter 2 (9x5x2-inch) loaf pans or one (10-inch) Bundt pan (or coat with a nonstick cooking spray).

3. Beat eggs; add oil, applesauce, sugar, vanilla, zucchini and carrot. Set aside.

4. Stir dry ingredients together and blend into liquid mixture. Stir in walnuts.

5. Divide evenly between the pans.

6. Bake loaf pans 1 hour (Bundt pan: 1 hour and 10 minutes) or until the center is puffed and a wooden toothpick inserted in the center comes out clean.

7. Remove from oven and cool 5 minutes in the pans. Carefully remove from pan and cool completely before slicing. Store leftovers in the refrigerator.

Diva Tips

[1]Freshly grated **nutmeg** has a superior flavor over ground nutmeg found in a can or jar. Whole nutmegs can be located in most spice sections. Use a very fine grater or a small nutmeg grater for best results. Whole nutmegs can be kept indefinitely in a jar in a cool, dark place.

[2]**Toasting nuts** adds crispness and intensifies the flavor. Spread in a single layer on a baking sheet or pan. Preheat oven to 350°; place pan in oven and bake 5-10 minutes, or until nuts release their aroma, being careful not to burn. A smaller portion of nuts will toast much quicker than a larger amount. Toast a larger amount than needed and freeze extras up to 1 year in a tightly sealed container. Four ounces of nuts equals about 1 cup.

Morning Glory Muffins

A glorious and delicious way to get extra servings of fruits and vegetables in your diet at breakfast or snack time.

24 muffins

2	**cups all-purpose flour**
2	**teaspoons baking powder**
½	**teaspoon baking soda**
½	**teaspoon salt**
2	**teaspoons cinnamon**
3	**large eggs**
1	**cup sugar**
½	**cup oil**
½	**cup applesauce**
2	**teaspoons vanilla extract**
2	**cups grated carrots (about 2 large or 4 medium)**
1	**large apple, peeled, cored, and finely chopped (1 cup)**
½	**cup raisins**
½	**cup pecans, toasted[1] and finely chopped[2]**
½	**cup sweetened coconut**

1. Preheat oven to 375°.

2. Lightly grease 24 medium (2-inch) muffin cups (or coat with a nonstick cooking spray or line with cupcake papers).

3. In a large bowl, mix flour, baking powder, soda, salt and cinnamon. Set aside.

4. In a separate bowl, beat the eggs, sugar, oil, applesauce and vanilla together. Add carrots, apple, raisins, pecans and coconut, stirring until well combined. Add the flour mixture and stir just until blended. Do not over mix.

5. Spoon batter into prepared muffin pan.

6. Bake 15-20 minutes until the tops are golden and spring back when lightly pressed. Cool 5 minutes in the pan. Remove from pan and cool on a wire rack. Store in the refrigerator or freeze up to 3 months.

Diva Tips

[1]**Toasting nuts** adds crispness and intensifies the flavor. Spread in a single layer on a baking sheet or pan. Preheat oven to 350°; place pan in oven and bake 5-10 minutes, or until nuts release their aroma, being careful not to burn. A smaller portion of nuts will toast much quicker than a larger amount. Toast a larger amount than needed and freeze extras up to 1 year in a tightly sealed container. Four ounces of nuts equals about 1 cup.

[2]To **chop nuts**, place ½ to 1 cup nuts in a plastic bag and smash with a meat pounder on a hard surface. Turn bag over and repeat on the other side. Smashing takes a fraction of the time chopping or slicing does.

Ham Breakfast Sandwich

Looking for something different for breakfast or snack? Try these raisin bread sandwiches.

6 servings

4   tablespoons (2-ounces) cream cheese, softened (can use low-fat if desired)
4   teaspoons apricot jam
2   teaspoons low fat yogurt or sour cream
6   slices raisin bread
3   slices deli ham
1   Granny Smith apple, cored and sliced into 3 rings

1. Combine cream cheese, apricot preserves, and yogurt.
2. Evenly divide among the 6 slices of bread, spreading on one side.
3. Top 3 slices of bread with ham and apple slice.
4. Cover with remaining bread slices. Cut into triangles and serve.

Kiss My Grits

Like fried foods, grits are synonymous with the South. Not content to leave well enough alone, we have dressed them up with shrimp and dressed them down with cheese. But, no thank you ma'am, I prefer mine plain with a big ole pat of butter. Eat up, ya'll.

6-8 servings

1   cup water
1   can (14-ounces) low-sodium chicken broth
¼   teaspoon salt
1   cup quick-cooking grits
1   cup half-and-half
½   pound uncooked **shrimp**[1], peeled and deveined (optional)
1   cup (4-ounces) shredded Cheddar cheese

1. Bring water, broth and salt to a boil.
2. Slowly stir grits into boiling liquid. Reduce heat and cook 3 minutes, stirring occasionally.
3. Add half-and-half and bring back to a boil, stirring constantly. Remove from heat and cover. (Add shrimp at this point, remove from heat and let sit 10-15 minutes).
4. When ready to serve, heat through. Remove from heat and stir in cheese until all melted. If too thick, stir in more half-and-half to desired consistency.

Diva Tips

[1]**Shrimp** are very perishable and must be eaten within 24 hours of purchasing. When buying shrimp, it should have no odor. Keep shrimp in a plastic bag surrounded by ice packs in the refrigerator. May be kept frozen up to 2 months. The best method for freezing is to completely submerge shrimp in water and freeze. Thaw in the refrigerator or under cold running water.

Homefries

This recipe gives equal time to potatoes for breakfast for all my friends up north.

4 servings

4 large potatoes (2 pounds), peeled and cut into ½-inch cubes

6 slices **bacon**[1,2], fried and crumbled, reserving drippings

3 tablespoons butter or margarine, divided

½ onion, chopped (½ cup)

½ red bell pepper, chopped
   salt and pepper, to taste
   sour cream, for garnish

1. Cover potatoes with cold water in a medium saucepan. Season with salt if desired. Bring to a boil, lower the heat and simmer just until potatoes are barely fork-tender, about 5-6 minutes. Drain thoroughly and set aside.

2. Heat 1-tablespoon bacon drippings and 1-tablespoon butter in a large skillet over medium heat. Add the onion and pepper and cook until onion is golden about 8-10 minutes. Remove onion and pepper and set aside.

3. To the same skillet, heat remaining bacon drippings and butter over medium heat. Add the well-drained potatoes in a single layer and season with salt and pepper to taste.

4. Cook without disturbing until golden brown on the underside, about 5-7 minutes. Turn potatoes over with a large spatula and continue cooking until potatoes are well browned all over.

5. Gently stir in the onions, peppers and crispy bacon and heat through. Serve immediately.

6. Top with a dollop of sour cream if desired.

Diva Tips

[1] If you only use **bacon** occasionally, separate into individual slices, wrap each piece in plastic wrap, and place wrapped pieces in a zip top freezer bag. When a recipe calls for a few slices of bacon, remove only as many as needed.

[2] To cook **bacon**, remove desired number of slices from package in one piece. Chop or cut through all slices into small pieces with kitchen scissors or a knife. Fry over medium-high heat, separating pieces as they cook. Cook until crisp and golden brown.

Cheese and Sausage Polenta

Polenta is to Italians what grits are to Southerners. Fancy restaurants serve polenta as a side dish and charge and exorbitant fee for it even though it's just ground corn. This recipe makes a delicious side dish for brunch. Or impress your friends by serving it at your next dinner party.

8 servings

1   can (14-ounces) chicken broth
⅔   cup yellow cornmeal
1   pound breakfast sausage
1   clove **garlic, crushed**[1] (½ teaspoon)
½   teaspoon salt
⅛   teaspoon pepper
½   cup half-and-half
1   cup (4-ounces) shredded Cheddar cheese
2   tablespoons butter or margarine, melted
2   large eggs, lightly beaten
1   can (4-ounces) chopped green chilies

1. Preheat oven to 350°.

2. Bring chicken broth to a boil. Slowly add cornmeal, stirring constantly to prevent lumps.

3. Reduce heat; simmer 5-8 minutes, stirring occasionally. Remove from heat, cover and let stand 5 minutes.

4. Meanwhile, brown sausage, breaking apart into small pieces. Drain off fat. Add garlic, salt and pepper; cook an additional minute. Remove from heat.

5. Blend cornmeal mixture with half-and-half with a mixer or blender.

6. Mix cornmeal mixture with sausage, stirring until well mixed. Add remaining ingredients.

7. Pour mixture into a well-greased (9-inch) square baking dish. Bake 30-40 minutes until center is set.

8. Remove from pan and cut into 4 squares and each square into 2 triangles.

9. If desired, coat the bottom of a skillet with additional butter or margarine; lightly brown triangles on both sides. Serve hot.

Diva Tips

[1]To **crush garlic,** peel off papery skin by whacking clove with the side of a knife; paper should slip right off. Place the clove between two sheets of plastic wrap and smash with a meat pounder or the bottom of a heavy pan until pulverized. Scrape garlic off plastic wrap and use in recipe as directed.

Buttermilk Waffles

If we are not eating pancakes for weekend breakfasts, my husband, Jim, and I enjoy waffles. This recipe also makes a fun Sunday night supper.

16 (4-Inch) waffles

2   large **eggs, separated**[1]
1   cup **buttermilk**[2]
1   cup heavy cream
2   cups all-purpose flour
3   teaspoons baking powder
½   teaspoon baking soda
1   tablespoon sugar

1. Heat waffle iron.
2. Beat egg yolks; add buttermilk and cream.
3. Mix dry ingredients together and add to egg mixture; stir just until smooth.
4. Beat egg whites until stiff but not dry.
5. Fold whites into batter.
6. Spoon batter onto waffle iron; cook according to manufacturers instructions.
7. Transfer to rack in a 250° oven to keep warm for a short time.

Diva Tips

[1]**Eggs separate** easier when cold. Break egg into a funnel or into your fingers over first bowl. The white will easily slip into the bowl and the yolk will remain in the funnel or your fingers (as long as it is not broken). Transfer white to a separate bowl and yolk to a third bowl. This keeps an accidentally broken yolk from contaminating the whites already separated. Whites with even a small amount of yolk will not beat up to soft peaks. Repeat with remaining eggs over the first bowl.

[2]No **buttermilk**? To make a good substitute, stir 1-tablespoon vinegar into enough milk to measure 1 cup.

Lighter-Than-Air-Pancakes

I could make these pancakes in my sleep. My husband, Jim, loves pancakes and we treat ourselves almost every weekend. Forget the pancake mix; these are better, lighter and just as easy.

10-12 (4-inch) pancakes

2	large eggs
2	cups **buttermilk**[1]
1	tablespoon sugar
2	tablespoons vegetable oil
2	cups **self-rising flour**[2]

1. Beat the eggs in a medium bowl; stir in buttermilk, sugar and oil.

2. Add flour and stir just until flour is moistened.

3. Preheat a nonstick griddle over medium-high heat. Wipe griddle generously with vegetable oil. Be sure griddle is very hot to begin cooking. Griddle is ready when drops of water "dance" on the surface.

4. Spoon or pour ¼-⅓ cup batter onto griddle. When pancakes are golden on the underside and bubbles have risen to the surface, turn over and cook an additional 1-2 minutes until golden on the other side. (Do not turn pancake more than once or mash down as it cooks or pancakes will become tough).

5. Remove to a wire rack or stack on serving plates. Repeat until all pancakes are cooked.

6. Pancakes can be kept warm in a low oven for a short time.

7. For pancake varieties, fold in 1 cup fresh or well-drained blueberries to the batter or sprinkle each pancake with a few chocolate chips after spooning batter onto the griddle.

Diva Tips

[1]No **buttermilk?** To make a good substitute, stir 1-tablespoon vinegar into enough milk to measure 1 cup and let sit 5 minutes.

[2]To make **self-rising flour**, add 1 teaspoon baking powder, ½ teaspoon baking soda and ¼ teaspoon salt to every cup of flour; mixing thoroughly.

Bananas Foster Pancakes

Mardi Gras for breakfast. Who needs a trip to the Big Easy when you can make this dish reminiscent of that famous New Orleans' restaurant?

10-12 (4-inch) pancakes

¼ cup (½ stick) butter or margarine
4 (slightly green, under ripe) bananas, sliced ½-inch thick
½ cup maple syrup
½ cup **pecans, toasted**[1] and **chopped**[2]
1 batch Lighter-Than-Air-Pancakes
½ cup heavy cream, (optional)

1. Melt butter in a large nonstick skillet. Add bananas and stir until golden, but not mushy, 2-3 minutes. Add brown sugar and stir until melted. Add maple syrup and heat through.

2. Spoon bananas over pancakes and sprinkle with pecans.

3. Whip cream until soft peaks form. Top pancakes with whipped cream, if desired. Serve immediately.

Diva Tips

[1]**Toasting nuts** adds crispness and intensifies the flavor. Spread in a single layer on a baking sheet or pan. Preheat oven to 350°; place pan in oven and bake 5-10 minutes, or until nuts release their aroma, being careful not to burn. A smaller portion of nuts will toast much quicker than a larger amount. Toast a larger amount than needed and freeze extras up to 1 year in a tightly sealed container. Four ounces of nuts equals about 1 cup.

[2]**To chop nuts**, place ½ to 1 cup nuts in a plastic bag and smash with a meat pounder on a hard surface. Turn bag over and repeat on the other side. Smashing takes a fraction of the time chopping or slicing does.

Blintzes

12 blintzes

1 cup all-purpose flour
1½ teaspoons **baking powder**[1]
½ teaspoon salt
2 large eggs
1¼ cups milk
3 tablespoons butter or margarine, melted
1 cup ricotta cheese
1 package (3-ounces) cream cheese, softened
½ teaspoon salt
2 tablespoons butter or margarine
warm maple syrup (optional)
sliced strawberries (optional)
sour cream (optional)

1. Combine the first 6 ingredients in the container of an electric blender and process until smooth. Or beat with a mixer.

2. Let mixture stand 30 minutes-1 hour (makes crêpes more tender).

3. In a hot, well-buttered (6 or 8-inch) nonstick skillet (or crêpe pan), pour 3 tablespoons batter, swirling pan to distribute the batter evenly in the bottom of the pan. Cook until the top of the crêpe appears dry and the bottom is golden brown. Carefully remove from pan and repeat with remaining batter, greasing the bottom of the pan for every crêpe. (Crêpes can be made to this point, separated with wax paper and frozen for use later).

4. In a mixing bowl, blend the two cheeses and salt. Divide cheese mixture evenly among the crêpes, spooning mix across the center of the cooked-side of the crêpe.

5. Fold the two opposite edges over the cheese and roll into a cylinder shape, totally encasing the cheese.

6. Melt the remaining butter in a large skillet; add the blintzes, seam-side down, and brown on all sides.

7. Remove to a serving dish and add any optional topping desired.

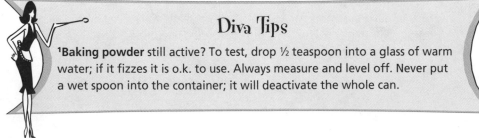

Diva Tips

[1]Baking powder still active? To test, drop ½ teaspoon into a glass of warm water; if it fizzes it is o.k. to use. Always measure and level off. Never put a wet spoon into the container; it will deactivate the whole can.

Blintz Puff

Dress up those blintzes in a casserole.

6-8 servings

4 large eggs
1⅓ cups sour cream
3 tablespoons butter or margarine,
   melted
1 teaspoon vanilla
1 tablespoon all-purpose flour
1 batch blintzes (12)
1 package (10-ounces) frozen
   strawberries with juice, thawed
¼ cup maple syrup
1 pint fresh strawberries¹, sliced

1. Preheat oven to 350°.

2. Beat eggs until light; add sour cream and mix together until light and fluffy.

3. Add butter, vanilla and flour, stirring until well blended.

4. Place blintzes, seam-side down, in a buttered (9x11-inch) baking dish (or coated with a nonstick cooking spray).

5. Pour sour cream mixture over blintzes.

6. Bake 45 minutes-1 hour or until puffed and golden.

7. While puff is baking, make strawberry syrup by placing thawed strawberries with the juice and maple syrup in a blender, mixing until liquefied. Toss with fresh strawberries.

8. Spoon blintz puff onto serving dishes and top with strawberries.

Diva Tips

¹Buy **strawberries** that are shiny and deep red with no visible decay or moldy spots. Green cap (leaves) should be flat. To store, leave in original container and enclose tightly in a plastic bag, removing as much air as possible. Place in the coldest part of your refrigerator (back, bottom shelf). If bought fresh, will keep for several days to a week. Wash strawberries only right before using and before removing the cap under running cold water. Never submerge berries in water: they absorb water like a sponge. Storing damp berries hastens decay.

Supreme Baked French Toast

What a great idea to make French toast ahead and bake it in the morning.

4-6 servings

¼ **cup (½ stick) butter or margarine, softened**

1 **French baguette, cut into 1-inch slices (or use Challah bread or croissants)**

6 **large eggs**

1½ **cups milk**

1½ **cups half-and-half**

¼ **cup sugar**

1 **teaspoon vanilla**

⅛ **teaspoon nutmeg[1]**

⅛ **teaspoon cinnamon**
   warm maple syrup

1. Spread the butter all over the inside of a (9-inch) square baking dish.

2. Fill the dish with bread slices to fill to the top.

3. Mix eggs, milk, half-and-half, sugar, vanilla, nutmeg, and cinnamon. Pour over bread slices. Cover and refrigerate overnight.

4. In the morning preheat oven to 350°.

5. Bake uncovered until puffed and golden 40-45 minutes.

6. Let stand 5 minutes before cutting and serving.

Diva Tips

[1]Freshly grated **nutmeg** has a superior flavor over ground nutmeg found in a can or jar. Whole nutmegs can be located in most spice sections. Use a very fine grater or a small nutmeg grater for best results. Whole nutmegs can be kept indefinitely in a jar in a cool, dark place.

Strawberry Stuffed French Toast

6-8 servings

1 package (8-ounces) cream cheese, softened
1 teaspoon vanilla extract
2 tablespoons strawberry jam
¼ cup chopped fresh **strawberries**[1]
½ cup **pecans, toasted**[2] and chopped
1 pound loaf French bread, cut into ½-inch slices
6 large eggs
1 cup half-and-half
½ teaspoon vanilla extract
⅛ teaspoon nutmeg
1 package (10-ounces) frozen strawberries with juice, thawed
¼ cup maple syrup
1 pint fresh strawberries, sliced

1. Combine cream cheese, vanilla, jam, strawberries and nuts. Spread 1½ tablespoons filling on one piece of bread. Top with second bread. Repeat with remaining cream cheese and bread.
2. Beat eggs until light; add half-and-half, vanilla and nutmeg. Dip "sandwiches" into egg mixture coating both sides.
3. Put on a baking sheet until all bread is dipped. Pour any remaining egg mixture over bread and let sit 15 minutes to absorb liquids. (To make the night before: cover dipped bread with plastic wrap and refrigerate.)
4. Lightly butter hot griddle; cook bread on both sides until golden brown.
5. Place on a buttered, foil-lined baking sheet in a single layer. Keep hot in a warm oven until ready to serve.
6. Make strawberry syrup by placing thawed strawberries with the juice and maple syrup in a blender and mixing until liquefied. Toss with fresh strawberries. Serve with toast.

Diva Tips

[1]Buy **strawberries** that are shiny and deep red with no visible decay or moldy spots. Green cap (leaves) should be flat. To store, leave in original container and enclose tightly in a plastic bag, removing as much air as possible. Place in the coldest part of your refrigerator (back, bottom shelf). If bought fresh, will keep for several days to a week. Wash strawberries only right before using and before removing the cap under running cold water. Never submerge berries in water: they absorb water like a sponge.

Storing damp berries hastens decay.

[2]**Toasting nuts** adds crispness and intensifies the flavor. Spread in a single layer on a baking sheet or pan. Preheat oven to 350°; place pan in oven and bake 5-10 minutes, or until nuts release their aroma, being careful not to burn. A smaller portion of nuts will toast much quicker than a larger amount. Toast a larger amount than needed and freeze extras up to 1 year in a tightly sealed container. Four ounces of nuts equals about 1 cup.

Breakfast Strata

When guests arrive for the weekend, turn your home into a Bed-and-Breakfast with this dish. Make it the night before and bake it in the morning. I always make it for holiday breakfasts: it's a great make ahead recipe.

6-8 servings

6   **slices white bread, crusts removed**

1   **package (1-pound) breakfast sausage, cooked, crumbled and drained**

2   **cups (8-ounces) shredded Cheddar cheese**

6   **large eggs, beaten**

2   **cups milk or half-and-half**

1   **teaspoon salt**

⅛   **teaspoon pepper**

1. Cut bread into cubes and place in the bottom of a buttered (9x13-inch) baking dish.

2. Layer sausage and cheese over bread.

3. Mix eggs with milk, salt and pepper. Carefully pour over sausage and cheese.

4. Cover and refrigerate overnight or let sit 1 hour for bread to absorb liquids.

5. Bake uncovered at 350° 45 minutes - 1 hour or until puffed in the center. Cut into squares and serve hot.

A Kitchen Diva is a gourmet with brains and moxie.

Artichoke Frittata

A frittata is an Italian omelet. Unlike its cousin, it is not folded but cut into wedges.

6-8 servings

1½ tablespoons vegetable oil (preferably extra virgin olive oil), divided

½ cup chopped green onions

5 large eggs

2 tablespoons sour cream

1 can (14-ounces) artichoke heart quarters, drained and chopped

1 small jar (2-ounces) diced pimentos

½ cup (2-ounces) grated Swiss cheese

2 tablespoons Parmesan cheese

1 tablespoon **chopped fresh parsley**[1-2] (optional)

1 teaspoon salt

   pepper to taste

1. Heat 1 tablespoon oil in a large nonstick skillet over medium heat; cook onions until tender. Remove from pan and set aside.

2. Beat eggs with sour cream until light and fluffy. Stir in onions and remaining ingredients.

3. Heat ½ tablespoon oil in the same skillet onions were cooked.

4. Pour in egg mixture. Cook 4-5 minutes until bottom is lightly browned and edges are set.

5. Slide frittata out of the pan onto a flat plate.

6. Place skillet over frittata and invert back into pan, uncooked side down. Cook an additional 2-3 minutes or until center is set. (Time will depend upon size of skillet). Slide onto a serving plate; cut into wedges and serve hot.

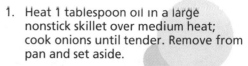

Diva Tips

[1]To **chop fresh herbs**, roll herbs into a tight bundle and finely chop crosswise with a sharp knife. Or snip with kitchen scissors.

[2]To **store fresh herbs** (parsley or cilantro), wash in plenty of cold water; drain on paper towels. Roll clean, damp herbs in dry paper towels and place in a tightly covered plastic container. Store 1-2 weeks in the coldest part of your refrigerator.

Omelet Soufflé

This omelet is baked in the oven.

2-4 servings

1	**tablespoon butter or margarine**
2	**tablespoons chopped onion**
1	**cup thinly sliced mushrooms**
4	**large eggs, separated[1]**
1	**tablespoon sour cream**
1	**tablespoon all-purpose flour**
	salt and pepper to taste
½	**cup (2-ounces) grated sharp Cheddar cheese**
½	**cup finely diced ham**
½	**cup diced tomatoes**
2	**tablespoons butter or margarine**

1. Preheat oven to 375°.

2. Melt the butter in a (10-inch) nonstick, ovenproof skillet over medium-high heat. Cook the onion until softened. Add the mushrooms and cook until tender and the liquid is absorbed. Remove the onions and mushrooms from skillet and set aside.

3. In a large bowl, beat the egg yolks with the sour cream; add the flour, salt and pepper. Stir in the onions, mushrooms, cheese, ham and tomatoes.

4. In a separate bowl, beat the egg whites to stiff peaks but not dry. **Fold[2]** into egg yolk mixture.

5. Over medium-high heat, melt 2 tablespoons butter in the same nonstick skillet, coating the entire pan.

6. Pour the egg mixture into the hot skillet, spreading it evenly.

7. Bake in the oven 7-9 minutes or until puffed and cooked through. Remove from the oven and flip onto a serving dish. Cut into wedges and serve hot.

Diva Tips

[1]Eggs separate easier when cold. Break egg into a funnel or into your fingers over first bowl. The white will easily slip into the bowl and the yolk will remain in the funnel or your fingers (as long as it is not broken). Transfer white to a separate bowl and yolk to a third bowl. This keeps an accidentally broken yolk from contaminating the whites already separated. Whites with even a small amount of yolk will not beat up to soft peaks. Repeat with remaining eggs over the first bowl.

[2]To fold ingredients together, insert large rubber spatula in the center of the mix; drag it across the bottom and then up the sides, rotating spatula and bringing some of the bottom of the mix to the top. Keep repeating this movement while turning the bowl to mix from all sides.

Veggie Quiche

Serve this delicious quiche for brunch, lunch or as an easy supper.

6 servings

- 2 slices white bread, crusts removed and cut into pieces
- ½ cup milk
- 2 slices **bacon¹**
- 1 cup sliced mushrooms
- 3 tablespoons butter or margarine
- 1 medium onion, finely chopped (¾ cup)
- 2 cloves garlic, crushed (1 teaspoon)
- 1 package (10-ounces) frozen broccoli cuts, thawed
- 1 package (3-ounces) cream cheese, softened
- 3 large eggs, room temperature
  dash hot sauce
- 1 teaspoon salt
- ¼ teaspoon pepper
- 2 large Roma **tomatoes²**, seeded and diced
- 1 cup shredded Swiss or Cheddar cheese
- 1 (9-inch) deep-dish pie crust
- 6 asparagus spears

1. Preheat oven to 350°.

2. Mix bread and milk; set aside.

3. Cook bacon until crisp. Crumble and set aside.

4. Cook mushrooms in bacon drippings until softened. Remove mushrooms and set aside.

5. Melt butter in the same skillet. Add onion and garlic and cook over medium heat until softened.

6. Remove onions from skillet and add to mushrooms.

7. Put broccoli in pan and cook over low heat, just long enough to completely dry broccoli, being careful not to scorch. Remove from pan and finely chop.

8. In a large mixing bowl, beat the cream cheese until smooth and light. Add the eggs, one at a time, mixing well. Mix in bread soaked in milk along with any liquid. Add the onions and garlic with their butter. Stir in dry broccoli and a dash of hot sauce. Mix thoroughly and season with salt and pepper. Stir in tomatoes, and cheese.

9. Pour mixture into pie crust. Place asparagus evenly in a spoke pattern extending from the center.

10. Bake 45-55 minutes or until center is set. (May need to cover with aluminum foil the last 15 minutes of baking to prevent excess browning.)

11. Remove from oven and cool slightly before cutting.

Diva Tips

¹If you only use **bacon** occasionally, separate into individual slices, wrap each piece in plastic wrap, and place wrapped pieces in a zip top freezer bag and store in the freezer up to 3 months. When a recipe calls for a few slices of bacon, remove only as many as needed.

²Buy **tomatoes** which are firm, but yield to gentle pressure and are deep red. A ripe tomato should smell like a garden. Tomatoes should be stored on your counter and not in the refrigerator. Cold temperature robs tomatoes of some of their flavor. Tomatoes will last for 3-5 days at room temperature.

Wild Rice Quiche

I have made this quiche so many times, I could make it in my sleep. Keep copies of the recipe handy. Even real men have asked for the recipe, but I promised not to divulge their names.

6 servings

2 slices **bacon**[1]
⅓ cup wild rice
¾ cup water
¼ cup chopped green onions (about 4)
½ cup chopped mushrooms
1 cup shredded Swiss cheese
½ cup diced **tomatoes**[2]
½ teaspoon salt
¼ teaspoon pepper
⅛ teaspoon cayenne pepper (optional)
3 large eggs
¾ cup heavy cream
1 (9-inch) deep-dish pie crust

1. Preheat oven to 375°.

2. Cook bacon until crisp; remove, reserving 2-tablespoon drippings. Crumble bacon and set aside.

3. Combine rice, water and 1 tablespoon bacon drippings in a heavy saucepan; bring to a boil; cover, reduce heat, and simmer 1 hour until water has been absorbed.

4. Heat remaining 1 tablespoon bacon drippings in a medium skillet over medium-high heat and sauté onions and mushrooms just until softened.

5. Combine, cooked rice, bacon, onions, mushrooms, cheese, tomatoes and spices. Set aside.

6. Beat eggs in a large mixing bowl until frothy; add cream. Beat at high speed 2 minutes. Stir in rice mixture. Spoon mixture into pie crust.

7. Bake 45-60 minutes or until center is set. (May need to cover with aluminum foil the last 15 minutes of baking to prevent excess browning.)

8. Remove from oven and cool slightly before cutting.

Diva Tips

[1]If you only use **bacon** occasionally, separate into individual slices, wrap each piece in plastic wrap, and place wrapped pieces in a zip top freezer bag and store in the freezer up to 3 months. When a recipe calls for a few slices of bacon, remove only as many as needed. To cook bacon, remove desired number of slices from package in one piece. Chop or cut through all slices into small pieces with kitchen scissors or a knife. Fry over medium-high heat, separating pieces as they cook. Cook until crisp and golden brown.

[2]**Tomatoes** should be stored on your counter and not in the refrigerator. Cold temperature robs tomatoes of some of their flavor. Tomatoes will last for 3-5 days.

California Mudslide

Be sure to nominate a designated driver if you plan to serve these drinks. This recipe makes 2 adult chocolate milkshakes.

2 servings

- **3 tablespoons vodka**
- **3 tablespoons Kahlúa (or any coffee liqueur)**
- **½ cup heavy cream**
- **1 scoop chocolate ice cream**
- **2 tablespoons chocolate syrup**
- **1 cup crushed ice**
- **1 teaspoon unsweetened cocoa powder**
- **1 teaspoon sugar**
- **whipped cream (optional)**
- **2 maraschino cherries with stems (optional)**

1. Measure vodka, Kahlúa and cream in a blender; add ice cream, chocolate syrup, and crushed ice. Process until smooth.

2. Mix cocoa and sugar on a saucer. Lightly wet the rim of a martini glass and dip rim in cocoa mixture.

3. Pour drink into glass; top with whipped cream and cherry. Serve immediately.

Texas Tornado

Beware: this drink is lethal. It is smooth like a milkshake and goes down just as easy.

2 servings

- **2 tablespoons crème de cocoa**
- **¼ cup Kahlúa (or other coffee liqueur)**
- **¼ cup rum or vodka**
- **½ cup heavy cream or half-and-half**
- **2 scoops vanilla ice cream**
- **½ teaspoon vanilla extract**
- **1 cup crushed ice**
- **whipped cream, for garnish**

1. Measure crème de cocoa, Kahlúa, rum and cream into a blender; add ice cream, vanilla and ice. Process until smooth.

2. Pour into a glass and top with whipped cream if desired.

> A Kitchen Diva is the high, holy priestess of the temple she calls kitchen.

Creamsicle

Not to be confused with your childhood frozen ice cream on a stick, but it does tastes just as good.

4 servings

¼ **cup Grand Marnier (or other orange liqueur)**
½ **cup vodka**
½ **cup heavy cream**
1 **can (6-ounces) frozen orange juice concentrate, unthawed and undiluted**
3 **scoops vanilla ice cream**
2 **cups crushed ice**
   orange slices (optional, for garnish)

1. Measure Grand Marnier, vodka, cream and frozen orange juice concentrate into a blender; add ice cream and ice. Process until smooth.

2. Serve in wine or high ball glasses with an orange slice for garnish, if desired.

Frozen Fuzzi Navel

Take a thermos of this drink to your own private beach; relax, read a book and enjoy the crashing of the waves on the sand.

20 servings

½ **cup sugar**
2 **cups water, divided**
1 **can (12-ounces) frozen lemonade concentrate, unthawed and undiluted**
1 **can (12-ounces) frozen orange juice concentrate, unthawed and undiluted**
2½ **cups peach schnapps**
1 **cup rum or vodka**
1 **package (10-ounces) frozen peaches, thawed**
   7-up or ginger ale, chilled
   fresh peach slices, strawberries, and orange slices (optional, for garnish)

1. Add sugar to 1 cup of water; bring to a boil, stirring until sugar has completely dissolved. Remove from heat and cool completely. Add remaining cup of water.

2. Pour sugar water into a blender and add lemonade mix, orange juice concentrate, peach schnapps and rum.

3. Add peaches and process until smooth (may need to process in batches).

4. Pour into a container and freeze.

5. To serve: scoop out ¼ cup into a glass and stir in chilled 7-up. Garnish with a skewer of a peach slice, strawberry and orange slice.

Cosmo Girl Cocktail

2 servings

1 cup crushed ice
¼ cup vodka
2 tablespoons cranberry juice (or more to taste)
1 tablespoon lime juice (or more to taste)
2 thin strips lime peel

1. Place the ice, vodka, and juices in a cocktail shaker. Shake to mix well.

2. Serve in martini glasses, garnished with lime peel.

Blue Velvet Margarita

Reminiscent of the blue skies over Acapulco.

2 margaritas

1 cup crushed ice
¼ cup tequila
1 tablespoon triple sec or Grand Marnier
¼ cup blue Curaceau
¼ cup freshly squeezed lime juice
1 teaspoon super fine sugar
2 lime wedges
  salt

1. Mix ice, tequila, triple sec, Curaceau, lime juice and sugar in a blender. Process until smooth.

2. Rub the rim of a margarita glass with the lime wedge and dip into salt. Pour mixture into glasses and serve immediately with a lime wedge.

Mexican Sunset

A stunning presentation. Sit with this drink outside on a warm summer night and watch the sun fall behind the horizon.

1 serving

1 cup chilled orange juice
  crushed ice
1½ tablespoons grenadine

1. Pour the orange juice in a tall glass over crushed ice.

2. Add grenadine and allow to settle on the bottom.

Recovery Bloody Mary

Delicious and spicy. A great eye-opener for the morning after or served with any brunch.

8 servings

2 cans (12-ounces each) tomato juice, chilled

2 cans (12-ounces each) V-8 vegetable juice, chilled

1 cup vodka

1 teaspoon lemon pepper

1 teaspoon celery salt

½ teaspoon garlic pepper (or substitute ¼ teaspoon garlic powder and ¼ teaspoon pepper)

1½ teaspoons **prepared horseradish**[1]

1 teaspoon Worcestershire sauce

1 teaspoon **chili oil**[2]

lime slices

celery stalks, for garnish

celery salt (optional glass garnish)

chili powder (optional glass garnish)

1. Mix first 9 ingredients thoroughly. Chill.

2. Serve over ice with a lime slice and a celery stalk for stirring.

3. If you are adventuresome, wet the rim of your glass with a lime slice and dip in a mixture of celery salt and chili powder before pouring drink into the glass.

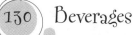

Diva Tips

[1]**Prepared horseradish** can be found in the dairy case of most grocery stores next to the kosher items. (Don't confuse with horseradish sauce next to the mayonnaise.) Or you can finely grate your own fresh, peeled horseradish root.

[2]**Chili oil** can be located in the Oriental section of the grocery store.

White Sangría

Allow this mixture to sit for several hours or overnight to reach its full taste potential.

6 servings

¼ cup brandy

¼ cup triple sec or Grand Marnier (or any orange liqueur)

½ cup orange juice

⅓ cup **superfine sugar**[1]

1 bottle (750 ml or 3 cups) dry white wine

2 apples, sliced

2 oranges, sliced

1 **mango**[2], peeled and sliced

1 bottle (28-ounces) club soda or sparkling water, chilled

sugar, for dipping the glass rim

fresh fruit slices, for garnish

1. Mix brandy, triple sec, and orange juice in a large pitcher; add sugar, stirring until thoroughly dissolved.

2. Stir in wine.

3. Add fruit slices and refrigerate at least 2 hours or overnight (the longer it sits-the better).

4. To serve: lightly wet rim of glass with a cut piece of fruit and dip into sugar. Pour mixture over crushed ice, filling glass ⅔'s full. Top off with chilled club soda. Garnish with skewered fresh fruit.

Diva Tips

[1]**Superfine sugar** has very fine crystals and dissolves quickly. Do not confuse it with powdered sugar.

[2]Ripe **mangoes** should be mostly red and yield to a gentle squeeze. To ripen, place in a paper bag at room temperature. Once ripe, store in a plastic bag in the refrigerator for several days. Without peeling, stand the mango on its end, with the stem end pointing up. With a sharp knife, cut straight down on one "flat" side, just grazing the pit. Repeat on the other "flat" side. Trim off the remaining flesh from the pit. Carefully score the cut side of the mango halves in a crisscross pattern through the flesh, just down to the peel. Bend the peel back, turning the halves inside out; cubes of fruit will pop out allowing them to be cut off the peel.

Magnolia Blossoms

A courtly drink to be enjoyed on the veranda with your favorite southern belle.

6 cups

1 **can (6-ounces) frozen orange juice concentrate, thawed**

1 **bottle (750 ml or 3 cups), dry white wine chilled**

1½ **cups cold water (or substitute chilled club soda for a sparkly beverage)**

½ **cup triple sec**
   orange slices
   sliced strawberries

1. Combine first 4 ingredients, mixing well.

2. Serve over ice and garnish with orange slices and strawberries.

Georgia Peach Punch

20 servings

2 **cans (10-ounces each) frozen peach daiquiri mix, thawed**

1 **can (12-ounces) frozen orange juice concentrate, thawed**

1 **can (12-ounces) frozen limeade concentrate, thawed**

1 **quart club soda, chilled**

1 **bottle (2-liters) ginger ale, chilled**

1 **bottle (750 ml or 3 cups) white wine, chilled**

   fresh peach slices (optional)

1. Mix the frozen concentrates with the club soda.

2. Pour over ice in a pitcher or punch bowl; add ginger ale and white wine.

3. Garnish the glasses with peach slices, if desired.

Mock Champagne

My sister-in-law, Deana Robinson Stowe, shared this recipe with me. It is very refreshing, quick and easy (won't stain carpets or prom dresses).

20 servings

1 **bottle (64-ounces) white grape juice, chilled**

1 **bottle (2-liters) ginger ale, chilled**
   crushed ice

1. Pour juice and ginger ale over ice in a punch bowl or large pitcher.

2. Serve immediately.

Raspberry Tea

Southerners love their icetea (one word with an elongated "i") and drink it no matter what the weather outside. I have tweaked the standard a little, adding lemonade and raspberry flavoring.

1 gallon

1   quart water
3   small tea bags
1½ cups sugar
1   can (12-ounces) frozen lemonade concentrate, thawed
1   envelope raspberry Kool-aid

1. Bring water to a boil. Remove from heat; add tea bags, cover and brew 30 minutes.

2. Remove tea bags and discard.

3. Stir sugar into brewed tea until completely dissolved.

4. Pour into a pitcher. Add lemonade concentrate and Kool-aid, stirring until mixed.

5. Add enough cold water and ice to make 1 gallon. Serve over ice.

Hot Cocoa Mojo

Few things are scarier than a snowstorm (½-1-inches) or more likely, an ice storm, in the South. Since we have very little equipment to clear the roads, our freeways become free-for-alls, the grocery stores shelves empty upon the forecast and the city becomes paralyzed. Our friends in the north are always puzzled at our inability to function when nature sends a little cold our way, but we here in the South take it as a day to reflect on our great weather the other 364 days of the year. I make hot chocolate, harkening to the days of my child-hood, sit back, sip and watch the cars go sledding along the byways.

6 servings

½   cup sugar
⅓   cup unsweetened cocoa powder
**   dash salt**
⅓   cup water
⅓   cup chocolate syrup
4   cups (1 quart) milk (or 2 cups milk and 2 cups half-and-half)
¾   teaspoon vanilla

1. Combine sugar, cocoa, and salt in a large saucepan. Blend in water. Cook over medium heat, stirring constantly, until mixture comes to a boil. Boil and stir 2 minutes.

2. Add chocolate syrup and milk; heat until hot, but do not let it boil.

3. Remove from heat; stir in vanilla.

4. Beat with a whisk (or an electric mixer) until foamy. Serve hot.

Sunny Beach Sipper

This drink will transport your senses to the tropics no matter what time of the year. Go ahead, wear your straw hat and samba across the kitchen floor.

4 servings

2   cups orange juice
1   cup **pineapple juice**[1]
1   banana, sliced
1   cup crushed ice

1. Place juices and banana in a blender; process until smooth.

2. Add ice and blend a few seconds longer. Serve immediately.

Diva Tips

[1]To minimize waste, buy **pineapple juice** in small, individual, 6-pack containers. Or reserve and freeze the juice from unsweetened, canned pineapple and use in recipes calling for pineapple juice.

Breakfast Smoothie

Nutritious breakfast or snack for people on the go.

2 servings

¼   cup orange juice
1   container (8-ounces) vanilla or peach yogurt (or your favorite flavor)
1   large ripe banana
1   cup fresh **strawberries**[1]
½   cup crushed ice
1   tablespoon honey

1. Place all ingredients into a blender and process until smooth.

2. Pour into a glass and serve immediately.

Diva Tips

[1]Buy **strawberries** that are shiny and deep red with no visible decay or moldy spots. Green cap (leaves) should be flat. To store, leave in original container and enclose tightly in a plastic bag, removing as much air as possible. Place in the coldest part of your refrigerator (back, bottom shelf). If bought fresh, will keep for several days to a week. Wash strawberries only right before using and before removing the cap under running cold water. Never submerge berries in water: they absorb water like a sponge. Storing damp berries hastens decay.

Tahitian Fruit Smoothie

5 cups

1½ cups sliced **strawberries**[1]
1 banana, sliced
¼ cup crushed pineapple
1¼ cups **pineapple juice**[2], chilled
1 cup orange juice, chilled
1 carton (8-ounces) vanilla yogurt (or substitute your favorite flavor)
1 cup crushed ice
2 tablespoons honey

1. Place all ingredients in a blender and process until smooth.
2. Serve immediately.

Diva Tips

[1]Buy **strawberries** that are shiny and deep red with no visible decay or moldy spots. Green cap (leaves) should be flat. To store, leave in original container and enclose tightly in a plastic bag, removing as much air as possible. Place in the coldest part of your refrigerator (back, bottom shelf). If bought fresh, will keep for several days to a week. Wash strawberries only right before using and before removing the cap under running cold water. Never submerge berries in water: they absorb water like a sponge. Storing damp berries hastens decay.

[2]To minimize waste, buy **pineapple juice** in small, individual, 6-pack containers. Or reserve the juice from unsweetened, canned pineapple and use in recipes calling for pineapple juice.

Peach Smoothie

4 servings

3   medium ripe **peaches**[1], peeled and pit removed (or use frozen peaches)

1   can (12-ounces) peach or apricot nectar, divided

1   container (8-ounces) peach yogurt (or substitute vanilla)

2   tablespoons honey

¼   teaspoon almond extract

1   cup crushed ice

   additional peach slices for garnish

1. Slice peaches and place in a blender; add 1 cup peach nectar and process until smooth.

2. Add remaining nectar, yogurt, honey, almond extract and ice. Process again until smooth.

3. Pour into glasses and garnish with peach slices if desired.

Diva Tips

[1]A ripe **peach** will be a deep golden color with a strong perfumy aroma. For the fullest flavor store peaches (and all fruit with a pit) at room temperature.

A best friend is like a four-leaf-clover: hard to find and lucky to have.

Entrées

Entrées

Poultry

Beef

Pork

Veal

Lamb

Seafood

Pasta

10-Minute Chicken

This chicken cooks up so quickly, the rest of your dinner should be prepared before beginning this dish.

4 servings

2 tablespoons vegetable oil (preferably extra virgin olive oil)

1½ pounds **chicken tenders**[1] or boneless, skinless chicken breasts

4 cloves garlic, crushed (2 teaspoons)

pinch red pepper flakes

½ cup white **wine**[2]

2 tablespoons freshly squeezed lemon juice

¼ cup chopped fresh parsley (optional)

salt and pepper to taste

1. Heat oil in a large skillet over medium-high heat. Add chicken (if using whole breasts, cut each into 4 long, thin strips) and brown quickly on all sides, about 5-6 minutes.

2. Add garlic and pepper flakes and cook an additional minute.

3. Add wine and lemon juice to the pan; reduce heat to medium. Cook until liquid is reduced to a glaze, about 3-4 minutes.

4. Remove from heat and stir in parsley. Taste and adjust seasonings with salt and pepper if desired.

Diva Tips

[1]To remove the white tendon in the **chicken tenders**, grasp the end of the tendon with a paper towel. Pull the tendon towards you while holding the chicken with the edge of a knife.

[2]Cook with an inexpensive **wine** that you would drink. Cooking wine found in the vinegar section of the grocery store is poor quality and high in sodium.

New Age Chicken

This recipe cooks up quickly: from the freezer to the table in less than 30 minutes.

4 servings

4 **boneless and skinless chicken breasts**
2 **teaspoons lemon pepper**
1 **teaspoon butter or margarine**
¼ **cup low-sodium chicken broth**

1. Place chicken between two sheets of plastic wrap; pound to ¼-inch uniform thickness. Sprinkle lemon pepper on one side of breast. Repeat with remaining breasts. (If breasts are too large, cut in half.)

2. Heat a nonstick grill pan or skillet over medium-high heat until pan is hot. Coat the bottom of the pan with butter and immediately add chicken breasts, being careful not to crowd pan. Cook 3-4 minutes until edges turn white and bottom is golden brown. Turn and repeat on the other side. Remove chicken to a dish and tent with foil to keep warm. Repeat with remaining chicken breasts if necessary.

3. Stir in chicken broth, scraping up the browned bits on the bottom of the pan; continue cooking until juice has reduced and slightly thickened. Add chicken back to pan just to coat with juice, turning to coat both sides. Do not over cook! Serve at once.

A Kitchen Diva is nothing less than a magician: transforming fruits of the earth into nutriments that will eventually disappear.

Chicken Parmesan

4 servings

1 clove **garlic, crushed**[1] (½ teaspoon)

⅓ cup butter or margarine, melted

2 tablespoons sour cream

1 cup finely **crushed buttery crackers**[2] (like Ritz) (1 stack)

⅓ cup Parmesan cheese

2 tablespoons finely chopped fresh parsley (optional)

½ teaspoon pepper

4 boneless, skinless chicken breasts

1. Preheat oven to 400°.

2. Combine garlic, butter, and sour cream in a shallow dish. In a separate dish, combine cracker crumbs, Parmesan cheese, parsley and pepper.

3. Place chicken between two sheets of plastic wrap; pound to ¼-inch uniform thickness. Cut breasts in half if too big. Dip each breast in butter/sour cream mixture; coat with the cracker crumbs.

4. Arrange chicken in a lightly greased, shallow baking pan, being careful not to crowd pan (use an additional pan if necessary). Bake uncovered 20-30 minutes until cooked through and golden brown.

Diva Tips

[1]To **crush garlic**, peel off papery skin by whacking clove with the side of a knife; paper should slip right off. Place the clove between two sheets of plastic wrap and smash with a meat pounder or the bottom of a heavy pan until pulverized. Scrape garlic off plastic wrap and use in recipe as directed.

[2]To make **cracker crumbs**, place crackers in a plastic bag and finely crush with a rolling pin, wine bottle, meat pounder or with hands. Or put crackers in the bowl of a food processor or blender and pulse until crackers are finely crushed.

Lemon Pepper Roasted Chicken

4 servings

1 (4-pound) whole **chicken**[1]
2 tablespoons lemon pepper
2 tablespoons butter, melted

1. Preheat oven to 450°.

2. Remove bag of giblets from chicken cavity. Discard liver; save and freeze the rest for making chicken stock, if desired. Rinse and dry chicken inside and out. Sprinkle generously with lemon pepper including the inside cavity.

3. Place on a standing roaster or in a pan with a rack. Bake 20 minutes. Baste with melted butter.

4. Reduce oven temperature to 350° and continue baking an additional 25-35 minutes or until juices run clear when pierced (or an instant-read meat thermometer reads 170° inserted into the thigh portion of the chicken).

5. Remove from oven and let rest for 10 minutes before carving into serving pieces.

Diva Tips

[1]If possible, **chicken** should be removed from the refrigerator 1 hour before cooking to come to room temperature so that chicken will cook evenly.

Mustard Chicken

4 servings

4 boneless, skinless **chicken**[1] breasts
4 tablespoons butter or margarine
1 **shallot**[2], minced (2 tablespoons)
1 clove garlic, crushed (½ teaspoon)
½ cup Dijon mustard
1 cup heavy cream
1 container (8-ounces or 1 cup) sour cream

1. Preheat oven to 350°.

2. Pound chicken breasts between 2 sheets of plastic wrap to ½-inch even thickness. Heat butter in a large skillet over medium high heat. Cook chicken in butter 2-3 minutes on both sides until golden brown. Remove chicken to a 9x13-inch baking dish.

3. Add shallots and garlic into the same skillet and sauté until clear. Stir in mustard and cream until smooth. Cook 5 minutes until thick and velvety. Remove from heat and stir in sour cream.

4. Coat chicken generously with the mustard sauce and bake 20-25 minutes until sauce is thick, bubbly, and chicken is cooked through.

Diva Tips

[1]If possible, **chicken** should be removed from the refrigerator 1 hour before cooking to come to room temperature so that chicken will cook evenly.

[2]**Shallots** look like a cross between garlic and onions. Buy shallots that are tight, with papery-looking skins and no green sprouts. They are mild and are used to season foods in which onions would be too strong. Substitute an equal amount of scallions. Store in a cool, dry place for weeks.

Hawaiian Chicken

4 servings

4 boneless, skinless chicken breasts
2 cloves garlic, crushed (1 teaspoon)
½ cup soy sauce
1 cup unsweetened pineapple juice
½ cup **dry sherry**[1]
¼ cup apple cider vinegar
¼ cup brown sugar
2 tablespoons fresh grated **gingerroot**[2]
¼ cup vegetable oil
4 pineapple slices, fresh or canned

1. Pound chicken breasts between 2 sheets of plastic wrap to ½-inch even thickness.

2. Measure next 8 ingredients in a bowl; mix together well. Marinate chicken for at least 2 hours or overnight (better).

3. Remove chicken from marinade and discard marinade. Preheat grill to high. Place chicken breasts on grill and cook 5-7 minutes on each side (total 10-14 minutes) or until a meat thermometer inserted in the chicken registers 180° internal temperature.

4. At the same time, grill pineapple slices, 2-3 minutes per side. Serve hot chicken topped with a pineapple slice.

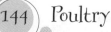

Diva Tips

[1]Cook with an inexpensive **sherry** that you would drink. Cooking sherry or cooking wine found in the vinegar section of the grocery store is poor quality and high in sodium.

[2]To measure fresh **gingerroot**, 1 ounce = 3 tablespoons minced; 1-inch x 1-inch piece = 1 tablespoon minced. Store extra ginger peeled or unpeeled in the freezer in 1-inch slices. While still frozen, grate or cut into small cubes and push through a garlic press. Or cover fresh, peeled ginger with vodka and store in the refrigerator.

Easy Chicken Pot Pie

6 servings

1 small onion, finely chopped (½ cup)

2 stalks celery, finely chopped (1 cup)

2 medium carrots, peeled and cut in small dice (1 cup)

2 tablespoons butter or margarine

1 medium potato, peeled and cut into small dice (1 cup)

1 can (14-ounces or 2 cups) low-sodium chicken broth

1 can (10-ounces) cream of chicken soup

1 can (14-ounces) green peas, drained

2 cups diced **cooked chicken**[1]

1 package refrigerated pie crusts, (2 pie crusts)

1. Preheat oven to 350°.

2. Sauté onions, celery, and carrots in butter until crisp-tender, about 5 minutes. Add potatoes and chicken broth. Cook over medium heat until chicken broth is reduced by half. Stir in soup, peas and chicken.

3. Line a (9-inch) pie pan with one pie crust; pour in filling. Top with remaining pie crust. Seal the two crusts by pressing together with a fork or pinching with fingers. Cut several vents in the top of the crust to allow steam to escape.

4. Bake 30-45 minutes until golden brown and filling is bubbly.

Diva Tips

[1]To **cook chicken** for use in any recipe requiring cooked chicken, sprinkle lemon pepper (or season with salt and pepper) on chicken breasts (boneless or rib-in) and place inside a baking bag (smaller version of the kind used to bake turkeys at Thanksgiving) or tightly seal in aluminum foil. Put on a baking sheet in a 350° oven about 1 hour. Remove from oven and cool in the bag. Remove and chop chicken as recipe directs. Reserve any accumulated juices in the cooking bag by pouring into a container and storing in the refrigerator up to 2 days or 3 months in the freezer. These juices are "liquid gold". Use in any recipe that requires chicken broth or bouillon.

Almond Chicken and Rice

This dish is great for sharing with a friend in need because it is simple, can be made ahead and children as well as adults love it.

4-6 servings

Casserole

4   chicken breasts, cooked and chopped (4 cups)

1   cup **cooked rice**[1]

1   can (10-ounces) cream of chicken soup

2   tablespoons minced onion

1   tablespoon lemon juice

¾   cup mayonnaise

¾   cup sour cream

½   teaspoon lemon pepper

Topping

1   cup corn flakes, crushed

½   cup slivered **almonds, toasted**[2]

2   tablespoons butter or margarine, melted

1. Combine all ingredients for the casserole.

2. Pour into a lightly greased (8-inch) square, over-proof dish. Cover dish with plastic wrap. Refrigerate overnight.

3. When ready to bake, toss corn flakes and almonds with melted butter. Remove plastic wrap and sprinkle corn flakes evenly over casserole. Bake at 300° 1 hour.

Diva Tips

[1]If you do not have leftover **rice**, mix ⅓ cup rice with ⅔ cup water in a small saucepan; heat to boiling over medium heat. Cover with a tight-fitting lid and lower heat to simmer. Cook 14 minutes without lifting lid. Remove from heat, and fluff with a fork. Proceed with recipe.

[2]**Toasting nuts** adds crispness and intensifies the flavor. Spread in a single layer on a baking sheet or pan. Preheat oven to 350°; place pan in oven and bake 5-10 minutes, or until nuts release their aroma, being careful not to burn. A smaller portion of nuts will toast much quicker than a larger amount. Toast a larger amount than needed and freeze extras up to 1 year in a tightly sealed container. Four ounces of nuts equals about 1 cup.

Chicken Piccata

Substitute an equal amount of veal scaloppine for the chicken in this recipe for a delicious Veal Piccata dish.

8 servings

8   boneless, skinless chicken breasts

2   teaspoons salt

½   teaspoon pepper

⅓   cup all-purpose flour

1   can (14-ounces) low-sodium chicken broth

6   tablespoons butter or margarine, softened, divided

2   tablespoons all-purpose flour

4   tablespoons vegetable oil (preferably extra virgin olive oil)

1   clove garlic, crushed (½ teaspoon)

⅔   cup dry white **wine**[1]

½   cup freshly squeezed lemon juice

⅛   teaspoon crushed red peppers (optional)

2   tablespoons **capers**[2] (optional)

¼   cup chopped fresh parsley

1. Pound chicken breasts between 2 sheets of plastic wrap to ¼-inch even thickness. Season with salt and pepper. Dredge breasts in ⅓-cup flour, shaking to remove excess. Set aside.

2. Bring chicken broth to a boil in a medium saucepan. Lower heat to medium and simmer until reduced to ½ cup.

3. Stir 2 tablespoons butter with 2 tablespoons flour until smooth. Set aside to use in the sauce later.

4. Heat 1 tablespoon oil in a large skillet over medium-high heat. Cook chicken breasts in batches (do not crowd the pan) until golden, about 3-4 minutes per side using only as much vegetable oil as needed. Transfer chicken to a warmed dish; tent with foil to keep warm.

5. In the same skillet, sauté garlic 1 minute. Add wine, lemon juice and reduced chicken broth and bring to a boil over medium-high heat, scraping up the browned bits in the bottom of the pan. Whisk in butter-flour mixture and continue simmering until sauce thickens slightly, about 2 minutes. Remove from heat and stir in remaining butter, crushed red peppers, capers, and parsley. Taste and season with salt and pepper if needed. Spoon sauce over chicken and serve immediately.

Diva Tips

[1]Cook with an inexpensive **wine** that you would drink. Cooking wine found in the vinegar section of the grocery store is poor quality and high in sodium.

[2]**Capers** can be found in the pickle aisle of your local grocery store.

Barbecue Chicken

My barbecue sauce is tart with sweet overtones.

4-6 servings

1	whole **chicken**[1], cut into pieces (or substitute your favorite pieces)
2	teaspoons lemon pepper
2	cups apple cider vinegar
2	cups catsup
¼	cup sugar
¼	cup brown sugar
1	teaspoon salt
¼	teaspoon pepper
¼	teaspoon garlic powder
	dash Tabasco sauce

1. Rinse and dry chicken pieces well. Season with lemon pepper. Place chicken in a baking bag or wrap air tight with aluminum foil. Bake at 325° 1 hour.

2. Meanwhile make barbecue sauce: bring vinegar to boil over medium-high heat in a saucepan. Reduce heat and simmer until reduced to 1 cup. Mix in remaining ingredients and simmer an additional 30 minutes.

3. Remove chicken from the bag or foil; heat grill to medium heat (or place chicken under the broiler of the oven). Baste with barbecue sauce and cook an additional 10-12 minutes until lightly charred. (Watch chicken carefully; the sugar in the barbecue sauce will cause it to burn.)

Diva Tips

[1]If possible, **chicken** should be removed from the refrigerator 1 hour before cooking to come to room temperature so that chicken will cook more evenly.

Sour Cream Chicken Enchiladas

Another recipe from friends in Dallas, Texas. These enchiladas are so delicious and easy, you will never have to order them out again.

6 servings

2 tablespoons butter or margarine
1 medium onion, chopped (1 cup)
½ cup chopped green bell pepper
2 cups chopped, cooked chicken
1 can (4-ounces) **chopped green chilies**[1]
3 tablespoons butter or margarine
¼ cup all-purpose flour
½ teaspoon **coriander**[2]
¾ teaspoon salt
2½ cups chicken broth
1 carton (8-ounces) sour cream (1 cup)
1½ cups (6-ounces) shredded Monterey Jack cheese, divided
12 (6-inch) flour tortillas
salsa for garnish (optional)

1. Preheat oven to 350°.

2. Melt 2 tablespoons butter in a large skillet. Sauté onion and bell pepper, until limp. Remove from skillet and combine with chicken. Add green chilies. Set aside.

3. In the same skillet, melt 3 tablespoons butter; blend in flour, coriander and salt. Cook over medium-high heat 1 minute, stirring constantly. Slowly stir in chicken broth; bring to a boil and cook until thick and bubbly, stirring constantly. Remove from heat and stir in sour cream and ¾ cup cheese.

4. Stir 1 cup of the sauce into the chicken mixture.

5. Dip a tortilla into remaining sauce. Spoon ¼-cup chicken mixture on the top one-third of the tortilla. Fold top of tortilla over filling; fold in sides and continue rolling tortilla to totally encase filling.

6. Place seam side down in a lightly greased (9x13-inch) baking dish. Repeat with remaining tortillas and filling. Pour any remaining sauce over tortillas. Cover pan with aluminum foil and bake 20 minutes. Remove foil, sprinkle with remaining cheese and return to oven for 5 additional minutes or until cheese is melted.

Diva Tips

[1]Canned **green chilies** can be located with the Mexican foods in your grocery store.

[2]**Coriander** can be located in the spice aisle of your grocery store.

Coq Au Vin

Most recipes for chicken in wine use red wine and the sauce is thickened with flour. I like this recipe, because it uses white wine and has a few short cuts.

4 servings

- **4** **boneless, skinless chicken breasts**
- **1** **teaspoon salt**
- **¼** **teaspoon pepper**
- **1** **can (14-ounces) low-sodium chicken broth**
- **4** **slices of bacon**
- **1** **small onion, diced (½ cup)**
- **1** **clove garlic, crushed (½ teaspoon)**
- **1** **cup (4 ounces), sliced mushrooms**
- **½** **cup dry white wine**[1]
- **1** **can (10-ounces) cream of mushroom soup**
- **½** **cup half-and-half or milk**
- **¼** **cup chopped fresh parsley**[2]

1. Preheat oven to 350°.

2. Pound chicken between 2 sheets of plastic wrap until ½-inch even thickness. Season with salt and pepper.

3. In a medium saucepan, bring broth to a boil; reduce heat and continue to simmer until broth is reduced to ⅓ cup.

4. Cook bacon until crisp in a large skillet. Remove bacon from pan, crumble and set aside. Drain off fat, reserving 2 tablespoons in the pan. Brown chicken in bacon fat until golden on both sides, about 3-4 minutes per side. Remove chicken to a (9x13-inch) baking pan that has been lightly greased or coated with a nonstick cooking spray.

5. In the same skillet, sauté onions until limp and golden, about 5 minutes. Add garlic and continue cooking for an additional minute. Add mushrooms to the pan and cook just until they lose their liquid, about 2 minutes. Place onions and mushroom mixture on top of chicken.

6. Mix wine, reduced chicken broth, soup, and half-and-half in the skillet. Heat to boiling, scraping the pan to remove any browned bits. Pour sauce over chicken; cover and bake 25-30 minutes until tender. Remove from oven, sprinkle chopped parsley and crisp bacon over dish and serve.

Diva Tips

[1]Cook with an inexpensive **wine** that you would drink. Cooking wine found in the vinegar section of the grocery store is poor quality and high in sodium.

[2]To store fresh herbs (**parsley** or cilantro), wash herbs in plenty of cold water; drain on paper towels. Roll clean, damp herbs in dry paper towels and place in a tightly covered plastic container. Store in the coldest part of your refrigerator 1-2 weeks.

Chicken Elegante

This chicken dish makes a delicious cream sauce. Complete the meal with a crisp salad and cooked rice.

6 servings

- **6 boneless, skinless chicken breasts**
- **1 teaspoon salt**
- **½ teaspoon pepper**
- **2 tablespoons butter or margarine**
- **1 small onion, diced (½ cup)**
- **1 clove garlic, crushed (½ teaspoon)**
- **1 package (8-ounces) mushrooms[1], sliced**
- **½ cup dry white wine[2] (or substitute chicken broth)**
- **1 can (10-ounces) cream of chicken soup**
- **1 container (8-ounces or 1 cup) sour cream**
- **2 tablespoons chopped green onion tops or chives (optional)**

1. Pound chicken between 2 sheets of plastic wrap until ½-inch even thickness. Season with salt and pepper.

2. Heat a large skillet over medium-high heat and melt butter. Add chicken breasts and brown all over (chicken does not have to be cooked all the way through). Remove chicken to a (9x12-inch) baking dish that has been lightly greased or coated with a nonstick cooking spray.

3. Add onion to the same skillet and sauté until clear and limp. Stir in garlic and cook for an additional minute, being careful not to burn. Add mushrooms and cook until mushrooms release their liquid. Add wine (or chicken broth) and stir, scraping the bottom of the pan to release any browned bits. Remove pan from heat and stir in soup and sour cream until mixed thoroughly.

4. Pour sauce mixture over chicken. Cover with aluminum foil and bake at 350° 20-30 minutes until sauce is bubbly and chicken is done. Sprinkle with chopped onions and serve.

Diva Tips

[1]Never immerse **mushrooms** in water; they will absorb liquid like a sponge. The best way to clean mushrooms is to wipe with a damp paper towel. Store mushrooms in a paper bag in the refrigerator.

[2]Cook with an inexpensive **wine** that you would drink. Cooking wine found in the vinegar section of the grocery store is poor quality and high in sodium.

Thai Peanut Chicken

4 servings

2 tablespoons vegetable oil

2 skinless, boneless **chicken breasts**[1], sliced into ½-inch pieces

1 large green bell pepper, cut into ¼-inch slices

¾ cup **chicken broth**[2]

¼ cup chunky peanut butter

1 tablespoon soy sauce

1½ teaspoons lemon pepper

3 cups **cooked rice**[3]

1. Heat vegetable oil in a large nonstick skillet or wok over medium-high heat.

2. Working in batches, cook chicken until no longer pink, about 4-6 minutes. Remove chicken to a separate dish and set aside.

3. Add bell pepper to the pan (adding an additional tablespoon vegetable oil if necessary) and cook 3-4 minutes until limp.

4. In a small bowl, whisk together broth, peanut butter, soy sauce, and lemon pepper.

5. Stir into the skillet with the cooked pepper. Bring to a boil; reduce heat, add chicken and stir together until well coated. Serve over cooked rice.

Diva Tips

[1]**Chicken** or meat slice easier and thinner when partially frozen.

[2]If using **canned broth**, freeze any leftovers to use in another recipe calling for chicken broth.

[3]To **cook rice**, heat 1 tablespoon vegetable oil in a medium saucepan over medium-high heat. Add 1 cup long grain rice; cook and stir until rice becomes white. Add 2 cups water or chicken broth (or a combination) and 1 teaspoon salt. Bring to a boil; reduce heat and cover with a tight-fitting lid. Cook 14 minutes or until all the liquid is absorbed. Remove from heat and let stand 5 minutes covered. Fluff with a fork.

Chicken with Thai Green Curry Sauce

A little spicy, but so delicious. Most grocery stores carry Thai seasonings, coconut milk and fish sauce in the Oriental food section.

4 servings

Green Curry Sauce

- 1 tablespoon Thai green curry paste
- 1 can (14-ounces) coconut milk
- ½ tablespoon sugar
- 2 tablespoons fish sauce (nam pla)
- 2 tablespoons freshly squeezed lime juice

Stir-Fry

- 2 tablespoons vegetable oil
- 4 boneless, skinless **chicken breasts[1]**, cut into thin strips
- ½ teaspoon red pepper flakes (or to taste)
- 1 pound snow peas, sliced
- 1 bunch green onions, chopped
- 1 bunch fresh bok choy, sliced
- ½ cup chopped fresh cilantro
- ¼ cup chopped fresh basil
- 3 cups **cooked rice[2]**

1. To make the sauce, heat a skillet over medium-high heat. Add green curry paste and cook stirring constantly until fragrant, about 1 minute. Add the coconut milk. Keep stirring and cooking over medium-high heat until this mixture gets a fragrant, cooked aroma. Add the sugar, fish sauce and lime juice; reduce heat and simmer gently, stirring occasionally while preparing the stir-fry.

2. To make the stir-fry: heat a nonstick skillet or a wok over medium-high heat; add vegetable oil. Cook chicken in batches until no longer pink, about 4-6 minutes. Remove from skillet and set aside.

3. Add red pepper flakes to the pan; cook and stir 1 minute. Add snow peas, onions and bok choy. Cook and stir 1 minute more or until vegetables just begin to get limp.

4. Return chicken to the pan with the vegetables; add the sauce. Stir in the fresh cilantro and basil; serve immediately over hot rice.

Diva Tips

[1]**Chicken** or meat slice easier and thinner when partially frozen. Cut chicken slices the length of the breast.

[2]To **cook rice**, heat 1 tablespoon vegetable oil in a medium saucepan over medium-high heat. Add 1 cup long grain rice; cook and stir until rice becomes white. Add 2 cups water or chicken broth (or a combination) and 1 teaspoon salt. Bring to a boil; reduce heat and cover with a tight-fitting lid. Cook 14 minutes or until all the liquid is absorbed. Remove from heat and let stand 5 minutes covered. Fluff with a fork.

Fire Roasted Rosa Chicken

4 servings

Reduction Sauce

2 **cups dry white wine**[1]

1 **can (14-ounces or 2 cups) low sodium chicken broth**

1 **package (8-ounces) mushrooms, sliced**

3 **tablespoons butter or margarine, divided**

1 **teaspoon Worcestershire sauce**

⅛ **teaspoon garlic powder**

4 **tablespoons freshly squeezed lemon juice (1 lemon)**

2 **tablespoons chopped fresh basil**[2-3]

1. In a large skillet, mix wine and chicken broth. Bring to a boil, reduce heat and simmer until reduced by half.

2. Meanwhile place mushrooms in a microwave-safe dish. Top with 1 tablespoon butter, Worcestershire sauce and garlic powder. Microwave 3-4 minutes until mushrooms release their liquid and are tender.

3. Add the lemon juice and the juice from the mushrooms to the wine and chicken broth in the skillet and reduce to 1 cup. Remove from heat. When ready to serve, whisk in remaining 2 tablespoons butter. Add mushrooms and stir in fresh basil. Spoon over grilled chicken.

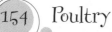

Diva Tips

[1]Cook with an inexpensive **wine** that you would drink. Cooking wine found in the vinegar section of the grocery store is poor quality and high in sodium.

[2]To **chop fresh herbs**, roll herbs into a tight bundle and finely chop crosswise with a sharp knife.

Or snip with kitchen scissors. To prevent fresh basil from darkening while cutting, sprinkle with a few drops of vegetable oil.

[3]**Basil** can be kept fresh for 3-4 days with the stems submerged in cool water in a container and kept on the counter. Refresh water every day.

Rosa Chicken

4 boneless, skinless chicken breasts

1 teaspoon lemon pepper

2 ounces fontina cheese, sliced

4 thin slices ham (preferably Black Forest or Praga)

4 tablespoons butter or margarine, melted

4 tablespoons freshly squeezed lemon juice (1 lemon)

dash Tabasco sauce

1. Pound chicken between 2 sheets of plastic wrap until ¼-inch even thickness. Season outside of chicken with lemon pepper.

2. Lay 1 slice cheese and 1 slice ham over bottom half of chicken breast. Fold the other half over ham enclosing completely. Whisk together melted butter, lemon juice and Tabasco. Set aside.

3. Heat grill to high heat. Place soaked hickory chips over coals (if using a gas grill, place on briquettes). Grill chicken over high heat, 6-7 minutes per side, being careful when turning not to disturb the ham and cheese. Remove from heat to a serving dish; top with mushrooms and sauce.

Chicken Parmigiana

4 servings

4 boneless, skinless chicken breasts

1 teaspoon salt

½ teaspoon pepper

1 cup all-purpose flour

1 large egg, beaten

1 tablespoon water

⅓ cup vegetable oil

2 cups good quality spaghetti sauce

4 tablespoons Parmesan cheese

2 ounces (½ cup) shredded imported provolone cheese (or mozzarella)

1. Pound chicken between 2 sheets of plastic wrap until ½-inch even thickness. Season with salt and pepper. If chicken pieces are too large, cut in half.

2. Dip seasoned chicken in flour, shaking to remove excess.

3. Mix beaten egg with water in a shallow dish. Dip floured chicken in egg and then in flour again.

4. Heat oil in a large skillet over medium-high heat. Fry chicken in hot oil in batches about 5 minutes per side or until golden brown. Remove chicken from skillet and place in a (9x13-inch) baking pan.

5. Spoon enough spaghetti sauce to cover chicken. Sprinkle with Parmesan cheese.

6. Bake in a preheated 350° oven 20 minutes. Top each chicken breast with provolone cheese. Return to oven and bake an additional 5 minutes or until cheese has melted and sauce is bubbly.

Chicken Crêpes

All components of this dish can be made ahead and assembled right before baking, making this recipe an easy, elegant dish to serve guests.

6 servings

Crêpes

1 cup all-purpose flour
¼ teaspoon salt
2 tablespoons butter or margarine, melted
2 large eggs
1⅓ cups milk
  melted butter (for coating the cooking pan)

1. Beat together all the crêpe ingredients until well mixed and no lumps remain (can be mixed in a blender). Refrigerate 1 hour up to 24 hours to allow the flour to absorb the liquid resulting in lighter crêpes.

2. Heat an (8-inch or 10-inch) nonstick skillet (or crêpe pan) over medium-high heat. Brush the bottom with just enough melted butter to coat. Pour 2 tablespoons batter in the center of the hot pan and quickly tilt the pan in all directions so batter covers the bottom with a thin film. Cook about 1 minute. Lift the edge of the crêpe to loosen. Crêpe is ready to flip over when the top is no longer wet looking or glossy. Flip crêpe over with a wide spatula and cook 30 seconds on the other side. Remove crêpe to a cooling rack or to a towel. Repeat until all the batter is used, brushing the bottom of the pan with additional butter before each crêpe is cooked. Makes 14-16 (6-inch) crêpes. (Crêpes can be made ahead and refrigerated up to 2 days or frozen up to 3 months).

> Kitchen Divas who live in glass houses should not cook naked.

Filling

2 tablespoons butter or margarine
1 shallot, finely minced (2 tablespoons)
½ cup finely chopped onion
1 clove garlic, crushed (½ teaspoon)
1 cup chopped mushrooms
2 packages (3-ounces each) cream cheese, softened
2 tablespoons **sour cream**[1]
2 tablespoons dry **sherry**[2]
2 cups cooked, chopped chicken

1. Melt butter in a large skillet over medium-high heat.

2. Sauté shallot, onions and garlic until clear and limp. Add mushrooms and cook until mushrooms are tender and all liquid released has been absorbed.

3. Remove from heat and stir in cream cheese, sour cream and sherry. Add chicken and stir just until mixed. (Can be made to this point and refrigerated up to 2 days.)

Sauce

6	tablespoons butter or margarine
6	tablespoons all-purpose flour
½	cup dry white wine or **sherry**[2]
1	can (14-ounces or 2 cups) low sodium chicken broth
1	cup milk
¾	cup Parmesan cheese
1	cup (4-ounces) grated Swiss cheese, divided

1. In a large saucepan, melt 6-tablespoons butter over medium heat; add flour, stirring until smooth. Cook 1 minute stirring constantly. Gradually add wine, chicken broth and milk; cook over medium heat, stirring constantly until thickened and bubbly. Remove from heat and stir in Parmesan and ½ cup Swiss until cheese melts.

To Assemble Crêpes

1. Place ¼-cup chicken mixture in the middle of the crêpe. Fold the top of the crêpe over the filling and then fold in the sides (like an envelope). Roll, totally encasing the filling in the crêpe.

2. Place seam side down in a lightly greased (9x13-inch) baking dish (or coated with a nonstick cooking spray). Repeat with remaining filling and crêpes.

3. Top with sauce.

4. Bake in a preheated 375° oven 15-20 minutes until sauce is bubbly and top is lightly browned. Top with remaining ½ cup Swiss cheese, return to oven and bake an additional 5-10 minutes or until cheese has melted.

Diva Tips

[1]Draining off any accumulated liquid in **sour cream** carton makes the sour cream thicker and creamier.

[2]Cook with an inexpensive **sherry** that you would drink. Cooking sherry or wine found in the vinegar section of the grocery store is poor quality and high in sodium.

Chicken Cordon Bleu

Another make ahead chicken dish, fancy enough for guests.

4 servings

- **4** boneless, skinless chicken breasts
- **4** thin slices of baked ham (preferably Black Forest or Praga)
- **2** ounces **fontina**[1] cheese, cut into 4 (1-inch) sticks
- **½** cup all-purpose flour
- **1** teaspoon salt
- **½** teaspoon pepper
- **1** cup dry **breadcrumbs**[2]
- **¼** cup Parmesan cheese
- **¼** teaspoon garlic powder
- **2** tablespoons finely chopped fresh parsley
- **1** large egg, lightly beaten
- vegetable oil (preferably extra virgin olive oil)

1. Pound chicken between 2 sheets of plastic wrap until ¼-inch even thickness.

2. Lay one ham slice on the inside of the chicken breast; top with a cheese stick.

3. Beginning with the short end, roll up chicken, tucking in the sides making a tight, neat package and pressing meat in place as necessary, totally encasing ham and cheese. Secure with a toothpick if necessary. Repeat with remaining chicken breasts.

4. Combine flour with salt and pepper. Dredge rolled chicken in flour, shaking to remove excess. Combine breadcrumbs with Parmesan cheese, garlic powder and parsley. Dip floured chicken in egg and then in breadcrumb mixture. Refrigerate for 1 hour. (Can be prepared up to this point, covered and refrigerated for up to 1 day.)

5. Heat enough oil in a large skillet to a depth of ¼-inch over medium-high heat. Cook chicken rolls in hot oil until golden brown all over, avoiding crowding the pan. Remove to a (9x13-inch) baking dish and bake in a preheated oven at 375° 20-25 minutes.

Diva Tips

[1]**Fontina** is a buttery-tasting Italian cheese (there are also American and Danish varieties). It tastes like a cross between a Swiss cheese and Brie.

[2]Save all your dried, leftover bread—baguettes, sandwich bread, bagels, crackers, rolls, etc.— and put into the bowl of your food processor or blender and pulse until you have fine crumbs. Or rub dried bread on a grater, catching the crumbs in a bowl. Store **crumbs** in a zip top plastic bag in the freezer and use as your recipe directs. Homemade breadcrumbs tastes superior to store prepackaged.

Picnic Chicken

*This recipe requires boneless chicken breasts with the skin. If they are unavailable, buy split chicken breasts and **debone**[1], leaving the skin intact. The result is well worth the effort because this chicken is delicious served hot, warm or cold making it ideal for a buffet or a picnic.*

6 servings

½   **cup chopped onion**
1   **clove garlic, crushed (½ teaspoon)**
1   **tablespoon butter**
½   **package (5-ounces) frozen chopped spinach, thawed**
1   **container (8-ounces) whole-milk ricotta cheese**
1   **large egg, lightly beaten**
2   **tablespoons chopped parsley[2]**
¼   **teaspoon dried Italian seasoning**
1   **teaspoon salt**
½   **teaspoon pepper**
    dash nutmeg
6   **boneless chicken breasts, with the skin**

1. Sauté onions and garlic in butter over medium-high heat until softened. Remove from heat.

2. Squeeze spinach in a paper towel until completely dry. Mix with onions. Add remaining ingredients (except chicken).

3. Place chicken breast, skin side up on the work surface (cover surface with plastic wrap, if desired). Loosen the skin from one side and stuff about ⅓ cup of the filling under the skin. Tuck loose ends of chicken under the bottom, forming an even, round shape.

4. Put the breasts in a lightly greased (9x13-inch) baking pan. (Do not crowd pan). Season chicken with additional salt and pepper if desired.

5. Bake in a preheated 350° oven 30-35 minutes or until skin is crispy and golden brown, being careful not to overcook.

6. Remove from pan and cool to room temperature. Slice diagonally in half with a serrated knife for prettier presentation. Serve hot (leave whole), room temperature or cold. Can be made totally the day ahead, covered and refrigerated. Can easily be doubled or tripled for a large crowd.

Diva Tips

[1]To **debone** chicken breast, slip a thin knife or fingers under the breastbones and pull away from the flesh. Slit the flesh around the larger bones with a knife and carefully lift out bone avoiding taking too much flesh with the bone.

[2]To store fresh herbs (**parsley** or cilantro), wash herbs in plenty of cold water; drain on paper towels. Roll clean, damp herbs in dry paper towels and place in a tightly covered plastic container. Store 1-2 weeks in the coldest part of your refrigerator.

Thanksgiving Turkey a l'Orange

This turkey bakes up quicker than conventional, and is so moist and delicious that this recipe will easily become one your family will pass down to generations to come. The juices from roasting make excellent gravy, too!

10-12 servings

1 (12-pound) turkey[1]
1½ tablespoons salt
1 teaspoon pepper
2 large onions, sliced
4 ribs celery, leaves included, roughly chopped
2 oranges, cut into quarters
4 cloves garlic
½ cup beer (any kind or substitute dry white wine)
¼ cup orange juice
1 turkey-size baking bag
cornstarch for thickening gravy (optional)

1. Defrost turkey 3-4 days in the refrigerator in the original plastic.

2. Preheat oven to 400°.

3. Remove plastic bag surrounding turkey. If turkey legs are tied together with a metal or plastic lock, untie. Remove plastic bag of giblets from the cavity of the bird and the neck from the neck cavity. Wash the giblets and neck and set aside, discarding the liver. Wash the inside of the turkey thoroughly. Wash the skin and remove any pinfeathers or hairs. Remove any lumps of visible fat. Dry thoroughly. Generously salt and pepper the inside and outside, including the neck cavity. Twist the end sections of the wings behind its back (it will look like it is reclining).

4. Stuff some of the onions and celery into both cavities; squeeze 4 orange quarters into the cavities, leaving the rinds inside as well. Retie the legs together with the metal or plastic lock. Place the garlic cloves inside the baking bag and crush. Layer the rest of the onions, celery and oranges (squeezing the juice over the vegetables) over the garlic. Place the turkey, breast side up, on top of the vegetables and scatter the giblets and neck around the turkey.

5. Heat the beer and orange juice together in a small saucepan to boiling. Carefully pull back the baking bag, exposing the turkey and pour the boiling liquid over all the skin. (This seals the pores, eliminating basting.) Close the bag airtight and seal with the tie provided by the manufacturer. Puncture a small 1-inch hole in the top of the bag. Place the turkey in a

A **Kitchen Diva's** journey in the kitchen begins with one measuring cup.

baking pan and place the pan in the lowest one-third of the hot oven. It may be necessary to remove all other racks of the oven.

6. Roast the turkey for 1 hour. Reduce oven to 375°. Carefully slice open the bag and fold back to expose the turkey. (Caution: steam will be hot!) Bake an additional hour or until a meat thermometer registers 180° when inserted into the thickest portion of the thigh. (Bake 5 minutes extra per pound over 12 pounds; subtract 5 minutes per pound under 12 pounds.)

7. Remove from oven and let **turkey rest**[2] at least 15 minutes before carving. Remove vegetables from the cavities. Strain juices from the bag, discarding solids. Juices can be used as is or can be thickened by adding 1½ tablespoons cornstarch to every cup of liquid. (To prevent lumps, mix cornstarch with ¼ cup cold water before adding to hot liquid.) Stir cornstarch mix into juices and bring to a boil in a medium saucepan. Cook until thickened.

Diva Tips

[1]General rule is to buy 1 pound of **turkey** per person.

[2]For juicier meat, let cooked **meat**, no matter what the cut or kind, **rest** 10-15 minutes before slicing or carving to allow the juices to settle back into the meat and prevent them from "flooding" out when meat is cut.

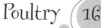

Barbecue Meatloaf

My husband, Jim, asks for this meatloaf at least once a week! It is his very favorite meal.

4 servings

- **1 pound extra lean ground sirloin**
- **½ cup dry breadcrumbs[1]**
- **¼ cup Parmesan cheese**
- **1 large egg, slightly beaten**
- **½ teaspoon salt**
- **¼ teaspoon pepper**
- **½ cup sweet, thick barbecue sauce (or catsup)**
- **⅛ teaspoon garlic powder**
- **1 teaspoon Worcestershire sauce**
- **1 teaspoon parsley flakes (optional)**
- **½ cup sweet, thick barbecue sauce or catsup (for topping)**

1. Preheat oven to 350°.

2. Measure all ingredients (except ½ cup barbecue sauce for topping) into a mixing bowl. Mix together with your hands or a large spoon.

3. Line a small, shallow baking pan with aluminum foil; lightly grease or coat with a nonstick cooking spray.

4. Make a free form loaf (9x4x2-inches) of the meat mixture on the baking pan. Spread the remaining barbecue sauce evenly over the top of the loaf. Bake 45-60 minutes or until done (meat thermometer should read 165°-170°). Remove from oven and cool slightly before slicing.

Diva Tips

[1]Save all your dried, leftover bread—baguettes, sandwich bread, bagels, crackers, rolls, etc.—and put into the bowl of your food processor or blender and pulse until you have fine **crumbs**. Or rub dried bread on a grater, catching the crumbs in a bowl. Store crumbs in a zip top plastic bag in the freezer and use as your recipe directs. Homemade breadcrumbs tastes superior to store prepackaged.

Hamburger Steak TV Dinner

My mom and I adapted this recipe from Julia Child's cooking show from the 1960's just when TV dinners were first introduced. We prepared this recipe quite often when she worked and I was in school because it is easy and delicious.

4 servings

1½ pounds extra lean ground sirloin
   salt and pepper, to taste
1   medium onion, sliced
4   carrots, sliced into ½-inch coins
4-5 medium potatoes, peeled and sliced
   ¼-inch thick
4   tablespoons butter or margarine
   Worcestershire sauce or your favorite
   steak sauce

1. Preheat oven to 350°.

2. Make 4 hamburger steaks from ground sirloin. Season with salt and pepper. Heat a large skillet over medium-high heat. Brown steaks on both sides.

3. Cut 4 pieces of foil each 18-inches long. Place 1 steak on the bottom half of each piece of foil.

4. Divide the onion into fourths; top each steak with ¼ of the onions. Top onions with carrot and potato slices. Season with additional salt and pepper if desired. Dot each packet with 1 tablespoon butter.

5. Fold foil over steak and veggies and seal all the edges together by folding over several times and firmly pressing into place.

6. Place packets on a baking sheet and bake 45-60 minutes. Remove from oven and carefully slit open the top of the packet, avoiding the steam that will be released. Season with Worcestershire sauce or your favorite steak sauce.

A Kitchen Diva who worries about calories is like a fish that worries about water.

Southwest Fajitas

These fajitas are so easy, needing only a day or so to marinate. Served with your favorite margarita, who needs to visit a Mexican restaurant?

6 servings

- 4 **cloves garlic (2 teaspoons)**
- 2 **pounds skirt steak[1]**
- ¼ **cup Dale's Steak Seasoning[2]**
  (or soy sauce)
- 1 **teaspoon Worcestershire sauce**
- ¼ **cup freshly squeezed lime juice**
  (1 lime)
- ¼ **cup tequila**
- ¼ **cup vegetable oil**
- 1 **teaspoon ground cumin**
- 1 **small onion, chopped (½ cup)**
- ½ **cup fresh cilantro[3], roughly chopped**
- 1 **tablespoon vegetable oil (optional)**
- 1 **large onion, thinly sliced (optional)**
- 1 **green bell pepper, sliced (optional)**
- 12 **flour tortillas**

1. Crush garlic in a large zip top bag.

2. Place skirt steak in bag. Mix the next 8 ingredients and pour over steak in the bag. Seal bag tightly. Marinate meat 12-48 hours in the refrigerator.

3. Preheat grill to high heat. Remove meat from bag and discard marinade. Grill over hot coals 3-5 minutes per side. Remove meat from grill to a cutting board and let rest at least 10 minutes before cutting into thin slices across the grain.

4. Heat 1 tablespoon vegetable oil in a large skillet over medium-high heat. Cook onions and peppers until lightly brown and wilted, if desired.

5. Roll meat in warm tortillas with peppers and onions and your choice of toppings (guacamole; pico de gallo; sour cream; salsa or shredded Cheddar cheese).

Diva Tips

[1]**Skirt steak** is a cut from the flank section and is long, flat and stringy. Cook for a short time and slice across the grain for tenderness.

[2]**Dale's Steak Seasoning** can be found near the steak marinades and Worcestershire sauces.

[3]To store fresh herbs (parsley or **cilantro**), wash herbs in plenty of cold water; drain on paper towels. Roll clean, damp herbs in dry paper towels and place in a tightly covered plastic container. Store 1-2 weeks in the coldest part of your refrigerator.

Sirloin Botanas Platter

We went through withdrawal from authentic Mexican food when we moved from Texas to Tennessee (there were not a lot of authentic Mexican restaurants in Memphis while we lived there). I had to become creative and learn how to cook Mexican dishes we missed so dearly. We loved the Botanas platters served in South Texas. Here is my version of the steak and cheese rolled in flour tortillas.

4 servings

1   **pound sirloin or skirt steak[1]**
1   **pound baby Jack cheese, cut into cubes (or substitute Velveeta®)**
1   **can (8-ounces) Rotel® tomatoes with chilies, chopped**
¾   **cup thick salsa (bought or homemade)**
1   **teaspoon chopped fresh jalapeños (optional)**
8   **(6-inch) flour tortillas**
     additional salsa, for serving if desired

1. Heat grill (or oven broiler) to high heat.

2. Grill (or broil) sirloin very quickly over high heat until browned on the outside and medium-rare on the inside (4-5 minutes per inch thickness, per side).

3. Remove from grill and let meat **rest[2]** for 10 minutes. Slice into thin slices across the grain.

4. Meanwhile make the queso sauce: melt cheese in a double boiler. Strain the Rotel® tomatoes, reserving the juice. Add strained tomatoes, salsa and jalapeños to melted cheese, thinning with the reserved juice if sauce gets too thick.

5. Place grilled meat slices on a serving plate and drizzle with cheese sauce. To serve, roll meat in warmed flour tortillas and serve with additional salsa if desired.

Diva Tips

[1]Remove **meat** from refrigerator 1 hour before cooking to allow it to come to room temperature so meat cooks more evenly.

[2]Allow cooked meat, no matter what cut or kind, to **"rest"** for 10-15 minutes before slicing or carving to allow the juices to settle back into the meat and prevent them from "flooding" out when meat is cut.

Filets of Beef

These steaks make a special dinner for your someone special.

4 servings

4 **beef**[1] **tenderloin filets**
2 **tablespoons vegetable oil (preferably extra virgin olive oil)**
salt and pepper, to taste
4 **tablespoons butter**
1 **tablespoon soy sauce**

1. Heat grill to medium-high temperature (or oven broiler).

2. Remove all the silver skin from filets by cutting with a sharp knife or kitchen scissors. Rub oil all over filets and season with salt and pepper. Place filets on grill (or under broiler) and cook 3-5 minutes per inch thickness per side or until desired doneness (test with a meat thermometer: 140° is rare; 150° is medium; do not overcook). **Meat**[2] will continue to cook after removing from heat.

3. Meanwhile prepare sauce: heat butter in a small skillet or saucepan over medium-high heat until foamy, being careful not to burn. Add soy sauce and immediately remove from heat. When steaks are done, baste with sauce and serve.

   (Note: to prepare meat 1-2 hours ahead of time, grill steaks on both sides for about ¾'s of the total grill time. Remove to a platter and keep loosely covered with aluminum foil. Five minutes before serving time, melt an additional 1 tablespoon butter in a large skillet over high heat. Add filets and cook for an additional 1-2 minutes per side to desired doneness. Add any accumulated pan juices to sauce; baste filets with sauce and serve immediately.)

Diva Tips

[1]Remove **meat** from refrigerator 1 hour before cooking to allow it to come to room temperature so that meat cooks more evenly.

[2]For juicier **meat**, let cooked meat, no matter what the cut or kind, rest 10-15 minutes before slicing or carving to allow the juices to settle back into the meat and prevent them from "flooding" out when meat is cut.

Marinated Flank Steak with Citrus Salsa

6 servings

Marinade

3 cloves garlic, crushed (1½ teaspoons)
1 medium onion chopped (1 cup)
¼ cup vegetable oil
¼ cup red wine vinegar
3 tablespoons soy sauce
¼ cup vodka (or any clear liquor or wine)
2 tablespoons catsup
¼ cup chopped fresh **cilantro**[1]
1 teaspoon Tabasco sauce
½ teaspoon dried tarragon
½ teaspoon black pepper, (freshly ground preferred)
1½ pounds flank steak (or London Broil steak)
Citrus Salsa

1. Combine all ingredients for the marinade in a zip top plastic bag. Score the flank steak with a knife, place in the bag and seal. Marinate in the refrigerator at least 8 hours up to 2 days.

2. Preheat the grill (or oven broiler) to high heat. Remove steak from bag and discard marinade. Grill (or broil) 5-7 minutes per side. (Do not over cook or meat will be dry.) Remove from heat and let rest 10 minutes before thinly slicing across the grain. Serve with Citrus Salsa.

Citrus Salsa

1½ cups

1 cup **orange sections**[2], coarsely chopped
¼ cup red onions, finely chopped
¼ cup fresh chopped cilantro
¼ teaspoon ground cumin
¼ teaspoon salt
2 tablespoons freshly squeezed lime juice
1 small jalapeño pepper, finely chopped (or to taste)
1 tablespoon vegetable oil

1. Combine all ingredients, stirring well. Cover and chill at least 1 hour up to 8 hours ahead for flavors to meld.

Diva Tips

[1]To store fresh herbs (parsley or **cilantro**), wash herbs in plenty of cold water; drain on paper towels. Roll clean, damp herbs in dry paper towels and place in a tightly covered plastic container. Store 1-2 weeks in the coldest part of your refrigerator

[2]To **section an orange**, slice off the top and bottom. Stand the fruit on one of the cut ends. Following the contour of the fruit, slice off all the peel and white pith in thick strips. After all peel has been removed, cut along each side of the membrane and orange section while holding the orange over a bowl to catch the sections and any juice. When all sections have been removed, squeeze all the remaining juice from the membranes into the bowl. Discard membranes.

Mom's Pot Roast

What could be better comfort food than a Sunday pot roast? For family gatherings, my mother, Hazel Stowe, always makes her pot roast in her large cast iron pan.

6-8 servings

1 (3-pound) **chuck** or **shoulder roast**[1]
   salt and pepper to taste
4 **tablespoons vegetable oil, divided**
2 **large onions, quartered**
1 **clove garlic, crushed (½ teaspoon)**
1 **can (14-ounces) beef or chicken broth**
6 **potatoes, quartered**
6 **carrots, coarsely sliced**

1. Season meat on all sides with salt and pepper.

2. Heat 2 tablespoons of vegetable oil in a heavy, ovenproof pan on top of the stove over medium-high heat. Brown the roast thoroughly on all sides.

3. Remove meat from pan and add 1 quartered onion and the garlic; stir and cook 1 minute.

4. Return meat to the pan on top of the onions. Pour broth in the pan. Cover tightly and put in a 350° oven. Bake 1-1½ hours.

5. Toss the potatoes, carrots and remaining onion with the remaining 2 tablespoons vegetable oil. Season with salt and pepper. Remove pan from oven and add vegetables around the meat. Cover **tightly**[2] and continue baking for an additional 1-2 hours.

6. Carefully remove vegetables from the pan. Remove meat, reserving drippings. Set aside to **cool**[3]. Add drippings (with any onions) to the Brown Mushroom Gravy and serve over sliced meat.

Kitchen Divas approach the kitchen with good tools and a sense of humor.

Mom's Brown Mushroom Gravy

1 can (14-ounces or 2 cups) chicken or beef broth

½ cup red wine (optional)

1 package (1.75-ounces) brown gravy mix

½ cup water

1 package (8-ounces) mushrooms, sliced

2 tablespoons butter or margarine

1. Bring broth and wine, if using, to a boil in a medium saucepan. Reduce heat to medium and simmer 10 minutes.

2. Stir gravy mix into water. Slowly mix into broth, stirring constantly until thickened.

3. Put sliced mushrooms in a microwave-safe dish and top with butter. Microwave on high for 2-3 minutes until mushrooms begin to loose their liquid. Stir mushrooms and any juices into the brown gravy. Add any meat drippings and serve over the sliced meat.

Diva Tips

[1]The **chuck** and **shoulder roasts** are tougher cuts and need to be cooked with liquid for a long period of time to tenderize.

[2]If **lid** does not fit snuggly, cover the pan tightly with aluminum foil and place the lid over the foil.

[3]Meat will slice neater when **cool**. Reheat meat with hot gravy.

Roasted Beef Tenderloin

This recipe is very elegant and can be served for special occasions or holiday dinners. Tenderloin is the tenderest cut of beef. Avoid overcooking: serve medium rare or medium.

6-8 servings

1 (4 to 6-pounds) whole tenderloin, trimmed
salt and pepper to taste
¼ cup melted butter or margarine
¼ cup brandy (or substitute beef broth)

1. To prepare tenderloin, remove from plastic vacuum pack; rinse under cold water and pat dry. Remove "head" (the large end) by slipping fingers under and loosening fibers. Pull away from the loin and reserve for other uses (cut into shish kebabs or grill separately). Remove all the silver skin from the loin with a sharp knife or with kitchen scissors. With the edge of the knife, scrape off the excess fat. (Or ask your butcher to prepare tenderloin.) Season with salt and pepper.

2. Coat beef with the melted butter. Preheat oven to 400°. Place in an open, shallow roasting pan. Tuck thin end underneath. Without covering, roast meat 45-60 minutes or until a meat thermometer registers 130° (medium-rare) to 140° (medium). (Meat will continue to cook after it is removed from the oven.)

3. Remove meat from oven; place tenderloin on a serving dish and loosely tent with foil to keep warm.

4. Pour brandy in baking pan and scrape up any browned bits from the bottom of the pan.

Tomatoes and oregano make it Italian.

Wine and tarragon make it French.

Sour cream makes it Russian.

Soy sauce makes if Chinese.

Garlic makes it good.

Red Wine Sauce

2   medium shallots, finely chopped
2   tablespoons butter or margarine
1   cup red **wine**[1]
1   can (10-ounces) condensed beef broth
     (in the canned soups section)
1   tablespoon cornstarch
⅓   cup tomato sauce
1   tablespoon **B-V** beef concentrate
     (or **Kitchen Bouquet**)[2]
     salt and pepper, to taste
1   tablespoon butter or margarine

1. Sauté shallots in butter. Add wine; stir in brandy mixture from baking pan. Bring to a boil and cook until liquid is reduced to ¼ cup.

2. Stir broth with cornstarch. Slowly add to wine mixture, stirring constantly. Bring to a boil; stir in tomato sauce and B V beef concentrate.

3. Taste and adjust seasonings with salt and pepper if necessary.

4. Stir in 1 tablespoon butter. Coat tenderloin with some of the sauce, reserving the rest.

5. Slice tenderloin into ½-inch slices. Serve with reserved wine sauce.

Diva Tips

[1]Cook with an inexpensive **wine** that you would drink. Cooking wine found in the vinegar section of the grocery store is poor quality and high in sodium.

[2]**B-V** or **Kitchen Bouquet** is located near the bouillon cubes in most grocery stores.

Baked Brisket au Jus

Plan to make a brisket ahead of time. Because the meat is so fibrous, it must be cooked a low temperature for a few hours. For ease of slicing, chill the meat thoroughly.

8-10 servings

1 (4-pound) beef **brisket**[1]
   seasoned salt
2 **tablespoons vegetable oil**
2 **large onions, sliced**
2 **cloves garlic, crushed**
1 **large baking bag**[2]
1 **can (12-ounces) beer (any kind or substitute dry white wine)**
1 **cup barbecue sauce**
¼ **cup apricot jam**
½ **teaspoon dry mustard**
2 **tablespoons cider vinegar**

1. Remove brisket from vacuum-seal bag; rinse with cold water and pat dry.

2. Cut away most of the fat, leaving a thin layer for flavor. Sprinkle seasoned salt all over the meat.

3. Heat oil in a large skillet and brown brisket on all sides. Remove from skillet and place in the baking bag. Put half of onions and garlic on top of the meat and half underneath. Pour beer into the bag and seal tightly with the tie provided by the manufacturer. With the tip of a knife, pierce a half-inch hole in the top of the bag (otherwise, bag will pop).

4. Put bag on a baking sheet and bake at 300° 4-4½ hours.

5. Remove from oven and cool. Refrigerate in the bag overnight or until thoroughly chilled. Carefully remove meat from bag. Pour juices from bag (may need to reheat juices to bring them back to a liquid state) and strain or (place juices and solids in a blender to make a smooth sauce). Return juices to a saucepan; add barbecue sauce, jam, mustard, and vinegar and heat together. **Slice cold**[3] brisket across the grain. Heat meat with some sauce in a large skillet. Serve with remaining heated sauce.

Diva Tips

[1]Tough meats need to cook by braising – cooking in a small amount of liquid at a low temperature for a long time to tenderize. Leftover **brisket** can be frozen in the sauce up to 3 months.

[2]**Baking bags** can be found in the grocery aisle with aluminum foil and plastic wrap. These are a smaller version of the same bags used to bake turkeys.

[3]Fibrous meats will **slice** better **cold**.

Braciola al Pomodoro

These are little, stuffed meat bundles cooked in tomato sauce. They make a delicious change from meatballs and really flavor the sauce.

6 servings

1½	pounds top sirloin beef, cut into 12 small, thin slices, pounded very thin
3	cloves garlic (1½ teaspoons), crushed
2	tablespoons chopped fresh parsley
1	tablespoon chopped fresh **rosemary**[1]
¼	cup Parmesan cheese
6	thin slices proscuitto (¼ pound) cut in half
⅓	cup vegetable oil (preferably extra virgin olive oil)
1	cup dry red **wine**[2]
1	can (14-ounces) imported Italian tomatoes with their juice
1	can (8-ounces) tomato paste
2	cans water (use tomato paste can)
	salt and pepper, to taste
1	teaspoon dried oregano
1	tablespoon fresh chopped **basil**[3]
2	tablespoons fresh chopped parsley
	cooked pasta

1. Put meat on the work surface (cover with plastic wrap to protect the surface, if desired). Mix together garlic, 2 tablespoons fresh parsley, rosemary, and cheese. Divide evenly among the meat slices.

2. Place a half slice of proscuitto over each piece of meat and roll into a small bundle. Secure each bundle with a toothpick.

3. Heat oil in a large skillet over medium-high heat. Add bundles, being careful not to crowd the pan, and thoroughly brown on all sides, 3-4 minutes. Transfer bundles to a plate.

4. Pour off most of the fat from the skillet. Add the wine to the hot pan and stir to pick up any browned bits stuck to the bottom of the skillet.

5. Put tomatoes in a blender or chop with a knife.

6. When the wine is reduced by half, 3-4 minutes, add chopped tomatoes, tomato paste and water; stirring to mix well. Season with salt and pepper. Stir in oregano.

7. Return meat to the sauce. Cook until sauce has thickened, 15-20 minutes, stirring occasionally. Remove toothpicks from the meat bundles and add back to sauce. Add basil and parsley and cook an additional 1-2 minutes. Serve over cooked pasta.

Diva Tips

[1]**Rosemary** is a woody herb. Before chopping, strip the green leaves off the woody stems.

[2]Cook with an inexpensive **wine** that you would drink. Cooking wine found in the vinegar section of the grocery store is poor quality and high in sodium.

[3]**Basil** can be kept fresh for 3-4 days with the stems submerged in cool water in a container and kept on the counter. Refresh water every day.

Italian Roast Beef au Jus

Jim and I first had this roast beef in Chicago. The meat is sliced very thin and served on crispy, French rolls with au jus and marinated celery and jalapeños. I asked for the recipe for the celery and peppers but was denied, so I had to come up with my own. Deliciouso!

6-8 servings

Italian Roast Beef

1 (3-pound) bottom round rump **roast[1]**
 seasoned salt
2 tablespoons vegetable oil
1 large **baking bag[2]**
7-8 cloves garlic, crushed
1 large onion, sliced
2 teaspoons dried basil
2 teaspoons dried oregano
1 teaspoon red pepper flakes
 (or to taste)
1 teaspoon pepper
1 can (12-ounces) beer, any kind
1 can (14-ounces) low-sodium beef
 broth
 crispy French rolls

1. Rinse meat with cold water and pat dry. Cut away most of the fat, leaving a thin layer for flavor. Sprinkle seasoned salt all over the meat.

2. Heat oil in a large skillet and brown roast on all sides. Remove from skillet and place in the baking bag. Put half of onions and garlic on top of the meat and half underneath.

3. Pour beer into the bag and seal tightly with manufacturer's tie. With the tip of a knife, pierce a half-inch hole in the top of the bag (otherwise, bag will pop). Put bag in a baking pan and bake at 300° 4-4½ hours.

4. Remove from oven and cool. Carefully remove cooled meat from bag; strain juice and discard solids; add beef broth to juices. Cover meat tightly and refrigerate meat in the juices overnight or until cold. Remove meat from juices and **slice[3]** meat across the grain as thinly as possible (a very sharp knife or electric knife works best). Heat juices in a large skillet. Remove from heat and add sliced meat into hot juice to reheat. Serve meat in crisp, hard rolls with juice (au jus) and Marinated Celery and Jalapeños.

Life is a party and you are invited. Wear your best dress and have a ball!

Marinated Celery and Jalapeños

1 cup sliced celery
2 medium jalapeno peppers, sliced
2 cloves garlic, thinly sliced
1 cup vegetable oil

1. Stuff celery, peppers and garlic in a heat proof container (like a canning jar).

2. Bring vegetable oil to a boil; pour hot oil over celery mix. Let sit uncovered until cool. Cover and store in the refrigerator. Will keep refrigerated 2-3 weeks. (When celery and peppers are gone, use the flavored, spicy oil for sautéing or in any salad dressing recipe.)

Diva Tips

[1]Tough **meats** need to cook by braising – cooking in a small amount of liquid at a low temperature for a long time to tenderize. Leftover beef can be frozen up to 3 months in the au jus.

[2]**Baking bags** can be found in the grocery aisle with aluminum foil and plastic wrap. These are a smaller version of the same bags used to bake turkeys.

[3]Fibrous meats **slice** easier when cold.

Roasted Pork Loin

Put pizzazz in your next pork loin.

6-8 servings

1 (3 to 4-pound) **rolled**, boneless **pork loin**[1]

   salt and pepper
3 **cloves garlic, slivered into 12 pieces**
½ **tablespoon vegetable oil**

1. Season roast generously with salt and pepper.

2. Make 12 small slits in the bottom of the roast (opposite the fat side) with the tip of a sharp knife. Push garlic all the way into the meat into the slits.

3. Heat an oven-proof, heavy skillet over medium-high heat. Spread the vegetable oil over the bottom of the hot skillet. Place meat fat side down in the hot skillet and brown, rendering some of the fat. Turn roast over to brown on all sides, ending with fat side up. Place skillet (or transfer meat to a roasting pan if skillet is not oven-proof) in a 325° oven and bake 30 minutes per pound until a meat thermometer registers 160°. (Do not add water and do not cover.) Remove from oven and let meat **rest**[2] 10-15 minutes before slicing.

Diva Tips

[1]A **rolled pork roast** is two loins from the rib section that are tied together and sold as a roll.

[2]For juicier meat, let cooked meat, no matter what the cut or kind, **rest** 10-15 minutes before slicing or carving to allow the juices to settle back into the meat and prevent them from "flooding" out when meat is cut.

Jerk Marinated Pork Tenderloin

Jerk is a spicy flavoring from the Caribbean, especially Jamaica, used in ancient times as a means for preserving and cooking meats. Most jerk rubs or sauces contain peppers (to add fire to your dish) and Caribbean spices, like cinnamon and allspice (to add flavor). Jerk is especially delicious on chicken, pork and ribs. Try it on chicken wings too!

4-6 servings

2 pounds **pork tenderloin**
½ cup commercially prepared **jerk marinade**[1]
3 **cloves garlic**, crushed (1½ teaspoons)
1 tablespoon grated fresh **gingerroot**[2]
¼ cup chopped fresh **cilantro**
½ teaspoon ground **cumin**

1. To prepare tenderloins: remove from plastic vacuum pack; rinse unto cold water and pat dry. Remove all the silver skin with a sharp knife or with kitchen scissors. With the edge of the knife, scrape off the excess fat. (Or ask your butcher to prepare tenderloin.)

2. Combine remaining ingredients and coat tenderloins. Seal in a zip top bag and marinate in the refrigerator at least 4 hours or overnight.

3. Preheat charcoal grill (or oven broiler) to medium-high heat. Remove tenderloins from bag and cook over hot coals (or under broiler) 10 minutes per side or until an instant-read thermometer reads 160°. Remove from grill, and let meat rest for at least 10 minutes before cutting into serving-size pieces.

Diva Tips

[1]**Jerk marinade** can be located with other steak marinades in the grocery store.

[2]To measure fresh **gingerroot**, 1 ounce = 3 tablespoons minced; 1-inch x 1-inch piece = 1 tablespoon minced or grated. Store extra ginger peeled or unpeeled in the freezer in 1-inch slices. While still frozen, grate or cut into small cubes and push through a garlic press. Or cover fresh, peeled ginger with vodka and store in the refrigerator.

Slow-Cooked Baby Back Pork Ribs

These ribs will rival (and surpass) any barbecue joint that boasts of tender, fall-off-the-bone ribs.

6-8 servings

Ribs

6-7 pounds baby back ribs
¼ cup dry spice rub (or your favorite dry spice rub)
heavy duty aluminum foil
your favorite barbecue sauce

Dry Spice Rub

½ **cup chili powder**
2 **tablespoons sweet paprika**
½ **tablespoon garlic powder**
1 **teaspoon onion powder**
½ **teaspoon ground cumin**
1½ **teaspoons salt**
1 **teaspoon pepper**
¼ **teaspoon cayenne pepper**
1 **tablespoon sugar**

1. Rinse ribs with cold water and pat dry.

2. Mix all ingredients for spice rub and store in a tightly covered container in a dry place until ready to use.

3. Rub dry spice rub into all surfaces of the ribs.

4. Tear two pieces of heavy-duty aluminum foil into equal lengths, 12-inches longer than the length of the ribs. Place two pieces of foil on top of another one. Fold one long edge together several times and seal, pressing edges firmly to form a larger rectangle.

5. Place the ribs in the center of one piece of foil. Fold the foil over top of the ribs. Again fold remaining 3 edges of the foil together pressing firmly to form a tightly sealed packet around the ribs. Place packet in a baking pan. (If time allows, refrigerate ribs 1 hour up to 1 day to let the spices work magic into the meat.)

6. Bake in a 300° oven 3-4 hours. Remove ribs from oven; heat a charcoal grill to medium. Remove ribs from foil and grill over hot coals 15-20 minutes, while basting with your favorite barbecue sauce, being careful not to let ribs burn. Cut into serving size pieces and be sure to have extra napkins, because these ribs are bone sucking good!

Believe in love at first sight: I fell in love with chocolate the first time I laid eyes on it and we have been a happy couple ever since.

Chris' Special Pork Chops

My son, Chris, surprised me by making these pork chops for dinner one night when he was home from college. They were so delicious, moist and tender that I made him write down the recipe for me the next time he made them. He confided that his secret is massaging all the spices into the meat.

6-8 servings

- **8 pork chops, ¾-inch thick**
- **8 teaspoons dry spice rub (see Slow-Cooked Baby Back Ribs recipe)**
- **½ cup Dale's steak Seasoning[1] (or soy sauce)**
- **1 cup beer (any kind)**

1. Rub ½ teaspoon dry rub onto each side of the pork chop, gently massaging spices into meat.

2. Mix together Dale's steak sauce and beer. Put pork chops in a zip top bag and pour beer mixture over meat. Marinate in the refrigerator for at least 1 hour or overnight.

3. Heat a charcoal grill to medium-high heat. Remove chops from the bag and discard marinade. Place chops over medium-hot coals and cook 10-12 minutes per side or until an instant-read meat thermometer registers 165° internal temperature.

Diva Tips

[1]**Dale's steak seasoning** is a soy sauce based sauce and is found in most grocery stores next to other steak sauces.

Apple Pork Tenderloins

Cooked apples are a delicious compliment to pork.

4-6 servings

Pork Cutlets

2 **pounds pork tenderloins**

1 **teaspoon salt**

½ **teaspoon pepper**

3 **tablespoons butter or margarine, divided**

2 **tablespoons vegetable oil (preferably extra virgin olive oil), divided**

3 **medium shallots[1], finely chopped**

1 **clove garlic, crushed (½ teaspoon)**

1 **cup low-sodium chicken broth**

2 **tablespoons apple brandy[2] (Calvados) (or apple juice)**

1 **cup heavy cream**

1. To prepare tenderloins: remove from plastic vacuum pack; rinse under cold water and pat dry. Cut away all the silver skin with a sharp knife or with kitchen scissors. With the edge of the knife, scrape off the excess fat. (Or ask your butcher to prepare tenderloin.)

2. Cut each tenderloin crosswise into 4-5 medallions about 2-inches thick. Place cut side up between two sheets of plastic wrap and pound until cutlet is ¼-inch thick. Season with salt and pepper.

3. Melt 1 tablespoon butter in a large skillet over medium-high heat. Add 1 tablespoon vegetable oil. When oil is hot, sauté cutlets in batches until browned on each side, 2-4 minutes. Do not crowd the pan. Add more butter and oil as needed for additional batches. Transfer to a plate and tent with aluminum foil to keep warm.

4. Add shallots and garlic to skillet and stir 1 minute. Add broth and apple brandy to pan. Stir and scrape up any browned bits stuck to the bottom of the pan. Cook until mixture is reduced by half, about 6-8 minutes. Add cream and simmer until sauce thickens enough to coat the back of a spoon, about 10 minutes. Taste and adjust seasonings, adding more salt and pepper if necessary. Spoon sauce over cutlets and top with spiced apples.

Laugh often, long, and loud. Laugh until people around you question your sanity.

Spiced Apples

3   medium tart apples, cored and cut into rings
3   tablespoons butter or margarine
½   teaspoon cinnamon
2   teaspoons sugar
2   cups apple juice or cider
2   tablespoons apple **brandy**[2] (Calvados) (optional)

1. Heat butter in a heavy skillet over medium-high heat. Fry one layer of apple rings until golden on both sides. Remove from pan and keep warm while frying remaining rings (adding more butter as needed). Set apples aside.

2. Mix sugar and cinnamon; sprinkle over apples.

3. Pour in apple juice and optional brandy into the skillet and simmer until thick and syrupy.

4. Return apples to the skillet and glaze with the apple syrup.

Diva Tips

[1]**Shallots** look like a cross between garlic and onions. Buy shallots that are tight, with papery-looking skins and no green sprouts. They are mild and are used to season foods in which onions would be too strong.

Substitute an equal amount of scallions. Store in a cool, dry place for weeks.

[2]Small bottles (airline serving size—about 3 tablespoons) of **liqueurs** can be purchased at most liquor stores.

Sherry's Veal

Thank you Sherry and Conrad Hale for such a tasty recipe.

4 servings

1	**pound (eight ⅛-inch) veal cutlets**
	salt and pepper to taste
¼	**cup all-purpose flour**
2	**tablespoons butter or margarine**
2	**tablespoons vegetable oil (preferably extra virgin olive oil)**
2	**shallots, finely minced**
2	**cups sliced mushrooms[1]**
1	**cup white wine[2]**
1	**cup chicken broth**
½	**cup heavy cream**
1	**lemon, cut into wedges**

1. Pound veal until very thin, being careful not to break through the fibers. Season with salt and pepper; dip in flour and shake to remove excess.

2. Heat butter and olive oil in a large skillet until hot. Brown cutlets 1-2 minutes per side. Remove to a dish and tent with a piece of foil to keep warm while preparing sauce.

3. Add shallots to the browning pan and cook for 2-3 minutes. Add mushrooms and cook just until mushrooms release their liquid. Remove mushrooms and shallots to a separate dish.

4. To the same pan, add wine and chicken broth. Bring to a boil stirring and scraping up any browned bits in the bottom of the skillet. Cook until liquid is reduced by half. Add cream and cook an additional 5-10 minutes.

5. Return mushrooms and shallots to sauce. Squeeze lemon over warm veal and spoon mushroom sauce over cutlets. Serve immediately.

Diva Tips

[1]Never immerse **mushrooms** in water; they will absorb liquid like a sponge. The best way to clean mushrooms is to wipe with a damp paper towel. Store mushrooms in a paper bag in the refrigerator.

[2]Cook with an inexpensive **wine** that you would drink. Cooking wine found in the vinegar section of the grocery store is poor quality and high in sodium.

Veal Marsala

Why order out when this recipe is so easy and quick?

4 servings

1 **pound (about eight ⅛-inch thick) veal cutlets**

salt and pepper to taste

¼ **cup all-purpose flour**

1-2 tablespoons butter or margarine

1-2 tablespoons vegetable oil (preferably extra virgin olive oil)

1 **cup Marsala wine[1]**

½ **cup chicken broth**

1. Pound veal until very thin, being careful not to break through fibers. Season with salt and pepper.

2. Dredge both sides of veal in flour, shaking to remove excess.

3. Heat 1 tablespoon butter and 1 tablespoon oil in a large skillet over medium-high heat. Cook cutlets in batches in hot oil, 1-2 minutes per side until golden (use extra butter and oil if needed). Do not crowd the pan. Remove cutlets to a separate dish and tent with aluminum foil to keep warm while preparing sauce.

4. Add Marsala to the pan. Stir to scrape up any browned bits from the bottom of the pan. Add chicken broth and reduce by half. Pour sauce over warm veal and serve immediately.

Diva Tips

[1]Cook with an inexpensive **wine** that you would drink. Cooking wine found in the vinegar section of the grocery store is poor quality and high in sodium.

Roast Rack of Lamb

A rack of lamb (a strip of 7 uncut rib chops) can be expensive, but is a very impressive, rich treat that is incredibly easy to prepare.

4 servings

Lamb

2   **(2-pound) racks of lamb**
    salt and pepper
1   **tablespoon finely chopped fresh rosemary[1]**
1   **tablespoon finely chopped fresh thyme[2]**
2   **cloves garlic, crushed (1 teaspoon)**
2   **medium shallots[3], finely minced**
2   **tablespoons vegetable oil (preferably extra virgin olive oil)**

1. Prepare the racks by trimming off most of the excess fat leaving ¼-inch.

2. Scrape ("french") the bones (extending out of the meat) clean. Season the meat with salt and pepper.

3. Mix the herbs, garlic and shallots together with the olive oil. Rub generously all over the lamb; cover and refrigerate 1 hour up to 2 days.

4. Preheat the oven to 450°. Cover ends of the bones with aluminum foil to prevent excess browning. Place the lamb in a roasting pan and cook 10 minutes. Lower heat to 350° and continue cooking 20-25 minutes or until a meat thermometer registers 135° (for medium) or until desired doneness (125° is rare; 160° is well).

5. Remove from oven and let rest for at least 10 minutes before carving. For impressive presentation, cut meat in between each bone and rest each chop, bone side up, on a bed of garlic mashed potatoes in a pool of brown sauce.

The perfect age for a Kitchen Diva is somewhere between old enough to know better and too young to care.

Brown Sauce

1 cup

1 medium carrot, chopped
1 medium onion, chopped
1 stalk celery, chopped
1 bay leaf
2 sprigs fresh thyme
3 black peppercorns
2 cups good quality no-sodium beef stock or broth
　 salt and pepper, if necessary

1 When the lamb is cooked, remove from roasting pan to a dish and tent with foil to keep warm. If there is a lot of fat in the pan, remove most of it, leaving 1-2 tablespoons to cook the vegetables.

2. Add the carrot, onion and celery to the roasting pan and cook on the top of the stove over medium heat for about 5 minutes or until vegetables are golden brown, stirring constantly. Add the bay leaf, thyme and peppercorns. Stir in 1 cup of the broth. Bring to a boil scraping the pan to loosen any browned bits stuck to the bottom. Pour in the remaining cup of stock and bring back to a boil. Reduce heat to a simmer and cook 5-10 minutes or until reduced by half. Taste and season with salt and pepper if necessary. Strain the sauce, pressing on the solids to remove all the liquid. Serve immediately.

Diva Tips

[1,2]Thyme and **rosemary** are woody herbs. Strip the green leaves off the woody stems and chop leaves.

[3]Shallots look like a cross between garlic and yellow onions. Buy shallots that are tight, with papery-looking skins and no green sprouts. They are mild and are used to season foods in which onions would be too strong. Substitute an equal amount of scallions. Store in a cool, dry place for weeks.

 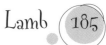

Boiled Shrimp with Cocktail Sauce

Soooo easy. Once you make this cocktail sauce, you will never buy it buy it in a jar again.

6 servings

Shrimp

8   **cups water**
2   **garlic cloves, crushed (1 teaspoon)**
1   **tablespoon Old Bay Seasoning**[1]
1   **tablespoon salt**
1   **small onion, quartered**
1   **lemon, quartered**
2   **pounds fresh, large shrimp**

Cocktail Sauce

1   **cup catsup**
2-3 **tablespoons prepared horseradish**[2]
    (or to taste)
1   **tablespoon lemon juice**
1   **teaspoon Worcestershire sauce**

1. In a large saucepan, mix water, garlic, Old Bay seasoning, salt, onion and lemon; bring to a boil and simmer for 4-5 minutes.

2. Add shrimp to boiling, seasoned liquid. Bring back to a boil. Remove from heat, cover and set aside for 6 minutes.

3. Drain shrimp and immediately spread in a single layer on a large pan in the refrigerator; cool completely. Peel and devein shrimp. Stir together all sauce ingredients. Dip shrimp in sauce.

(Note: Shrimp should be served cold. Can be prepared ahead of time and refrigerated up to 6 hours after cooling and draining. To create an ice block for serving and keeping shrimp cold: fill a large, deep rectangular pan one-half full with water. Place on a level surface in the freezer and freeze completely (24 hours). Dampen the top of the block of ice, and decorate the edges with fresh herbs or anything edible. Fill with additional water to secure the decoration. When ready to serve, carefully remove ice block from pan. Place ice block on a larger serving tray or on a rack over a pan to catch the melting ice; arrange shrimp over the top of the ice.)

Diva Tips

[1]**Old Bay seasoning** can be found in the spice aisle of the grocery store.

[2]**Prepared horseradish** can be found in the dairy case of most grocery stores next to the kosher items. (Don't confuse with horseradish sauce next to the mayonnaise.) Or you can finely grate your own peeled fresh horseradish root.

Lemon Scampi

6 servings

2 pounds fresh, large **shrimp**[1]
½ cup (1 stick) butter or margarine
4 cloves garlic, crushed (2 teaspoons)
3-4 tablespoons lemon juice (1 lemon)
1 teaspoon lemon **zest**[2]
  dash hot sauce (like Tabasco)
½ teaspoon salt (or to taste)
1 tablespoon finely chopped green onion (1 onion)
¼ cup chopped fresh parsley, optional (do not use dried parsley)

1. Peel and devein shrimp. Set aside.

2. Melt butter in a large skillet; sauté garlic for 30 seconds just until garlic releases its aroma. Remove from heat and add lemon juice, zest, hot sauce and salt. Toss with shrimp.

3. Preheat oven to 350°. Arrange shrimp with lemon sauce in a single layer in a (9x13-inch) pan. Top with green onions. Bake 15 minutes until shrimp turns pink and cooked through. Remove from oven and toss with parsley.

Diva Tips

[1]**Shrimp** is very perishable and must be eaten within 24 hours of purchasing. When buying shrimp, it should have no odor. Keep shrimp in a plastic bag surrounded by ice packs in the refrigerator. May be kept frozen up to 2 months. The best method for freezing is to completely submerge shrimp is water and freeze. Thaw overnight in the refrigerator or under cold running water.

[2]To **zest** lemon, lime or orange, wash fruit in hot water. Before cutting or juicing, remove zest (the very outermost layer of the fruit-the thin, colored part, avoiding the white pith which is bitter) with the finest part of a grater, or by peeling with a vegetable peeler and finely chopping with a knife or removing with a special tool called a zester.

Barbecue Shrimp

This shrimp is zesty and spicy. Dip French bread in the sauce to enjoy every ounce of this dish.

4 servings

½ **cup (1 stick) butter or margarine**

¼ **cup vegetable oil**

3 **tablespoons Worcestershire sauce**

¼ **teaspoon cayenne pepper (or to taste)**

¼ **cup fresh squeezed lemon juice (1 lemon)**

¼ **teaspoon hot sauce (like Tabasco)**

½ **teaspoon Italian seasoning[1] (or ¼ teaspoon oregano and ¼ teaspoon basil)**

2 **cloves garlic crushed, (1 teaspoon)**

½ **teaspoon sweet paprika**

1 **teaspoon salt**

½ **cup dry white wine**

2 **pounds fresh, large shrimp[2] in the shell**

crusty French bread, for dipping

1. Preheat oven to 350°.

2. Mix all ingredients, except shrimp, in a large ovenproof skillet or pan. Heat to a boil; lower heat, add shrimp and simmer 5 minutes until shrimp are just pink.

3. Place skillet in a preheated 350° oven and bake 10 minutes.

4. Remove from oven and stir shrimp and sauce. Return to oven and bake an additional 10 minutes.

5. Divide shrimp into 4 bowls, including the sauce. Serve with crusty French bread for dipping in the sauce.

Diva Tips

[1]Always crush **dried herbs** between your fingers before adding them to your recipe for optimum flavor.

[2]**Shrimp** is very perishable and must be eaten within 24 hours of purchasing. When buying shrimp, it should have no odor. Keep shrimp in a plastic bag surrounded by ice packs in the refrigerator. May be kept frozen up to 2 months. The best method for freezing is to completely submerge shrimp is water and freeze. Thaw in the refrigerator or under cold running water.

Margarita Shrimp

A fiesta on skewers.

4-6 servings

2	tablespoons fresh lime juice (1 lime)
2	tablespoons tequila (or white wine)
3	cloves garlic, crushed
1	teaspoon **Old Bay seasoning**[1] (or seasoned salt)
2	tablespoons chopped fresh cilantro
2	tablespoons vegetable oil
1½	pounds large **shrimp**[2] (20 per pound) peeled and deveined
12-16	(10-inch) wooden skewers (soaked 30 minutes in water)
3	tablespoons butter, melted

1. Mix lime juice, tequila, garlic, Old Bay seasoning and cilantro. Stir in oil.

2. Thread 2 skewers into each shrimp, one through the head end and one through the tail end (to keep shrimp level on the grill). Repeat until each double skewer is full (about 5 shrimp) Lay shrimp flat in a deep glass dish. Cover with marinade. Marinate for 1 hour at room temperature (or 2 hours refrigerated. Do not let shrimp sit in mixture too long or it could toughen the shrimp).

3. Preheat grill (or broiler) to medium-high heat. Remove shrimp from marinade; stir butter into mixture. Grill (or broil) shrimp 2 minutes per side basting with butter marinade until pink and cooked through (do not overcook).

Diva Tips

[1]**Old Bay seasoning** can be found in the spice aisle of the grocery store.

[2]**Shrimp** is very perishable and must be eaten within 24 hours of purchasing. When buying shrimp, it should have no odor. Keep shrimp in a plastic bag surrounded by ice packs in the refrigerator. May be kept frozen up to 2 months. The best method for freezing is to completely submerge shrimp is water and freeze. Thaw overnight in the refrigerator or under cold running water.

Fish Fast Facts

1. Fresh fish is virtually odorless or should only have a mild, fresh odor. The flesh should spring back when touched and not leave an impression. The eyes of whole fish should be clear and bright; the gills should be bright red.

2. Make fish the last purchase on your list before returning home. Be prepared to keep it cold by surrounding the fish with a bag of ice. (Most fish counters or fish mongers will provide the ice if requested.)

3. Store fish in the refrigerator up to 1 day surrounded by packs of ice. (Keep ice in tightly sealed plastic bags to prevent fish from becoming soggy.)

4. Thaw frozen fish in the refrigerator and not at room temperature. To quickly thaw, run fish under cold water and pat dry.

5. Serve: 4-6 ounces fillets per person

    6-8 ounces steaks per person

    12-16 ounces whole fish per person

6. Leftover, cooked fish can be refrigerated 2-3 days. Creatively use these leftovers in omelets, salads, or soups.

Life—everyone's life—is filled with challenges. The best way to handle obstacles is head-on, with a smile, and a handful of Hershey kisses.

Fish Substitution/Cooking Methods

TEXTURE	FLAVOR			BEST COOKING METHODS
	Mild	Medium	Full	
Delicate/ Flaky	Catfish Cod (Scrod) Flounder Lake White Fish Pollock (Alaska) Sole	Orange Roughy Pink Salmon	Herring Sardines Smelt	Bake Broil Deep Fry En Papillote Microwave Poach Sauté
Moderately Firm	Butterfish Grouper Haddock Halibut Snapper Striped Bass Tilapia	Amberjack Black Drum Mahi Mahi Ocean Perch Red Snapper Rock Fish Salmon (Atlantic) (Chum) (Coho) (King) Chilean Sea Bass Trout (Brook) (Rainbow)	Mackerel (Atlantic) (King) (Spanish) Yellow Tail	Bake Broil Deep Fry En Papillote Grill Microwave Poach Sauté Steam
Firm	Monkfish (Poor Man's Lobster)	Black Sea Bass Bluefish Shark	Sturgeon Swordfish Tuna Marlin	Broil Grill Microwave Poach Pickle Sauté Steam Stew

Fish by Ritz

4 servings

1   **large egg, lightly beaten**
1   **tablespoon fresh lemon juice (½ lemon)**
1   **teaspoon dark sesame oil[1]**
1   **teaspoon chili oil[2]**
2   **cups cracker crumbs (like Ritz) finely crushed**
2   **tablespoons sesame seeds, toasted[3]**
¼   **cup pecans, toasted and finely chopped**
¼   **cup Parmesan cheese**
8   **(4-ounce) fish filets (catfish or orange roughy)**

1. Preheat oven to 400°.

2. Beat egg with lemon juice, sesame oil, and chili oil. Set aside.

3. In a separate bowl, mix cracker crumbs, sesame seeds, pecans and cheese.

4. Dip dried fish filets in egg mixture. Coat fish with cracker mix.

5. Line a baking sheet with parchment paper and lightly butter paper. Place filets on prepared sheet. Bake 15 minutes or until done.

Diva Tips

[1,2]**Sesame oil** and **chili oil** can be found in the Oriental food section of the grocery store or in specialty shops.

[3]To **toast sesame seeds**, spread in a preheated, dry skillet in a single layer. Shake pan or stir seeds over medium-high heat until seeds turn a golden color for about 2-3 minutes, being careful not to burn. Toasting intensifies the flavor. Store sesame seeds in the refrigerator 6 months or freeze up to 1 year.

Ginger Soy Grilled Fish

6 servings

6 filets (2 pounds) **sea bass**[1], 1-inch thick
6 tablespoons extra virgin olive oil
    salt and pepper
1 (1-inch) piece of **gingerroot**[2], grated
1 medium shallot, finely minced
¼ cup rice wine vinegar
¼ cup fresh lime juice (2 limes)
2 tablespoons soy sauce
1 tablespoon dark sesame oil
⅓ cup extra virgin olive oil
2 tablespoons finely chopped fresh
    cilantro

1. Rub each filet with 1 tablespoon olive oil, season with salt and pepper. Set aside.

2. Mix remaining ingredients to make a sauce and let sit 30 minutes for flavors to meld.

3. Heat grill to high. Grill 4 minutes per side (8-10 minutes per inch).

4. Strain sauce, pressing on solids until all juice is extracted. Remove fish from grill and drizzle each filet with 2-3 tablespoons of sauce. Serve immediately.

Diva Tips

[1]Buy **fish** that is odor-free. Filets should lay flat and look moist. Fish is highly perishable and should be cooked the day of purchase. Store in a plastic bag surrounded by ice packs in the refrigerator to keep fish at its maximum freshness. Serve 6-8 ounce filet or 8-ounce fish steak per person.

[2]To measure fresh **gingerroot**, 1 ounce = 3 tablespoons minced; 1-inch x 1-inch piece = 1 tablespoon minced or grated. Store extra ginger peeled or unpeeled in the freezer in 1-inch slices. While still frozen, grate or cut into small cubes and push through a garlic press. Or cover fresh, peeled ginger with vodka and store in the refrigerator.

Jack Marinated Grilled Salmon

My son, Alex, was always the pickiest eater in my family. Imagine my amazement when he came home from college and asked me to make fish for him! Now he cooks fish for himself all the time.

4-6 servings

¾ cup pineapple juice

⅓ cup **Dale's steak seasoning**[1]
    (or substitute soy sauce)

¼ cup brown sugar

2 tablespoons whiskey
    (like Jack Daniel's)

½ teaspoon black pepper

3 cloves garlic, crushed (1½ teaspoon),

1 teaspoon **sesame oil**[2]

1 teaspoon **chili oil**[3]

½ cup vegetable oil

6 (6-ounces) salmon **fish**[4] filets

1. Combine first 9 ingredients in a medium bowl, stirring well to dissolve sugar. Reserve ¼ cup marinade for brushing on fish as it grills.

2. Rinse and dry filets and place in a zip top plastic bag. Pour marinade over fish and close bag tightly. Place bag in a glass dish and refrigerate 1 hour, up to 4 hours.

3. Preheat barbecue grill to medium-high heat. Remove fish from marinade and place on grill (or cook under the broiler). Cook 8 minutes without turning, brushing occasionally with reserved marinade. Serve immediately.

Diva Tips

[1]**Dale's steak seasoning** is a soy sauce based sauce and is found in most grocery stores next to other steak sauces.

[2-3]**Sesame oil** and **chili oil** can be found in the Oriental food section of the grocery store or in specialty shops. Store in the refrigerator.

[4]Buy **fish** that is odor-free. Filets should lay flat and look moist. Fish is highly perishable and should be cooked the day of purchase. Store in a plastic bag surrounded by ice packs in the refrigerator to keep fish at its maximum freshness. Serve 6-8 ounce filet or 8-ounce fish steak per person. Refer to the fish chart (page 191) for substitutions.

Shrimp and Crab-Stuffed Fish

6 servings

Stuffing

4   tablespoons butter or margarine
½   cup finely chopped onion
½   cup finely diced celery (1-2 stalks)
¼   cup finely diced green bell pepper
¼   cup finely chopped fresh mushrooms
½   pound shrimp, chopped
½   teaspoon **Old Bay Seasoning**[1]
¼   teaspoon **dried thyme**[2]
½   teaspoon salt
¼   teaspoon pepper
1   tablespoon Worcestershire sauce for
       chicken (white wine Worcestershire)
¼   cup white wine
¼   cup heavy cream
1   can (6-ounces) white crabmeat, drained
½   cup soft **breadcrumbs**[3]
12 (3-ounce) Flounder fish filets

Basting Sauce

4   tablespoons butter or margarine
¼   cup fresh lemon juice
½   teaspoon dried tarragon
1   teaspoon Worcestershire sauce for
       chicken (white wine Worcestershire)

1. Preheat oven to 350°.

2. Melt butter in a large saucepan over medium-high heat. Sauté onion, celery and green pepper until soft. Add mushrooms and cook until mushrooms release their liquid; continue cooking until liquid is absorbed. Add shrimp and cook an additional 2 minutes or until shrimp are barely pink. Remove from heat and season with Old Bay seasoning, thyme, salt and pepper; taste and adjust seasonings as necessary. Stir in Worcestershire sauce, wine and cream. Gently stir in crab. Add enough breadcrumbs to make thick stuffing.

3. Line a baking sheet with parchment paper or aluminum foil. Grease lightly with butter or margarine.

4. Place 6 fish filets on prepared baking sheet. Divide stuffing evenly among the filets. Top with remaining filets. Press down lightly to enclose stuffing.

5. Melt butter for basting sauce; stir in lemon juice, tarragon and Worcestershire sauce. Spoon or brush basting sauce over fish. Bake 10-15 minutes or until fish is done and flakes easily with a fork. Use a large spatula to remove fish to serving dishes.

Diva Tips

[1]**Old Bay seasoning** can be found in the spice aisle of the grocery store.

[2]Always crush **dried herbs** between your fingers before adding them to your recipe for optimum flavor.

[3]2 slices of bread = 1 cup **fresh breadcrumbs**. Put bread in the bowl of an electric blender or food processor and pulse until finely grated.

Fish En Papillote

4 servings

4	squares (14-inch) **parchment paper**[1]
1	clove garlic, cut in half
4	(6-ounces) white **fish filets**[2], ¾-inch thick
	salt and pepper, to taste
2	tablespoons butter or margarine, melted
4	tablespoons lemon juice, divided
2	medium zucchini, coarsely shredded
2	medium carrots, coarsely shredded
4	green onions, chopped
4	teaspoons vegetable oil

1. Preheat oven to 375°.

2. Fold parchment paper squares into triangles. Open paper and spray the inside with a nonstick cooking spray (or lightly butter). Rub garlic over inside of paper. Place a fish filet next to the inside fold of each square. Season each filet with salt and pepper; drizzle with ½ tablespoon butter and 1 tablespoon lemon juice.

3. Divide zucchini, carrots and green onions evenly over the fish. Drizzle oil over vegetables.

4. Fold triangle over fish to encase the filets. Fold the edges together, folding over 4 times. Press firmly to seal. Repeat with remaining side. Hold points of the paper together with a paper clip or staple.

5. Place packets on a baking sheet and bake 25 minutes.

6. Remove from oven and cut the top of the paper open to serve.

Diva Tips

[1]**Parchment paper** can be purchased in some grocery stores (check near the wax paper and foil aisle) or specialty shops.

[2]Buy **fish** that is odor-free. Filets should lay flat and look moist.

Fish is highly perishable and should be cooked the day of purchase. Store in a plastic bag surrounded by ice packs in the refrigerator to keep fish at its maximum freshness. Serve a 6-8 ounce filet or an 8-ounce fish steak per person.

Crab Quiche

6 servings

1   (9-inch) pie crust
1   can (6-ounces) white crabmeat, drained
1   cup (4-ounces) shredded Swiss cheese
¼   cup Parmesan cheese
¼   cup chopped green onions
1   jar (2-ounces) diced pimentos, drained
3   large eggs
1   cup milk or half-and-half
½   teaspoon salt
⅛   teaspoon pepper

1. Preheat oven to 350°.

2. Press pie crust into a pie pan.

3. In even layers place crab, Swiss cheese, Parmesan cheese, onion and pimento into pie crust.

4. In a small bowl, beat eggs with milk, salt and pepper. Pour over layers.

5. Bake 45-50 minutes or until a knife inserted halfway between side and center comes out clean. Remove from oven and let stand 10 minutes before cutting.

There are no mistakes in the kitchen, only lessons.

Which Pasta to Use...

Pair the right pasta with the right sauce. Use this chart as a general guideline.

SHAPE	PASTA	RECOMMENDED SAUCE
Short Shapes	farfalle (bow ties) fusilli (corkscrews) gemelli gnocchi orecchiette (hats) radiatore (radiators) rotelle (wheels) shells	butter cheese chunky light oil based meat use in salads seafood vegetable
Short Tubes	cavatappi elbow millerighe penne rigatoni ziti	butter cheese chunky tomato use in salads vegetable
Long	capellini (angel hair) fusilli lunghi (long springs) linguine spaghetti vermicelli	oil based seafood (except capellini) smooth tomato
Long Tubes	bucatini perciatelli	cheese cream sauce pesto
Wide (Ribbons)	fettuccine lasagna mafalda pappardelle tagliatelle	cheese cream seafood tomato thick meat
Stuffed	cannelloni cappelletti ravioli tortellini	butter cream pesto smooth tomato

Pasta Fast Tips:

1. To make pasta ahead, cook according to package directions, undercooking for 2 minutes. Drain. Plunge into cold water to cool quickly. Drain thoroughly. Toss with a few tablespoons cream or extra virgin olive oil. Store in a zip top bag in the refrigerator up to 3 days or freeze up to 6 weeks. Refresh and reheat in boiling water 1 minute.

2. Cook pasta uncovered in a large pot in plenty of salted, boiling water (4 quarts water plus 1 tablespoon salt for 1 pound pasta).

3. Cook just to al dente (firm to the bite). Overcooking makes pasta mushy.

4. When pasta has cooked, drain thoroughly and toss with some of the sauce to coat well. (Unless cooking ahead of time, do not rinse.)

5. Pasta will not wait. Once it is cooked, drain it, sauce it and serve it.

6. For the best flavor, use freshly grated Parmesan cheese for recipes calling for cheese topping.

Don't forget to make time and take every opportunity to make memories every day.

Macaroni and Cheese Soufflé

The lightest and fluffiest mac & cheese you will ever make.

6 servings

1	package (8-ounces) elbow macaroni (about 1½ cups)
2	tablespoons cornstarch
1	cup cream, half-and-half, or milk
½	teaspoon salt
1	teaspoon dry mustard
2	large **eggs, separated**[1]
1	package (3-ounces) cream cheese, cut into cubes, softened
2	cups (8-ounces) shredded sharp Cheddar cheese
2	tablespoons Parmesan cheese

1. Preheat oven to 375°.

2. Cook macaroni according to package directions.

3. While macaroni is cooking, mix cornstarch, cream, salt and dry mustard in a large saucepan. Bring to a boil over medium-high heat and cook 1 minute.

4. In a separate bowl lightly beat egg yolks.

5. Mix half of the hot cream mixture into the yolks, stirring constantly. Add yolk mixture back into saucepan with remaining cream. Stir and cook an additional minute. Remove from heat and stir in cheeses until melted and mixture is smooth.

6. Thoroughly drain macaroni and stir into cheese mixture.

7. Beat egg whites until stiff but not dry. **Fold**[2] into macaroni/cheese mixture.

8. Pour into a lightly greased (2-quart) baking dish.

9. Bake 25 minutes or until puffed and golden brown. Remove from oven. As it cools, it may fall just like a soufflé.

Diva Tips

[1]**Eggs separate** easier when cold. Break egg into a funnel or into your fingers over first bowl. The white will easily slip into the bowl and the yolk will remain in the funnel or your fingers (as long as it is not broken). Transfer white to a second bowl and yolk to a third bowl. This keeps an accidentally broken yolk from contaminating the whites already separated. Whites with even a small amount of yolk will not beat up to soft peaks. Repeat with remaining eggs over the first bowl.

[2]To **fold** ingredients together, insert large rubber spatula in the center of the mix; drag it across the bottom and then up the sides, rotating spatula and bringing some of the bottom of the mix to the top. Keep repeating this movement while turning the bowl to mix from all sides.

Amalfi Pasta

6-8 servings

1 package (1-pound) spaghetti or fettuccini
3 tablespoons vegetable oil (preferably extra virgin olive oil)
2 cloves garlic, crushed (1 teaspoon)
1 pound fresh medium shrimp, peeled and deveined
  salt and pepper to taste
2 roasted red bell peppers[1] (or substitute one 8-ounce jar roasted red peppers), cut into 1-inch pieces
1 cup heavy cream
1 tablespoon chopped fresh parsley[2]
  freshly grated Parmesan cheese

1. Cook spaghetti or fettuccini according to package directions, just until al dente.

2. While spaghetti is cooking, heat a large skillet over medium-high heat. Add oil and garlic and cook just until the garlic releases its aroma, about 1 minute.

3. Add the shrimp, season with salt, pepper, and cook, stirring frequently, until the shrimp have turned pink, about 1-2 minutes.

4. Stir in the roasted peppers; add cream. Cook until the cream has reduced by half. Add parsley.

5. Thoroughly drain the pasta; add to the skillet with the sauce. Toss the pasta over the heat until it is well coated. Serve at once topped with Parmesan cheese.

Diva Tips

[1]To **roast fresh red bell peppers**, heat grill to high heat. Place washed red bell peppers over high heat on the grill rack. Or place peppers on a foil-lined baking sheet and place under the oven broiler. As peppers blacken, rotate to cook on all sides. Remove and put in a tightly covered bowl for 30 minutes. Peel away blackened skin; remove seeds and scrape away the membranes inside. Use as directed in recipe.

[2]To store **fresh herbs (parsley** or cilantro), wash herbs in plenty of cold water; drain on paper towels. Roll clean, damp herbs in dry paper towels and place in a tightly covered plastic container. Store 1-2 weeks in the coldest part of your refrigerator.

Penne Puttanesca

I do not like anchovies, but I love this pasta. Fortunately for me, when anchovies are cooked, they add a salty-nuttiness and not a fishy taste to the dish to which they are added. Don't be like me and wait years to try this recipe. I am making up for lost time, though, because this has become one of my very favorite dinners.

6 servings

¼ cup vegetable oil (preferably extra virgin olive oil)

1 tin (2-ounces) anchovy filets in oil, drained

4 cloves garlic, crushed (2 teaspoons)

2 tablespoons chopped fresh **parsley**[1]

¼ teaspoon red pepper flakes, or to taste

1 pound ripe plum (Roma) tomatoes peeled and chopped (or substitute one 16-ounce can diced tomatoes)

20 kalamata **olives**[2], pitted and sliced (or substitute any black, oil-cured olives)

   salt and pepper to taste

1 pound penne pasta

1. Heat oil in a large skillet over medium heat. Add the anchovies. Cook and stir until anchovies have "melted" into the oil, 2-3 minutes. Add the garlic, parsley and red pepper flakes, sautéing until the garlic releases its aroma, about 1 additional minute.

2. Raise heat to medium-high. Add tomatoes and simmer, stirring often, until they break apart and form a sauce, about 15 minutes.

3. Reduce heat to low; stir in the olives. Taste and adjust the seasonings with salt and pepper, if desired.

4. Cook pasta according to package directions until al dente (firm but tender), about 12 minutes. Thoroughly drain; toss with the sauce and serve at once.

Diva Tips

[1]To store **fresh herbs (parsley** or cilantro), wash herbs in plenty of cold water; drain on paper towels. Roll clean, damp herbs in dry paper towels and place in a tightly covered plastic container. Store 1-2 weeks in the coldest part of your refrigerator.

[2]Avoid canned **olives** if at all possible. Brine-cured olives that are packed in oil have a superior taste. Some specialty stores offer olives from the deli counter.

Penne alla Destino

My husband, Jim, claims this recipe as his own.

6 servings

1 **pound penne pasta**

2 **tablespoons butter or margarine**

1 **small onion, finely diced (½ cup)**

1 **shallot¹, finely minced**

1 **clove garlic, crushed (½ teaspoon)**

1½ **pounds chicken tenders² or boneless, skinless chicken breasts (cut into thin pieces)**

2 **ounces proscuitto, sliced into thin strips**

2 **tablespoons sun-dried tomatoes, in oil, drained and chopped**

1 **cup heavy cream**

   salt and pepper to taste

¼ **cup Parmesan cheese**

1. Cook pasta according to package directions until al dente (firm but tender), about 12 minutes.

2. While pasta is cooking melt butter in a large skillet over medium-high heat. Add onion and cook just until it softens. Add shallot, garlic, and cook an additional minute or until garlic releases its aroma. Add chicken and cook on all sides until cooked through and golden brown, about 3-4 minutes.

3. Add proscuitto to chicken and cook until it begins to brown.

4. Add sun-dried tomatoes and cream to the skillet. Cook until cream is reduced by half.

5. Taste and adjust the seasonings with salt and pepper if desired.

6. Thoroughly drain pasta and toss with the sauce. Top with Parmesan cheese. Serve immediately.

Diva Tips

¹**Shallots** look like a cross between garlic and yellow onions. Buy shallots that are tight, with papery-looking skins and no green sprouts. They are mild and are used to season foods in which onions would be too strong. Substitute an equal amount of scallions. Store in a cool, dry place for weeks.

²To remove the white tendon in the **chicken tenders** grasp the end of the tendon with a paper towel. Pull the tendon towards you while holding the chicken with the edge of a knife.

Edith's Crêpe Lasagna

Edith Jaccarino, the mother of our friend, Peter, shared her recipe for lasagna made with crêpes. I make this recipe more than the traditional lasagna.

6-8 servings

8 Crêpes

8 **eggs**
2⅔ cups water
3 **cups all-purpose flour**
    dash salt
    vegetable oil or melted butter

1. Beat eggs in a large mixing bowl; stir in the water. Add the flour gradually, stirring with a whisk. Add a pinch of salt; stir and let sit for 30 minutes. (Or use a blender to mix crêpe batter.)

2. Heat a (10x10-inch) griddle pan over medium-high heat; brush with oil or melted butter.

3. Pour 1 scant cup of batter in the pan, tilting pan to spread crêpe batter in a thin layer. Cook about 30 seconds until the top of the crêpe is dry. Carefully remove and set aside. Repeat with remaining crêpes.

   (Note: Crêpes can be made 1-2 days in advance and refrigerated or frozen 3 weeks if wrapped well.)

Béchamel Sauce

4 **tablespoons (½ stick) butter or**
    margarine
2 **tablespoons all-purpose flour**
¾ **cup milk**
1 **large egg yolk, lightly beaten**
½ **cup Parmesan cheese**

1. Melt the butter in a saucepan over medium heat. Add the flour, mixing with a spoon or whisk until it is smooth. Cook 1-2 minutes, stirring constantly (don't let it brown).

2. Add milk a little at a time, stirring to keep smooth. Continue until all the milk has been added. Cook over medium heat, stirring, until sauce begins to thicken.

3. Pour a little of the sauce in with beaten egg yolk. Add yolk mixture back into saucepan with remaining sauce. Continue cooking for 1 minute. Remove from heat and stir in Parmesan cheese.

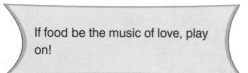

If food be the music of love, play on!

Lasagna

1 container (15 ounces) ricotta cheese
1 large egg, lightly beaten
2 tablespoons chopped fresh parsley
1 teaspoon sugar
  salt and pepper to taste
¼ cup Parmesan cheese
2 cups (8-ounces) shredded mozzarella cheese, divided
4 cups spaghetti sauce (plus extra for topping cooked lasagna)
6 tablespoons Parmesan cheese

1. Preheat oven to 350°.

2. In a mixing bowl combine ricotta, egg, parsley, sugar, salt, pepper, ¼ cup Parmesan and 1 cup mozzarella cheese. Stir until thoroughly mixed.

3. Lightly grease a (9x12-inch) baking dish (or coat with a nonstick cooking spray).

4. Spread 1 cup spaghetti sauce in the bottom of the pan.

5. Layer 1 whole crêpe over sauce; spread with ½ of ricotta mixture.

6. Layer another whole crêpe; top with 1 cup spaghetti sauce. Sprinkle with 2 tablespoons Parmesan cheese.

7. Layer crêpe; spread with ½ of béchamel sauce.

8. Layer crêpe; spread with remaining ricotta mixture.

9. Layer crêpe; spread with 1 cup spaghetti sauce. Sprinkle with 2 tablespoons Parmesan cheese.

10. Layer crêpe; spread with remaining béchamel sauce.

11. Layer crêpe; spread with 1 cup spaghetti sauce. Sprinkle with 2 tablespoons Parmesan cheese.

12. Cover pan with aluminum foil. Bake 1 hour.

13. Top with remaining 1 cup mozzarella cheese. Return to oven for 10 minutes until cheese has melted.

14. Remove from oven and let rest 10 minutes before cutting into serving pieces.

Ziti Bake

Makes enough for large parties, potluck dinners, or to share with a friend. Can be easily doubled.

8 servings

1 **pound package ziti pasta**
1 **container (15-ounces) ricotta cheese**
1 **cup sour cream**
½ **cup Parmesan cheese**
1 **large egg, slightly beaten**
1 **teaspoon sugar**
¼ **cup finely chopped fresh parsley¹**
¾ **teaspoon salt**
¼ **teaspoon pepper**
3 **green onions, finely chopped (optional)**
2 **cups (8-ounces) shredded mozzarella cheese, divided**
4 **cups of your favorite spaghetti sauce, divided (or more if needed as a garnish)**

1. Cook pasta according to package directions until al dente (firm but tender), about 12 minutes.

2. Mix ricotta cheese and next 8 ingredients. Stir in 1 cup mozzarella; set aside.

3. Drain pasta thoroughly; stir with 2 cups spaghetti sauce.

4. Spoon 1 cup of spaghetti sauce in the bottom of a (9x13-inch) pan; top with one-half of pasta. Spread ricotta cheese mixture evenly over pasta. Top with remaining pasta. Pour remaining spaghetti sauce evenly over pasta. (Can be made to this point and refrigerated).

5. Cover pan with foil and bake at 350° 1 hour or until center is bubbly (additional baking time may be needed if pasta is cold).

6. Remove foil and top with remaining mozzarella. Return to oven 10 minutes until cheese has melted.

7. Remove from oven and let rest 10 minutes before cutting into serving pieces. Serve with additional spaghetti sauce, if desired.

Diva Tips

¹To store **fresh herbs** (**parsley** or cilantro), wash herbs in plenty of cold water; drain on paper towels. Roll clean, damp herbs in dry paper towels and place in a tightly covered plastic container. Store 1-2 weeks in the coldest part of your refrigerator.

Vegetables,
Side Dishes
& Rice

Vegetables, Side Dishes & Rice

Cottage Fried Potatoes

This recipe is one of those from my Irish roots: a real comfort food.

2 servings

4   medium red potatoes, scrubbed
1   tablespoon butter or margarine
2   tablespoons bacon drippings
    (or use all butter)
    salt and pepper to taste
    bacon[1,2], cooked and crumbled,
    (optional)
    green onions, finely chopped,
    (optional)
    sour cream (optional)

1. Cover potatoes with cold water and bring to a boil; reduce heat and simmer until potatoes are just barely tender, 8-12 minutes.

2. Drain thoroughly; cool slightly and cut into ½-inch slices.

3. Melt butter and bacon drippings in a nonstick skillet over medium heat. Place slices into hot pan and season with salt and pepper. Brown slowly, turning as potatoes cook to a golden brown. Cook 15-20 minutes or until crisp on both sides.

4. To serve: top with crumbled bacon, green onions, and sour cream, if desired.

Diva Tips

[1]If you only use **bacon** occasionally, separate into individual slices, wrap each piece in plastic wrap, and place wrapped pieces in a zip top freezer bag. Store in the freezer up to 3 months. When a recipe calls for a few slices of bacon, remove only as many as needed.

[2]To cook **bacon**, remove desired number of slices from package in one piece. Chop or cut through all slices into small pieces with kitchen scissors or a knife. Fry over medium-high heat, separating pieces as they cook. Cook until crisp and golden brown.

Garlic Mashed Potatoes

These potatoes are better than any mashed potatoes served in the best steakhouses in America.

8 servings

4   **pounds potatoes, peeled**

2   **teaspoons salt**

1   **small onion, chopped**

6   **cloves garlic, crushed**

4   **tablespoons butter or margarine, melted**

1   **can (14-ounces) low-sodium chicken broth**

⅓   **cup cream, half-and-half, or milk[1]**

    salt and pepper to taste

1. Place potatoes in a large pot and cover with cold water; add salt, and onion. Bring to a boil. Reduce heat to a simmer and cook until potatoes are fork-tender about 15-20 minutes, being careful not to over cook (potatoes should still retain shape, but a chunk can be crushed with a pair of tongs).

2. Drain completely in a colander or strainer.

3. Return potatoes to the cooking pot and place back over low heat, shaking the pan so all the surface water can evaporate, being careful not to let the potatoes burn or scorch.

4. When dry, force the potatoes through a ricer, food mill or mash with a potato masher or fork.

5. Melt butter in a small saucepan; add garlic and cook over low heat just until garlic softens. Mash into a paste with butter. Set aside.

6. While potatoes are cooking, bring chicken broth to a boil. Lower heat and simmer until broth is reduced to ¼ cup. Add butter/garlic and milk; heat until hot.

7. Stir milk mixture into potatoes. Taste and adjust seasonings with salt and pepper as necessary. If potatoes are too stiff, add hot cream, 1 tablespoon at a time until desired consistency is reached.

8. Potatoes can be made ahead of time and reheated or kept hot in the oven.

   (Note restaurant secret: to prepare potatoes ahead of time, cook potatoes according to directions; dry and force through a ricer; cool. Place in a zip top plastic bag and store up to 1 day in the refrigerator. When ready to serve, microwave potatoes on medium power until hot. Mix in HOT liquid and proceed as directed above).

Diva Tips

[1]Making mashed potatoes is not an exact science because the amount of **liquid** to add is incumbent upon how much water the potatoes absorbed as they were cooking. But a good rule of thumb to follow is ¼ cup dairy (or liquid) per pound of potatoes.

Loaded Mashed Potatoes

This recipe is a marriage of my two favorite dishes: loaded baked potatoes and garlic mashed potatoes.

4-6 servings

4   Russet (baking) **potatoes**[1], peeled and cut into chunks

1½ pounds red potatoes, scrubbed clean and cut into chunks (the same size as Russets)

1½ teaspoons salt

¼   cup (½ stick) butter or margarine

4   cloves garlic, roughly chopped

½   cup heavy cream

¼   cup sour cream

1   cup (4 ounces) shredded Cheddar cheese

8   slices bacon, cooked crisp and crumbled

¼   cup chopped **chives**[2] or green onion tops

    pepper to taste

1. Place potatoes in a large pot and cover with cold water; add salt. Bring to a boil. Reduce heat to a simmer and cook until potatoes are fork-tender about 12-15 minutes, being careful not to over cook (potatoes should still retain shape, but a chunk can be crushed with a pair of tongs). Drain completely in a colander.

2. Return potatoes to the cooking pot and place back over low heat, shaking the pan so all the surface water can evaporate.

3. While potatoes cook, melt butter in a small saucepan; add garlic and cook over low heat just until garlic softens. Add cream to the garlic butter and heat through.

4. Remove cream mixture from heat and stir in sour cream.

5. When potatoes are cooked and dry, add butter/sour cream mixture to the pot while mashing with a potato masher to blend all the ingredients and achieve a light texture, being careful not to over mix (or potatoes may become gummy).

6. Taste and adjust the seasonings with salt and pepper. (Can be made to this point and kept warm in a double boiler over simmering water or covered and placed in a warm oven.)

7. Just before serving stir in cheese and bacon. Spoon into a serving dish and top with chives.

Diva Tips

[1]Making mashed **potatoes** is not an exact science because the amount of liquid to add is incumbent upon how much water the potatoes absorbed as they were cooking, but a good rule of thumb to follow is ¼ cup dairy (or liquid) per pound of potatoes.

[2]**Chives** are a member of the onion family but have a much milder flavor. Snip fresh chives with kitchen scissors to desired length. Store fresh chives in a plastic bag in the refrigerator up to 1 week.

Bavarian Potato Casserole

Take this potato dish to your next potluck, serve it for brunch or at your next cook out.

8-10 servings

1 **small onion, chopped (½ cup)**
2 **tablespoons butter or margarine**
2 **cloves garlic, crushed (1 teaspoon)**
1 **package (8-ounces) mushrooms[1], sliced**
1 **can (10-ounces) cream of mushroom soup**
1 **pint (2 cups) sour cream**
1 **teaspoon salt**
2 **cups (8-ounces) grated sharp Cheddar cheese**
¼ **cup Parmesan cheese**
1 **bag (2-pounds) frozen, cubed hash brown potatoes, thawed**
2 **cups cornflakes, crushed**

1. Sauté onion in butter in a large skillet over medium-high heat. Add garlic and cook an additional 30 seconds or until garlic releases it fragrance. Add mushrooms and cook until limp and all juices have been absorbed. Set aside.

2. Mix soup, sour cream, salt and cheeses in a large bowl. Stir in mushroom mixture. Add potatoes and mix thoroughly.

3. Pour into a lightly greased (2-quart) baking dish. (Can be made 1 day ahead to this point and refrigerated.)

4. When ready to bake, top with crushed cornflakes.

5. Bake in a preheated oven at 350° 45-60 minutes or until golden and bubbly. (Add 15 minutes to baking, if dish was refrigerated.)

Diva Tips

[1]Choose **mushrooms** with the caps closed around the stems, with smooth tops and without blemishes. Exposed black gills are signs of old age. Never immerse mushrooms in water; they will absorb liquid like a sponge. The best way to clean mushrooms is to wipe with a damp paper towel. Store mushrooms in a paper bag in the refrigerator.

Vegetables, Side Dishes & Rice

Cheesy Potatoes Gratin

I love potatoes, in fact, I can't think of any recipe containing potatoes that I don't like. This one is especially good.

8 servings

1 tablespoon butter or margarine

1 clove garlic, crushed (½ teaspoon)

8 medium potatoes, peeled and **thinly sliced**¹

2 tablespoons butter or margarine, melted

1 small onion, finely chopped (½ cup)

  salt and pepper to taste

4 tablespoons Parmesan cheese

1 cup (4-ounces) shredded Cheddar cheese

1 cup canned chicken broth

¼ cup heavy cream

1. Preheat oven to 350°.

2. Grease the bottom of a (9x13-inch) glass ovenproof dish with 1 tablespoon butter; rub the crushed garlic over the bottom of the dish.

3. Divide the potatoes into thirds.

4. Put a single layer of potatoes over garlic; drizzle with 1 tablespoon butter and sprinkle ½ onion over the layer. Season with salt and pepper. Sprinkle 2 tablespoons Parmesan and ½ cup Cheddar cheese over onions.

5. Continue with a second layer of potatoes and repeat with remaining butter, onion, salt and pepper, and cheeses.

6. Top with last layer of potatoes. Press down on the potatoes to even out.

7. Pour chicken broth down the side of the pan (liquid should fill about ⅓ depth of the pan).

8. Drizzle cream over the top of the potatoes to keep the top layer from drying out.

9. Bake uncovered 45-60 minutes or until potatoes are tender and most of the liquid is absorbed. Remove from oven and cool slightly before cutting into squares.

Diva Tips

¹The best kitchen tool to **thinly slice** potatoes is a mandolin. If you don't have one, use a food processor or a very sharp knife. If you slice with a knife, for safety, cut off a thin slice of potato to make a flat surface so that the potato will not roll around as you slice.

Twice Baked Potatoes Florentine

This recipe is a twist on an old classic and very versatile: serve with your favorite entrée or use as a vegetarian main dish. Add cubed smoked deli ham to the potatoes and serve with a crisp green salad to make a complete meal.

6 servings

6   **medium baking potatoes, scrubbed**
2   **tablespoons vegetable oil**
3   **tablespoons butter or margarine**
1   **small onion, chopped (½ cup)**
3   **cloves garlic, crushed**[1] **(1½ teaspoons)**
1   **package (9-ounces) frozen chopped spinach, thawed**
1   **tablespoon lemon juice**
1   **teaspoon salt**
½   **teaspoon pepper**
½   **cup cream, half-and-half, or milk**
½   **cup sour cream**
¼   **cup Parmesan cheese**
1   **cup (4-ounces) grated sharp Cheddar cheese**

1. Preheat oven to 350°.

2. Rub potatoes with oil.

3. Place on a baking sheet and bake for 1 hour or until potatoes are soft. Remove from oven and cool slightly.

4. Meanwhile, sauté onion in butter until clear; add garlic and cook an additional 30 seconds or until garlic releases it fragrance. Remove from heat.

5. Squeeze spinach until dry and no juices remain. Add to onion. Stir in lemon juice and season with salt and pepper. Set aside.

6. When potatoes can be safely handled, cut in half lengthwise and scoop out the pulp leaving a ¼-inch shell.

7. Mash the pulp; stir in cream and sour cream.

8. Add mashed potato mixture to onion/ spinach mixture, stirring to thoroughly mix. Stir in cheeses.

9. Spoon mixture back into shells, mounding in the center. (Can be made to this point and frozen).

10. Return to 350° oven and bake 20-30 minutes or until heated through and cheese has melted. Serve hot. (If baked frozen, add 25-30 minutes to baking time.)

Diva Tips

[1]To **crush garlic**, peel off papery skin by whacking clove with the side of a knife; paper should slip right off. Place the clove between two sheets of plastic wrap and smash with a meat pounder or the bottom of a heavy pan until pulverized. Scrape garlic off plastic wrap and use in recipe as directed.

Browned New Potatoes

4 servings

12 small (2-inches) red potatoes, scrubbed
1 teaspoon salt
1 tablespoon vegetable oil
1 tablespoon browning and seasoning sauce (like Kitchen Bouquet)
2 tablespoons freshly squeezed lemon juice
1 garlic clove, crushed (½ teaspoon)
½ cup Italian salad dressing

1. Place potatoes in a large pan and cover with water; add salt. Bring to a boil; reduce heat and simmer about 10-12 minutes until potatoes are barely tender. Drain thoroughly.

2. Heat oil in a large skillet. Add potatoes; cook over medium heat, shaking pan to brown potatoes on all sides.

3. Add browning sauce and continue cooking and shaking the pan to coat the potatoes evenly, about 1 minute.

4. Stir together, lemon juice, garlic, and salad dressing. Split potatoes open and drizzle with lemon vinaigrette.

Baked Sweet Potatoes

When I was a child, my mother would bake lots of sweet potatoes at one time and we would eat them cold as a snack the next day. No wonder I had such a healthy childhood.

2 servings

2 medium sweet potatoes, scrubbed clean
2 tablespoons butter or margarine
2 teaspoons sugar or brown sugar
½ teaspoon cinnamon

1. Preheat oven to 350°.

2. Place sweet potatoes on a foil-lined baking sheet.

3. Bake 45 minutes-1 hour or until soft.

4. Split open and fill with 1 tablespoon butter.

5. Mix sugar with cinnamon. Sprinkle 1½ teaspoons sugar mixture into each hot, buttered potato. Enjoy!

Sweet Potato Medallions

6 servings

2   tablespoons butter or margarine

3   large sweet potatoes (2 pounds),
    peeled and sliced ½-inch thick

1   cup apple juice or cider

½   teaspoon cinnamon

1   tablespoon sugar

1. Melt butter in a large skillet.

2. Fry potatoes in butter 1 minute; turn potato medallions over and cook an additional minute.

3. Pour apple juice into skillet; sprinkle potatoes with cinnamon and sugar. Cover tightly.

4. Cook until almost all the juice is absorbed and potatoes are tender.

5. Uncover and continue cooking until juice is reduced to a syrupy glaze.

6. Remove from heat and spoon glaze over potatoes. Serve hot.

Iced tea is appropriate to drink at all meals and you start drinking at age 6 months.

Praline Sweet Potatoes

There are certain dishes I always serve for the holidays. This is the one dish that my kids would never forgive me if it wasn't on the table at Thanksgiving, no matter where we celebrate.

8 servings

Potatoes

6   medium **sweet potatoes**[1]
     (about 3 pounds)
½   cup brown sugar
½   cup sugar
¼   cup (½ stick) butter or margarine,
     melted
½   cup cream, half-and-half, or milk
1   teaspoon vanilla extract
2   large eggs, slightly beaten
½   teaspoon salt
½   teaspoon cinnamon
⅛   teaspoon nutmeg

Praline Topping

½   cup brown sugar
¼   cup all-purpose flour
3   tablespoons butter or margarine,
     melted
1   cup **pecans, toasted**[2] and chopped

1. Wash and scrub the potatoes clean under cool running water. Dry with a paper towel.

2. Line a baking sheet with aluminum foil. Bake potatoes on the prepared baking sheet in a 350° oven for 1 hour or until potatoes are soft.

3. Remove from oven and cool to the touch; peel and mash potatoes (should equal about 4 cups).

4. Combine potatoes, sugars and next 7 ingredients in a large mixing bowl; beat at medium speed of an electric mixer (or stir by hand) until smooth.

5. Spoon mixture into a lightly greased (1½ quart) baking dish.

6. Mix topping ingredients until crumbly. Sprinkle evenly over potato mixture. Bake at 350° for 30 minutes or until thoroughly heated.

Diva Tips

[1]Canned **sweet potatoes** can be substituted for fresh. Three medium sweet potatoes are generally equivalent to one (16-ounces) can or 2 cups mashed.

[2]**Toasting nuts** adds crispness and intensifies the flavor. Spread in a single layer on a baking sheet or pan. Preheat oven to 350°; place pan in oven and bake 5-10 minutes, or until nuts release their aroma, being careful not to burn. A smaller portion of nuts will toast much quicker than a larger amount. Toast a larger amount than needed and freeze extras up to 1 year in a tightly sealed container. Four ounces of nuts equals about 1 cup.

Fall Roasted Vegetables

Roasting vegetables enhances their natural sweetness.

6-8 servings

1½ pounds sweet potatoes (2-3 medium), cut in ½-inch wedges

1 large red potato, cut in ½-inch wedges

1 zucchini, cut in 1-inch slices

1 yellow, crookneck squash, cut in 1-inch slices

1 large green or red bell pepper, cut into 1-inch strips

1 large onion, cut into wedges

6 cloves garlic

3 tablespoons vegetable oil (preferably extra virgin olive oil)

2 tablespoons **balsamic vinegar**[1]

salt and pepper to taste

1 tablespoon chopped fresh **rosemary**[2] (optional)

1 tablespoon chopped fresh oregano (optional)

1. Preheat oven to 450°.

2. Combine the first 8 ingredients in a large bowl; tossing well to coat.

3. Arrange vegetables in a single layer on a lightly greased foil-lined roasting pan or broiler pan (or coat with a nonstick cooking spray).

4. Roast 25-30 minutes or until well browned, stirring gently every 10 minutes.

5. Just before serving, drizzle with balsamic vinegar; season with salt and pepper and fresh herbs, if desired.

Diva Tips

[1]**Balsamic vinegar** is a dark-aged Italian vinegar fermented for 10-15 years, and has a slightly sweet taste. Buy the best you can afford (usually from Modena, Italy). Most balsamic vinegars sold in grocery stores are just caramel-colored vinegars.

[2]**Rosemary** is a woody herb. Strip off and chop the green leaves from the woody stems.

Lemon Asparagus

My friend and fellow member of National Charity League, Michelle Chapman, shared this recipe with me, which has become my daughter Lindsey's favorite way of eating asparagus.

4 servings

1 pound **asparagus spears**[1], tough ends removed

¼ cup vegetable oil (preferably extra virgin olive oil)

2 tablespoons freshly squeezed lemon juice

1 clove garlic, crushed

2 tablespoons chopped fresh basil

½ teaspoon dried oregano

½ teaspoon salt

4 tablespoons **pine nuts, toasted**[2]

1. Place 1-inch of water in a large skillet and bring to a boil; add asparagus and cook 2-3 minutes until crisp-tender. Drain thoroughly.

2. Mix the next 6 ingredients together; microwave on high 45 seconds.

3. Place asparagus in a serving dish; pour sauce over and top with pine nuts.

Diva Tips

[1]**Asparagus** is plentiful during its peak season February through June. Choose fresh, firm stalks, ½-inch in diameter with tightly closed caps. To remove tough ends, bend each spear until it snaps. For thicker stalks, peel the outer layer to the tender middle. To store, put ½-inch water in a tall, narrow jar or glass. Cut off ½-inch from the butt end of the asparagus and place in the jar. Make a tent with plastic wrap or plastic bag and refrigerate. Will keep fresh up to 1 week if the water is changed daily.

[2]**Toasting nuts** adds crispness and intensifies the flavor. Spread in a single layer on a baking sheet or pan. Preheat oven to 350°; place pan in oven and bake 5-10 minutes, or until nuts release their aroma, being careful not to burn. A smaller portion of nuts will toast much quicker than a larger amount. Toast a larger amount than needed and freeze extras up to 1 year in a tightly sealed container. Four ounces of nuts equals about 1 cup.

Roasted Asparagus

4 servings

1 pound fresh **asparagus spears**[1], tough ends removed

1-2 tablespoons vegetable oil (preferably extra virgin olive oil)

salt and pepper to taste

½ cup chicken broth

1 tablespoon butter or margarine

¼ cup finely grated Parmesan cheese

1. Preheat oven to 375°.

2. Place asparagus on a lightly greased baking sheet (or coat with a nonstick cooking spray).

3. Drizzle vegetable oil over asparagus, rolling the spears to completely coat with the oil.

4. Season with salt and pepper. Bake 5-6 minutes.

5. While asparagus is baking, bring chicken broth to a boil; reduce heat and simmer until broth is reduced to about 2 tablespoons.

6. Whisk butter into reduced broth and drizzle over cooked asparagus; sprinkle with cheese.

7. Return to oven and bake an additional 2-3 minutes until cheese has melted. Serve hot.

Diva Tips

[1]**Asparagus** is plentiful during its peak season February through June. Choose fresh, firm stalks, ½-inch in diameter with tightly closed caps. To remove tough ends, bend each spear until it snaps. For thicker stalks, peel the outer layer to the tender middle. To store, put ½-inch water in a tall, narrow jar or glass. Cut off ½-inch from the butt end of the asparagus and place in the jar. Make a tent with plastic wrap or plastic bag and refrigerate. Will keep fresh up to 1 week if the water is changed daily.

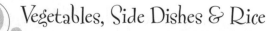

Cheesy Broccoli

My son, Alex, loves broccoli and this recipe is one of his favorites.

4 servings

1 bag (24-ounces) frozen broccoli flowerets
1 tablespoon butter or margarine
½ small onion, sliced (¼ cup)
1 clove garlic, crushed (½ teaspoon)
1 jar (5-ounces) **Old English cheese**[1]
2 tablespoons milk

1. Place broccoli into a deep microwave-safe dish. Cover tightly with plastic wrap (no need to add water). Cook in the microwave on high power 8-10 minutes, turning ¼ turn every 2 minutes.

2. Meanwhile, melt butter in a skillet and sauté sliced onion over medium heat 3-4 minutes until limp and clear; add garlic and cook for an additional 1-minute. Add cheese and stir until melted. Add enough milk to make a smooth, medium sauce to pour over broccoli.

3. Carefully remove plastic wrap from broccoli, letting built up steam escape. Thoroughly drain broccoli and place in a serving dish.

4. Pour cheese sauce over cooked broccoli and serve immediately.

Diva Tips
[1]Old English cheese is found near the Velveeta.

Roasted Broccoli with Pecan Sauce

4 servings

1 pound fresh **broccoli**[1]

2 tablespoons vegetable oil (preferably extra virgin olive oil)

 salt and pepper to taste

4 tablespoons butter

⅓ cup **pecans, toasted**[2] and chopped

1 teaspoon **chili oil**[3]

1 teaspoon lemon juice

1. Preheat oven to 450°.

2. Cut broccoli stems apart leaving about 2-inches of stem. Cut large stems in half or thirds. Rinse and thoroughly dry.

3. Cover a shallow baking dish with aluminum foil and lightly grease or coat with a nonstick cooking spray.

4. Lay broccoli in a single layer. Drizzle with vegetable oil. Season with salt and pepper to taste.

5. Roast 10-15 minutes until lightly browned.

6. Meanwhile, melt butter in a small skillet, over low heat. Add toasted pecans. Cook, stirring occasionally, until the butter is golden brown about 5 minutes. Add the chili oil and lemon juice.

7. Pour the sauce over the broccoli and serve.

Diva Tips

[1]Fresh **broccoli** will have firm stalks with tightly bunched heads. The florets should be a blue-green color. If broccoli shows signs of the buds beginning to turn yellow, it is past its prime. Refrigerate broccoli in a plastic bag up to 4 days. If broccoli becomes limp, trim the bottom off the stem and stand in a container of cool water. Refrigerate overnight.

[2]**Toasting nuts** adds crispness and intensifies the flavor. Spread in a single layer on a baking sheet or pan. Preheat oven to 350°; place pan in oven and bake 5-10 minutes, or until nuts release their aroma, being careful not to burn. A smaller portion of nuts will toast much quicker than a larger amount. Toast a larger amount than needed and freeze extras up to 1 year in a tightly sealed container. Four ounces of nuts equals about 1 cup.

[3]**Chili oil** can be found in the Oriental section of the grocery store or in specialty shops.

Greek Beans

This is a combined recipe from my Wisconsin sister-in-law, Kerry Destino, and a client, Lynne Pardue. Thanks to you both for a delicious recipe that is great for buffets or picnics.

6 servings

1½ **pounds fresh green beans**
⅓ **cup white wine vinegar**
1 **clove garlic, crushed (½ teaspoon)**
½ **teaspoon dried dill weed**
½ **teaspoon dried oregano**
¾ **teaspoon salt**
¼ **teaspoon pepper**
⅓ **cup vegetable oil (preferably extra virgin olive oil)**
1 **small red onion, chopped (½ cup)**
1 **cup crumbled feta cheese**
1 **cup pecans, toasted[1] and chopped**

1. Wash, trim and cut beans into 1-2 inch pieces.

2. Bring enough water to cover beans to a boil; add salt and beans. Cook until barely tender, 5-7 minutes. Drain and plunge in ice water to stop the cooking. Drain thoroughly and allow beans to dry (or pat dry with a paper towel).

3. Combine vinegar, garlic, dill, oregano, salt and pepper, whisking to blend well. Stir in vegetable oil.

4. Toss with beans; add onions, cheese and pecans. (If making ahead, add onions, cheese and pecans just before serving.)

Diva Tips

[1]**Toasting nuts** adds crispness and intensifies the flavor. Spread in a single layer on a baking sheet or pan. Preheat oven to 350°; place pan in oven and bake 5-10 minutes, or until nuts release their aroma, being careful not to burn. A smaller portion of nuts will toast much quicker than a larger amount. Toast a larger amount than needed and freeze extras up to 1 year in a tightly sealed container. Four ounces of nuts equals about 1 cup.

Almond Green Beans

Everyone has their version of this classic vegetable, but mine has a few surprise ingredients.

4 servings

1	**pound green beans, washed and strings removed, and snapped in half**
1	**small onion, chopped (½ cup)**
1	**teaspoon salt**
2	**tablespoons butter**
1	**clove garlic, crushed (½ teaspoon)**
1	**tablespoon walnut or almond oil**[1]
⅓	**cup sliced almonds, toasted**[2]
¼	**teaspoon almond extract**

1. Place beans and onion in a saucepan; cover with water and add salt. Bring to a boil; cover, reduce heat and simmer 7-10 minutes or until crisp-tender. Drain thoroughly. Place back over low heat, shaking the pan so all the surface water can evaporate.

2. Melt butter in a skillet and cook over low heat until a light, golden brown.

3. Sauté garlic in browned butter for 30 seconds or just until it releases it fragrance; do not brown garlic. Remove from heat and add walnut oil and sliced almonds. Stir until almonds are thoroughly coated.

4. Stir almond extract into garlic/almonds and immediately toss with hot green beans.

Diva Tips

[1]Small bottles of **almond** or **walnut oil** can be found in the grocery store with the vegetable oils. Nut oils become rancid very quickly; store in the refrigerator up to 6 months.

[2]**Toasting nuts** adds crispness and intensifies the flavor. Spread in a single layer on a baking sheet or pan. Preheat oven to 350°; place pan in oven and bake 5-10 minutes, or until nuts release their aroma, being careful not to burn. A smaller portion of nuts will toast much quicker than a larger amount. Toast a larger amount than needed and freeze extras up to 1 year in a tightly sealed container. Four ounces of nuts equals about 1 cup.

Rose's Green Beans and Artichokes

My mother-in-law, Rose, introduced me to "exotic" foods such as artichokes and squid. I wrote this recipe down years ago as I helped her cook a holiday dinner. I have made adjustments to the recipe and now I call it my own.

8 servings

2   packages (1-pound each) frozen Italian green beans (or the equivalent of fresh beans)

1   package (1-pound) frozen artichoke hearts (or substitute one 14-ounce can)

4   tablespoons vegetable oil, divided

2   medium shallots, finely chopped (2 tablespoons)

2   cloves garlic (1 teaspoon), crushed

1   package (8-ounces) white **mushrooms**[1], thinly sliced

salt and pepper to taste

6   tablespoons Parmesan cheese, divided

¼   cup dry **breadcrumbs**[2]

1. In separate pans, cook green beans and artichoke hearts according to package directions. Completely drain and set aside.

2. Heat 2 tablespoons vegetable oil in a large skillet over medium heat; add shallots and garlic. Cook and stir 1 minute or just until shallots soften, being careful not to let the garlic burn.

3. Turn the heat up to medium-high; add mushrooms and cook until mushrooms are softened and have absorbed all the liquid that has been released.

4. Lightly grease a (2-quart) baking dish (or coat with a nonstick cooking spray).

5. Layer one-half of the green beans in the prepared dish; season with salt and pepper.

6. Drizzle with 1 tablespoon oil and sprinkle with 2 tablespoons Parmesan cheese.

7. Next, layer artichoke hearts and season with salt and pepper.

8. Layer mushroom/shallots; sprinkle with 2 tablespoons Parmesan cheese.

9. Finally, cover with the remaining green beans, season with salt and pepper; drizzle with the remaining tablespoon oil and sprinkle the remaining cheese over. (Can be made to this point and refrigerated up to 1 day. Bring to room temperature before proceeding with baking). When ready to bake, top with breadcrumbs.

10. Bake at 350° 30 minutes or until heated through.

Diva Tips

[1]Never immerse **mushrooms** in water; they will absorb liquid like a sponge. The best way to clean mushrooms is to wipe with a damp paper towel. Store mushrooms in a paper bag in the refrigerator.

[2]Save all your dried, leftover bread—baguettes, sandwich bread, bagels, crackers, rolls, etc.—and put into the bowl of your food processor or blender and pulse until you have fine crumbs. Or rub dried bread on a grater, catching the crumbs in a bowl. Store crumbs in a zip top plastic bag in the freezer and use as your recipe directs. Homemade **breadcrumbs** taste superior to store prepackaged.

Lemon Sugar Snap Peas

Could this vegetable be so named because it cooks up in a "snap"?

4-6 servings

1½ pounds fresh **sugar snap peas**[1]
    (or substitute frozen sugar snap
    peas)
2   tablespoons butter or margarine
1   clove garlic, crushed (½ teaspoon)
2   teaspoons lemon **zest**[2] (1 lemon)
1   tablespoon freshly squeezed lemon
    juice
½   teaspoon salt
    freshly ground pepper

1. Cook peas in enough boiling salted water to cover, 3 minutes or until crisp-tender. Drain and plunge in ice water to stop the cooking. Drain thoroughly and allow peas to dry (or pat dry with a paper towel).

2. Melt butter in a skillet over medium-high heat; add peas and sauté for 2-3 minutes

3. Add garlic and cook an additional 30 seconds just until it releases it fragrance; stir in lemon zest and juice to the pan. Cook until thoroughly heated through. Serve immediately.

   (Note: To prepare peas ahead, cook, cool and drain. Wrap in paper towels and store in a zip top bag in the refrigerator. Proceed as recipe directs.)

Diva Tips

[1]**Sugar snap peas** are cross between an English pea and a snow pea. They are bright green with a crisp pod and tender pea seeds; both are edible. Generally, cook the pods intact without removing the peas.

[2]To **zest** lemon, lime or orange, wash fruit in hot water. Before cutting or juicing, remove zest (the very outermost layer of the fruit—the thin, colored part, avoiding the white pith which is bitter) with the finest part of a grater, or by peeling with a vegetable peeler and finely chopping with a knife or with a special tool called a zester.

Orange-Glazed Carrots and Sugar Snap Peas

A delicious addition to any holiday table.

6 servings

1	pound baby carrots
1	teaspoon salt
½	pound fresh **sugar snap peas**[1] (or substitute frozen)
1	cup low-sodium chicken broth
¼	cup orange juice
2	tablespoons butter or margarine
2	tablespoons **Grand Marnier**[2] (or substitute apple juice)
2	tablespoons orange marmalade

1. Place carrots in a large saucepan; cover with water and season with salt. Bring to a boil and cook 8-10 minutes until crisp-tender.

2. Add sugar snap peas to carrots and cook an additional 2-3 minutes until peas are crisp-tender. Drain thoroughly.

3. While carrots are cooking, place chicken broth and orange juice in a saucepan. Bring to a boil, reduce heat and simmer until liquid is reduced to ¼ cup. Stir butter in briskly until melted. Add Grand Marnier (or apple juice) and orange marmalade; heat through.

4. Toss with carrots and sugar snap peas and serve immediately.

Diva Tips

[1]**Sugar snap peas** are cross between an English pea and a snow pea. They are bright green with a crisp pod and tender pea seeds; both are edible. Generally, cook the pods intact without removing the peas.

[2]Small bottles (airline serving size—about 3 tablespoons) of **liqueurs** can be purchased at most liquor stores.

Corn Pudding

8 servings

1 package (20-ounces) frozen Southern-style creamed corn, thawed

2 cups frozen white corn kernels, thawed (or substitute one 14-ounce can corn, drained)

4 tablespoons butter or margarine, melted

2 teaspoons sugar

2 large eggs, lightly beaten

1 cup milk

salt to taste

1. Preheat oven to 350°.

2. Combine all ingredients in a medium bowl, mixing well.

3. Pour into a greased (2-quart) baking dish.

4. Bake uncovered 40-45 minutes until set in the middle.

Presto Mushrooms

2-4 servings

1 package (8-ounces) **mushrooms**[1], sliced

2 tablespoons butter or margarine

¼ teaspoon garlic powder

1 teaspoon Worcestershire sauce

1. Place mushrooms in a microwave safe dish.

2. Top with butter, garlic powder and Worcestershire sauce.

3. Cook on high power 2-3 minutes. Stir. Continue cooking in 1-minute increments until mushrooms are tender.

Diva Tips

[1]Choose **mushrooms** with the caps closed around the stems, with smooth tops and without blemishes. Exposed black gills are signs of old age. Never immerse mushrooms in water; they will absorb liquid like a sponge. The best way to clean mushrooms is to wipe with a damp paper towel. Store mushrooms in a paper bag in the refrigerator.

Grilled Artichokes

I love to order these appetizers from a famous cheesecake restaurant chain. Since they would not share their recipe with me, I had to make my own.

4 servings

2   large **artichokes**[1]
2   tablespoons balsamic vinegar
¼   cup white wine vinegar
1   teaspoon salt
½   teaspoon freshly ground pepper
2   cloves garlic, crushed (1 teaspoon)
1   small shallot, finely minced
1   teaspoon finely chopped fresh oregano (optional)
1   teaspoon finely chopped fresh **thyme**[2] (optional)
¼   cup vegetable oil (preferably extra virgin olive oil)

1. Wash artichokes under cold running water to remove any grit. Trim the thorny ends from the leaves with scissors. Trim ½-inch off the top and any tough leaves around the base. If stem is still intact, peel outside of stem down to the tender center.

2. Place prepared artichokes in a large pot; cover with water. Bring to a boil, reduce heat, cover, and simmer 30-35 minutes or until a leaf at the bottom will easily pull out.

3. Remove artichoke from water and turn upside down to drain.

4. Combine remaining ingredients, blending thoroughly.

5. When artichoke is cool enough to handle, cut in half, lengthwise and scoop out the fuzzy center.

6. Spoon marinade over artichoke halves, inside the leaves.

7. Marinate at least ½ hour, preferably up to 1 day.

8. Grill over hot coals until golden brown and heated through.

9. To eat: pull off the leaves one at a time. Draw the bottom of each leaf between your teeth to remove the sweet flesh. Discard the upper portion of the leaf.

Diva Tips

[1]Fresh **artichokes** should feel heavy with compact, deep green leaves and should "squeak" when lightly handled and gently squeezed. Avoid artichokes with bruised, brown leaves.

[2]**Thyme** is a woody herb. Strip off and chop the green leaves from the woody stems.

Stuffed Artichokes

This recipe came from Italy with my husband's family and each member makes their own variation.

2 servings

2   large **artichokes**[1]
¼   cup dry **breadcrumbs**[2]
¼   cup Parmesan cheese
⅛   teaspoon pepper
⅛   teaspoon garlic powder
¼   cup extra virgin olive oil

1. Wash artichokes under cold running water to remove any grit. Trim the thorny ends from the leaves with scissors. Trim ½-inch off the top and cut off the stem end so the artichoke will stand upright. Remove any loose bottom leaves.

2. Place prepared artichokes in a large pot; cover with water. Bring to a boil, cover, reduce heat and simmer 30-35 minutes or until a leaf at the bottom will easily pull out. Remove artichoke from water and turn upside down to drain.

3. Mix breadcrumbs, cheese, pepper and garlic. Carefully separate leaves and sprinkle this mixture in between. Drizzle with olive oil.

4. Place upright on a baking sheet. Bake in a preheated 350° oven 20-30 minutes or until heated through.

5. To eat: pull off the leaves one at a time. Draw the bottom of each leaf between your teeth to remove the stuffing and the sweet flesh. Discard the upper portion of the leaf. When all the leaves are gone, scoop the fuzzy choke out of the center with a spoon and discard. Quarter the heart and enjoy eating it.

Diva Tips

[1]Fresh **artichokes** should feel heavy with compact, deep green leaves and should "squeak" when lightly handled and gently squeezed. Avoid artichokes with bruised, brown leaves.

[2]Save all your dried, leftover bread—baguettes, sandwich bread bagels, crackers, rolls, etc.—and put into the bowl of your food processor or blender and pulse until you have fine crumbs. Or rub dried bread on a grater, catching the crumbs in a bowl. Store crumbs in a zip top plastic bag in the freezer and use as your recipe directs. Homemade **breadcrumbs** taste superior to store prepackaged.

Spinach and Artichokes

8 servings

1   **small onion, chopped (½ cup)**
½   **cup chopped celery**
½   **cup (1 stick) butter or margarine**
1   **clove garlic, crushed (½ teaspoon)**
2   **packages (10-ounces each) frozen, chopped spinach, thawed**
2   **cups sour cream**
2   **tablespoons mayonnaise**
1   **package (12-ounces) frozen artichoke hearts (or substitute one 14-ounce can, drained), chopped**
    dash hot pepper sauce
1   **teaspoon salt**
¼   **teaspoon pepper**
½   **cup Parmesan cheese**
1   **cup shredded Monterey Jack cheese**
¼   **cup dry breadcrumbs[1]**

1. Preheat oven to 350°.

2. In a skillet, cook onions and celery in the butter until vegetables are tender. Add garlic and cook just until fragrance is released, about 30 seconds. Remove from heat.

3. Squeeze all the liquid out of the spinach until dry.

4. Stir dried spinach with the onion mixture; add sour cream, mayonnaise, artichoke hearts, hot pepper, salt, pepper, and Parmesan cheese.

5. Pour into a lightly greased (2-quart) baking dish (or coat with a nonstick vegetable spray). (Can be made to this point, and refrigerated up to 1 day).

6. Top with shredded cheese and sprinkle with breadcrumbs. Bake 30-40 minutes or until edges are golden brown and heated through.

Diva Tips

[1]Save all your dried, leftover bread—baguettes, sandwich bread, bagels, crackers, rolls, etc.—and put into the bowl of your food processor or blender and pulse until you have fine crumbs. Or rub dried bread on a grater, catching the crumbs in a bowl. Store crumbs in a zip top plastic bag in the freezer and use as your recipe directs. Homemade **breadcrumbs** tastes superior to store prepackaged.

Zucchini Fans

This zucchini makes an impressive presentation.

4 servings

4   small (6-inch) zucchini
¼   cup (½ stick) butter or margarine, melted
1   teaspoon finely **chopped fresh tarragon**[1-2]
    salt and pepper, to taste

1. Wash zucchini and dry.

2. Slice zucchini into 4 or 5 slices, up to the stem, leaving pieces intact.

3. Mix butter and tarragon.

4. Carefully fan out zucchini slices without breaking from the stem by pressing down with the palm of your hand and slightly twisting.

5. Drizzle fans with butter mixture and season with salt and pepper.

6. Cook over hot coals on the grill (or under the broiler), 3-4 minutes per side just until tender.

7. Serve with additional tarragon butter if desired.

Diva Tips

[1]To **chop fresh herbs**, roll herbs into a tight bundle and finely chop crosswise with a sharp knife. Or snip with kitchen scissors. To prevent fresh tarragon from darkening while cutting, sprinkle with a few drops of vegetable oil.

[2]To **store fresh herbs (tarragon)**, wash in plenty of cold water; drain on paper towels. Roll clean, damp herbs in dry paper towels and place in a tightly covered plastic container. Store 1-2 weeks in the coldest part of your refrigerator.

  Vegetables, Side Dishes & Rice

Zucchini Boats Stuffed with Sausage

10-12 servings

- **6** medium zucchini, washed and ends trimmed
- **1** teaspoon salt
- **½** pound bulk sausage (breakfast or Italian)
- **1** medium onion, finely chopped (¾ cup)
- **2** cloves garlic, crushed (1 teaspoon)
- **1** cup chopped **mushrooms**[1]
- **¼** cup dry **breadcrumbs**[2]
- **1** cup shredded Cheddar cheese
- salt and pepper, to taste

1. Bring a pan of water to boil; add salt and whole zucchini. Cook 5-7 minutes, just until barely tender. Drain. When cool enough to handle, cut in half lengthwise. Scoop out pulp, leaving ¼-inch shell. Set aside reserving pulp.

2. In a skillet, brown the sausage separating into small pieces as it cooks (if using Italian, remove sausage from casings). Add onion and cook until tender. Add garlic and mushrooms. Cook until all liquid released from vegetables has been absorbed. Remove from heat.

3. Stir in zucchini pulp, breadcrumbs and cheese into sausage mixture. Taste and adjust seasonings as necessary.

4. Divide sausage mixture evenly into zucchini boats. Place on a foil-lined baking sheet; bake 15-20 minutes or until cheese is melted.

Diva Tips

[1]Never immerse **mushrooms** in water; they will absorb liquid like a sponge. The best way to clean mushrooms is to wipe with a damp paper towel. Store mushrooms in a paper bag in the refrigerator.

[2]Save all your dried, leftover bread—baguettes, sandwich bread, bagels, crackers, rolls, etc.—and put into the bowl of your food processor or blender and pulse until you have fine crumbs. Or rub dried bread on a grater, catching the crumbs in a bowl. Store crumbs in a zip top plastic bag in the freezer and use as your recipe directs. Homemade **breadcrumbs** taste superior to store prepackaged.

Eggplant Parmigiana

Another staple in the Destino household. I keep eggplant prepared and ready to go into active duty for this recipe in the freezer at all times.

4-6 servings

1	large **eggplant**[1]
	salt
1	large egg, lightly beaten
1	tablespoon water
1	cup all-purpose flour
½	teaspoon pepper
	vegetable oil
1	cup spaghetti sauce
6	tablespoons Parmesan cheese
2	ounces Provolone cheese, thinly sliced

1. Slice eggplant into ½-inch slices; sprinkle with salt and let "rest" for 30 minutes to draw out moisture.

2. Wipe all juices and salt off slices with a paper towel.

3. In a small bowl, mix egg with water.

4. In a separate dish mix flour and pepper.

5. Pour enough oil to measure ½-inch in a large skillet and heat almost to the smoking point. (If oil is very hot, eggplant will not absorb oil as it cooks.)

6. Coat eggplant slices with flour shaking or patting to remove excess. Dip in egg mixture and then again in the flour. Carefully place in hot oil. Fry until golden; turn over and cook until golden on the other side.

7. Remove from oil and drain on paper towels. Repeat as necessary until all slices have been cooked. (At this point, eggplant can be frozen in a single layer on a cookie sheet. Store in a zip top plastic bag.)

8. Place one layer of eggplant in a lightly greased baking dish (or coat dish with a nonstick cooking spray). Top with 2 tablespoons spaghetti sauce; sprinkle with Parmesan cheese. Cover with sliced Provolone cheese. Top with another layer of eggplant; spread 2 more tablespoons of sauce over and sprinkle with Parmesan cheese.

9. Repeat until all eggplant has been used.

10. Bake in a preheated 350° oven 20-30 minutes until bubbly and heated through. Serve hot or make sandwiches out of cold eggplant Parmigiana with crusty Italian bread the next day. Yum!

Diva Tips

[1]Fresh **eggplant** has a smooth, glossy, dark purple skin. Buy eggplant that feels heavy, has a green stem, and unblemished skin. Store in the refrigerator up to 2 days.

Barbecue Baked Beans

Thick, sweet and good enough to serve with your prized hamburgers.

6-8 servings

2 cans (14-ounces each) baked beans, drained

½ cup brown sugar

1 tablespoon dry minced onion

1 teaspoon dry mustard

1 cup sweet, thick barbecue sauce

4 slices **bacon**[1,2], cooked and crumbled (reserve bacon fat)

1. Preheat oven to 350°.

2. Mix all ingredients together, including bacon fat.

3. Pour into a lightly greased (2-quart) casserole (or coat dish with a nonstick cooking spray).

4. Bake 30 minutes or until bubbly and heated through.

Diva Tips

[1]If you only use **bacon** occasionally, separate into individual slices, wrap each piece in plastic wrap, and place wrapped pieces in a zip top freezer bag. Store in the freezer up to 3 months. When a recipe calls for a few slices of bacon, remove only as many as needed.

[2]To cook **bacon**, remove desired number of slices from package in one piece. Chop or cut all slices into small pieces with kitchen scissors or a knife. Fry over medium-high heat, separating pieces as they cook. Cook until crisp and golden brown.

Take time to laugh; laughter is the music of your soul.

Pinto Beans

8 cups or 16 servings

3   cups dried pinto beans

3   quarts water

6   slices **bacon**[1], cooked and crumbled

1   small onion, diced (½ cup)

4-6 cloves garlic, crushed (1-2 tablespoons)

1   tablespoon chili powder

1-2 teaspoons ground cumin

3   cans (14-ounces each) vegetable broth
     or chicken broth

1   tablespoon salt (added when beans
     are cooked)

1. Pick and sort through the beans to remove any small rocks. Rinse the dried beans to remove dust and dirt. Soak beans overnight in water (or bring water and beans to a boil, remove from heat and let sit for 1-2 hours covered until beans plump and absorb water).

2. Cook bacon in a skillet over medium-high heat until crispy, about 6-8 minutes.

3. Remove bacon to a dish and cook onion in bacon drippings about 4-5 minutes.

4. Add the garlic and cook an additional 1 minute, just until garlic releases its fragrance.

5. Stir in chili powder and cumin and cook for 1 minute more.

6. Add 1 cup of broth to the pan, stirring and scraping to loosen any brown bits adhered to the pan.

7. Strain soaked beans and rinse. Return beans to pot and add broth and enough water to cover the beans.

8. Add onion mixture to the beans.

9. Bring bean mixture to a hard boil; decrease heat to medium-low and simmer for 2-2½ hours or until beans are soft, adding more liquid or water as needed to keep beans from burning and sticking to the pan.

10. When beans are cooked through, season with salt and cook an additional 2 minutes.

11. Add reserved bacon. Keep warm until ready to serve or cool, cover and refrigerate up to 3 days.

    (Note: you may substitute 4 (14-ounce) cans of pinto beans for the dried beans. Rinse beans thoroughly, omit soaking and proceed with the recipe. Cook ½-1 hour and only add salt if necessary.)

Diva Tips

[1]If you only use **bacon** occasionally, separate into individual slices, wrap each piece in plastic wrap, and place wrapped pieces in a zip top freezer bag. Freeze up to 3 months. When a recipe calls for a few slices of bacon, remove only as many as needed.

Sausage Spinach Dressing

In the south we prefer to cook the "stuffing" outside the bird and we call it dressing.

8 servings

1	pound sausage (breakfast or Italian, casings removed)
4	tablespoons butter or margarine
1	large onion, finely chopped (1¼ cups)
2	stalks celery, finely chopped (½ cup)
2	cloves garlic, crushed (1 teaspoon)
1	apple, peeled, cored and diced (1-1½ cups)
½	pound fresh spinach leaves, thoroughly washed and chopped
1	package (8-ounces) frozen creamed spinach, thawed
2	large eggs, lightly beaten
2	cans (14-ounces each) chicken broth
½	cup heavy cream
1	package (8-ounces) dry cornbread stuffing
1½	teaspoons chopped fresh **thyme**[1]
1½	teaspoons chopped fresh **rosemary**[1]
½	teaspoon dry rubbed sage
1	teaspoon garlic pepper

1. Cook sausage over medium-high heat in a large skillet until brown and crumbly. Drain off fat.

2. Melt butter with sausage and add onion and celery. Cook until vegetables are tender. Add the garlic, apple, and chopped spinach. Cook and stir just until spinach is wilted, 1-2 minutes. Remove from heat and stir in creamed spinach.

3. In a large mixing bowl, mix eggs, chicken broth and cream.

4. Add cornbread stuffing and herbs.

5. Stir in sausage and spinach to the cornbread mixture. Season with garlic pepper.

6. Pour into a lightly greased (2½ or 3-quart) baking dish (or coat dish with a nonstick cooking spray).

7. Bake in a preheated 350° oven 45 minutes or until golden brown and set in the middle.

Diva Tips

[1]**Thyme** and **rosemary** are woody herbs. Strip off and chop the green leaves from the woody stems.

Wild Rice Dressing

Dressing is normally served with turkey during the holidays, but this recipe makes a great side dish for beef tenderloin.

8-10 servings

½   **pound bacon[1], cooked and crumbled**
½   **cup (1 stick) butter or margarine**
1   **large onion, finely chopped (1 cup)**
1   **cup finely chopped celery**
2   **cloves garlic, crushed (1 teaspoon)**
1   **package (6-ounces) long grain and wild rice, cooked according to package directions**
1   **package (8-ounces) herb-seasoned stuffing**
1   **can (14-ounces) chicken broth**
¼   **cup chopped fresh parsley[2]**
    salt and pepper, to taste

1. Preheat oven to 350°.

2. Fry bacon until crisp. Transfer to a bowl with a slotted spoon.

3. Drain off all but 2 tablespoons bacon drippings. Melt butter with the bacon drippings. Cook onion and celery until tender. Add garlic and cook an additional minute or just until garlic releases it fragrance.

4. Add cooked vegetables with any juices to bacon.

5. Stir remaining ingredients into bacon mixture. Taste and adjust the seasonings with salt and pepper, if necessary.

6. Spoon into a lightly greased (8x11-inch) baking dish (or coat dish with a nonstick cooking spray).

7. Bake covered 20 minutes; remove cover and bake an additional 15-20 minutes or until lightly browned.

Diva Tips

[1]If you only use **bacon** occasionally, separate into individual slices, wrap each piece in plastic wrap, and place wrapped pieces in a zip top freezer bag. Store in the freezer up to 3 months. When a recipe calls for a few slices of bacon, remove only as many as needed.

[2]To store **fresh herbs (parsley** or cilantro), wash herbs in plenty of cold water; drain on paper towels. Roll clean, damp herbs in dry paper towels and place in a tightly covered plastic container. Store 1-2 weeks in the coldest part of your refrigerator.

Stir-Fried Rice

This recipe is a great way to use leftover rice from last night's take out dinner.

4 servings

2	tablespoons vegetable oil
1	large carrot, shredded
3	green onions, thinly sliced
2	cups **cooked rice**[1]
2	tablespoons butter or margarine
1	large egg
2	tablespoons **sesame seeds, toasted**[2]
1	teaspoon dark **sesame oil**[3]
	salt and pepper, to taste

1. Heat oil in a large skillet over medium high heat. Sauté carrots and onions until tender, 2-3 minutes.

2. Add rice and stir until heated through.

3. Make a hole in the center of the rice; melt butter in the hole. Break egg into melted butter and stir until egg is cooked. Stir together with rice.

4. Add sesame seeds and sesame oil.

5. Taste and adjust seasonings with salt and pepper if desired. Stir until heated through. Serve hot.

Diva Tips

[1]To make **cooked rice**, bring 1⅓ cups water to a boil; add ⅔ cup long grain rice. Lower heat, tightly cover and simmer 14-18 minutes until all liquid has been absorbed. Cool completely before making stir-fried rice.

[2]**Toasting** intensifies the flavor of **sesame seeds**. Spread seeds in a preheated, dry skillet in a single layer. Shake pan or stir seeds over medium-high heat until seeds turn a golden color for about 2-3 minutes, being careful not to burn. Sesame seeds tend to go rancid very quickly. Store sesame seeds in the refrigerator 6 months or freeze up to 1 year.

[3]**Sesame oil** can be found in the Oriental food section of the grocery store or in specialty shops. Store in the refrigerator.

Mexican Red Rice

Make your own red rice to serve along with homemade tacos.

3 cups (6 servings)

1   **tablespoon vegetable oil**
1   **cup long-grain white rice**
1   **small onion, finely chopped (½ cup)**
1   **clove garlic, crushed (½ teaspoon)**
1   **tablespoon tomato paste**[1]
1   **can (14-ounces) low sodium chicken broth**
1   **teaspoon salt, or to taste**

1. Pour oil in a medium saucepan over medium-high heat; add rice. Sauté 2-3 minutes or just until rice begins to turn white.

2. Add the onions and garlic; cook 2 minutes more.

3. Stir in tomato paste and cook until rice is coated and tomato begins to roast.

4. Stir in chicken broth and salt; bring to a boil, reduce heat; cover tightly and simmer 14-16 minutes or until liquid is absorbed.

5. Remove from heat and fluff with a fork. Let stand covered until ready to serve.

Diva Tips

[1]Small quantities of **tomato paste** can be purchased in tubes in the tomato paste aisle of the grocery store. Or freeze remaining tomato paste from the can in 1 tablespoon increments on a flat sheet. When frozen transfer to a zip top plastic bag and store in the freezer up to 6 months.

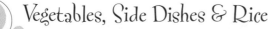

Yellow Rice Pilaf

6 (½-cup) servings

1 tablespoon butter or vegetable oil
1 cup **Basmati rice**[1]
1 envelope saffron powder
   (or 5-6 threads)
1 teaspoon curry powder
1 can (14-ounces) chicken broth
1 teaspoon salt
3 tablespoons chopped **fresh parsley**[2]
   (optional)

1. Melt butter in a heavy saucepan over medium-high heat. Add rice and sauté for 2-3 minutes or just until rice begins to turn white. Add saffron and curry powder, stirring to heat through.

2. Stir in chicken broth and salt; bring to a boil, reduce heat, cover tightly and simmer 14-16 minutes or until liquid is absorbed.

3. Remove from heat and fluff with a fork. Let stand covered until ready to serve. Toss with parsley just before serving.

Diva Tips

[1]**Basmati rice** has a distinctive, perfumy, nutty flavor and aroma. Used widely in Indian cuisines and pilafs.

[2]To store **fresh herbs** (**parsley** or cilantro), wash herbs in plenty of cold water; drain on paper towels. Roll clean, damp herbs in dry paper towels and place in a tightly covered plastic container. Store 1-2 weeks in the coldest part of your refrigerator.

Royal Rice Pilaf

An elegant side dish for a dinner party or delicious addition to a picnic.

6 (½-cup) servings

2 **tablespoons butter**
¼ **cup finely chopped celery**
1 **cup long-grain white rice**
¼ **cup wild rice**
1 **tablespoon dried minced onions**
1 **can (14-ounces) low-sodium chicken broth**
1 **cup water**
¼ **cup pecans, toasted[1] and chopped**
2 **tablespoons chopped chives[2] (or substitute chopped green onions)**

1. Melt butter in a heavy saucepan over medium-high heat. Sauté celery until softened, 2-3 minutes.

2. Add long-grain rice and sauté an additional 2-3 minutes or until rice begins to turn white.

3. Add wild rice and dried onions. Stir in chicken broth and water; bring to a boil, reduce heat, cover tightly and simmer 15-18 minutes or until liquid is absorbed.

4. Remove from heat and fluff with a fork. Let stand covered until ready to serve. Toss with pecans and chives just before serving.

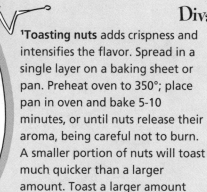

Diva Tips

[1]**Toasting nuts** adds crispness and intensifies the flavor. Spread in a single layer on a baking sheet or pan. Preheat oven to 350°; place pan in oven and bake 5-10 minutes, or until nuts release their aroma, being careful not to burn. A smaller portion of nuts will toast much quicker than a larger amount. Toast a larger amount than needed and freeze extras up to 1 year in a tightly sealed container. Four ounces of nuts equals about 1 cup.

[2]**Chives** are a member of the onion family but have a much milder flavor. Snip fresh chives with kitchen scissors to desired length. Store fresh chives in a plastic bag in the refrigerator up to 1 week.

Brown Rice Pilaf

Brown rice is more nutritious than white rice. It takes longer to cook and has a chewy, nutty taste.

6 (½-cup) servings

1 tablespoon vegetable oil
1 cup long-grain brown rice
1 can (10-ounces) condensed beef broth
1½ cups water
3 tablespoons butter or margarine
1 large carrot, shredded
3 green onions, thinly sliced
1 cup (4-ounces) fresh **mushrooms**[1], thinly sliced
1 can (8-ounces) sliced water chestnuts, roughly chopped
   salt and pepper to taste
2 tablespoons dry white **wine**[2]
2 tablespoons cold butter or margarine, cut into bits

1. Heat vegetable oil in a heavy saucepan over medium-high heat. Add brown rice and sauté for 2-3 minutes or just until rice begins to turn opaque.

2. Stir in beef broth and water; bring to a boil, reduce heat, cover tightly and simmer 30-45 minutes or until liquid is absorbed and rice is tender. (Add additional water as necessary to prevent sticking and burning if rice absorbs liquid before it is cooked.)

3. Remove from heat and fluff with a fork.

4. Melt 3 tablespoons butter in a large skillet. Add carrots, green onions, and mushrooms. Cook over medium-high heat until vegetables are tender and any liquid released is reabsorbed, about 3-5 minutes, stirring constantly.

5. Add chopped water chestnuts to carrot mixture.

6. Stir vegetables into rice. Taste and adjust seasoning with salt and pepper, if desired.

7. Spoon rice mixture into a (2-quart) baking dish. Drizzle with white wine and dot with butter. Cover and bake at 350° 20 minutes until heated through.

Diva Tips

[1]Never immerse **mushrooms** in water; they will absorb liquid like a sponge. The best way to clean mushrooms is to wipe with a damp paper towel. Store mushrooms in a paper bag in the refrigerator.

[2]Cook with an inexpensive **wine** that you would drink. Cooking wine found in the vinegar section of the grocery store is poor quality and high in sodium.

Milano Risotto

Offer this delicious, creamy dish for your first course or as a main dish for lunch or dinner.

4 main course servings or 6 side dishes

3 cans (14-ounces each) low sodium chicken broth

½ cup dry white **wine**[1]

6 tablespoons butter or margarine, divided

½ pound fresh, large shrimp, peeled deveined

1 small onion, finely chopped (½ cup)

2 cloves garlic, crushed (1 teaspoon)

¼ teaspoon crushed red pepper flakes (optional)

1½ cups **Arborio rice**[2]

salt and pepper to taste

2 tablespoons chopped fresh parsley

1. Bring broth and ¼ cup wine to simmer in a medium saucepan. Keep hot.

2. Melt 2 tablespoons butter in a large skillet over medium heat. Add shrimp and cook until shrimp begin to turn pink, about 2 minutes. Add remaining ¼ cup wine. Simmer another 2 minutes until shrimp are just cooked through. Remove from heat and set aside.

3. Melt remaining 4 tablespoons butter in a large heavy saucepan over medium heat. Add onion, garlic and red pepper flakes. Sauté until onion is golden, about 4 minutes.

4. Add rice and stir to coat with butter.

5. Add 2 cups hot broth. Simmer until liquid is absorbed, stirring often.

6. Continue adding broth 1 cup at a time to the rice, stirring often and simmering until liquid is absorbed before adding more, about 20-30 minutes.

7. Drain any liquid from shrimp and add to rice. Cook until rice is tender and creamy.

8. Remove from heat. Stir in shrimp. Season with salt and pepper, if needed.

9. Stir in parsley and transfer to serving bowls.

Diva Tips

[1]Cook with an inexpensive **wine** that you would drink. Cooking wine found in the vinegar section of the grocery store is poor quality and high in sodium.

[2]**Arborio rice** is a short-grain, Italian rice that forms a creamy sauce as it cooks. Look for it in the grocery store next to the regular rice. Use a short-grain rice when making risotto because of its high starch content.

Desserts

Desserts

Desserts

Cakes

Cookies

Candy

Southern Banana Pudding

This dessert has to be my all-time favorite. Who am I kidding? I haven't met a dessert yet that wasn't love at first bite.

8 servings (unless you make it for me, then it's one.)

⅔ cup sugar

3 tablespoons cornstarch

⅛ teaspoon salt

3 large **eggs, separated**[1]

3 cups milk

3 tablespoons, butter or margarine, softened

2 teaspoons vanilla extract

½ package (6-ounces or about 42) vanilla wafers, divided

6 medium bananas

¼ teaspoon cream of tartar

6 tablespoons sugar

1 teaspoon vanilla extract

1. Combine sugar, cornstarch and salt in a large, heavy saucepan.

2. Beat egg yolks; combine with milk, mixing well.

3. Slowly stir into sugar. Cook over medium heat, stirring constantly, until mixture comes to a boil. Boil and stir 1 minute or until smooth and thickened. Remove from heat and stir in butter and vanilla.

4. Line a (3-quart) glass baking dish with ⅓ of the vanilla wafers. Slice 2 bananas and layer over wafers. Pour ⅓ of custard over bananas. Repeat layers twice.

5. Beat egg whites and cream of tartar until foamy. Gradually add 6 tablespoons of sugar, beating in 1 tablespoon at a time. Continue beating until stiff peaks form and mixture is glossy. Do not under beat. Add vanilla.

6. Spread meringue over custard, sealing to the edge of the dish.

7. Bake in a preheated oven at 325° 10 minutes or until meringue is golden brown.

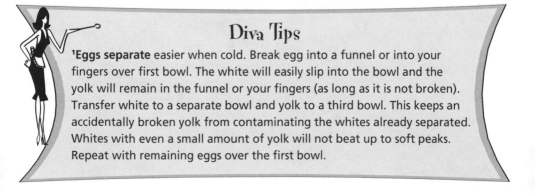

Diva Tips

[1]**Eggs separate** easier when cold. Break egg into a funnel or into your fingers over first bowl. The white will easily slip into the bowl and the yolk will remain in the funnel or your fingers (as long as it is not broken). Transfer white to a separate bowl and yolk to a third bowl. This keeps an accidentally broken yolk from contaminating the whites already separated. Whites with even a small amount of yolk will not beat up to soft peaks. Repeat with remaining eggs over the first bowl.

Snickers Pie

This pie is made with my favorite candy bar.

10-12 servings

Brownie Layer

½ cup (1 stick) butter or margarine

2 squares (2-ounces) unsweetened
    baking chocolate, coarsely chopped

1 cup sugar

2 large eggs, lightly beaten

½ cup all-purpose flour

½ teaspoon baking powder

½ teaspoon vanilla extract

2 cups (about 8-ounces or 10 mini)
    Snickers candy bars cut into ½-inch
    pieces

1. Preheat oven to 350°.

2. Lightly butter a (9-inch) pie pan
   (or coat with cooking spray).

3. In a medium saucepan over low heat,
   melt butter and chocolate. Remove
   from heat and stir in sugar. Mix in eggs
   until well blended. Add flour and
   baking powder, stirring to incorporate
   thoroughly. Stir in vanilla extract.

4. Pour into prepared pan and place in
   the oven. Bake 17-18 minutes. Remove
   from oven; cool 10 minutes.

5. Carefully place the Snickers candy bar
   pieces evenly over brownie layer.

Cheesecake Layer

1 package (8-ounces) cream cheese,
    softened

1 package (3-ounces) cream cheese,
    softened

⅓ cup sugar

1 large egg, slightly beaten

1 teaspoon vanilla extract

1. Beat the cream cheese in a large bowl
   of an electric mixer until light and
   fluffy.

2. Add sugar and beat on medium speed
   until the mixture is smooth about 1
   minute. Add the egg and vanilla and
   mix just until the mixture is well
   blended.

3. Pour the cream cheese mixture over
   the Snickers bar layer, spreading
   mixture evenly. Return to oven and
   bake 15 minutes. Remove from oven
   and cool pie 1 hour until the
   cheesecake layer is firm.

Topping

½ cup heavy cream

1 tablespoon butter or margarine

2 teaspoons light corn syrup

1 cup (6-ounces) semi-sweet chocolate chips

1 cup unsalted peanuts, roughly chopped

1. Heat the cream, butter and corn syrup in a medium saucepan until mixture come to a boil.

2. Remove from heat and add in chocolate chips. Let sit for a few minutes to soften. Stir until chocolate is melted and mixture is smooth. Cool 30 minutes until it thickens slightly.

3. Pour the topping over the pie. Using a thin spatula spread the topping completely over the pie.

4. Sprinkle with chopped peanuts. Cool pie completely before cutting into serving pieces.

Money talks; chocolate sings!

Chocolate Kahlúa Loaf

12 servings

- **3** cups **heavy cream**[1]
- ¼ cup Kahlúa, or any coffee-flavored liqueur
- ¼ cup sugar
- ¼ cup unsweetened cocoa powder
- **1** teaspoon vanilla extract
- **1** inner packet graham crackers **(11-double crackers)**

1. Combine cream, Kahlúa, sugar, cocoa and vanilla in a large mixing bowl.

2. Beat with an electric mixer on medium speed until mixture is stiff and good spreading consistency.

3. Spread ¼ cup (½-inch) of chocolate whipped cream evenly on a double cracker; stack with a second cracker.

4. Repeat spreading and stacking until 4 crackers are stacked together. Press together evenly.

5. Place the stack on a serving platter standing crackers on long edge. Repeat with remaining crackers, placing one stack in front of the other to make a (5x6½-inch) loaf.

6. Spread remaining chocolate cream over the top and sides of the loaf, rounding the ends and top.

7. Refrigerate several hours or overnight.

8. Cut long side into 6 slices (about 1-inch wide), and then cut each slice in half to make 12 servings.

Diva Tips

[1]**Heavy cream**, bowl and beaters should be very cold before whipping. If you over whip cream (it separates into solids and liquids), gently fold in a few tablespoons of milk or more cream.

5-Layer Dreamland Pie

Take a bite; close your eyes. This dessert is dreamy.

16 servings

½ cup (1 stick) butter or margarine, softened

1 cup all-purpose flour

1½ cups **pecans, toasted**[1] and finely chopped, divided

1 package (8-ounces) cream cheese, softened

1 cup powdered sugar

1 large container (12-ounces) Cool Whip, divided

3 medium bananas, sliced

2 small packages (3.4-ounces each) instant chocolate pudding mix

3 cups milk

1. Preheat oven to **350°**.

2. Cream butter; add flour, stirring just until mixed. Stir in ½ cup nuts.

3. Press mixture evenly into the bottom of a (9x13-inch) baking pan. Bake 20 minutes or until lightly browned. Remove from oven and cool completely.

4. Beat cream cheese in a large mixing bowl until smooth. Add powdered sugar. Fold in 1 cup Cool Whip. Spread over crust.

5. Slice bananas about ¼-inch thick; place evenly over cream cheese layer.

6. Beat pudding mix with milk according to directions on the package. Spread chocolate pudding over bananas. Let stand 5 minutes to set.

7. Spread remaining Cool Whip over chocolate pudding and refrigerate until set at least 2 hours.

8. Sprinkle with remaining toasted pecans just before serving. Cut into (2x3-inch) squares. Refrigerate any leftovers.

Diva Tips

[1]**Toasting nuts** adds crispness and intensifies the flavor. Spread in a single layer on a baking sheet or pan. Preheat oven to 350°; place pan in oven and bake 5-10 minutes, or until nuts release their aroma, being careful not to burn. A smaller portion of nuts will toast much quicker than a larger amount. Toast a larger amount than needed and freeze extras up to 1 year in a tightly sealed container. Four ounces of nuts equals about 1 cup.

Chocolate Meringue Pie

My brother, Wayne Stowe, expects this pie at all family gatherings!

8 servings

Meringue Topping

4	large **egg whites**[1]
¼	teaspoon cream of tartar
½	cup sugar
1	tablespoon cornstarch
½	teaspoon vanilla extract

1. Preheat oven to 325°.

2. In a large mixing bowl, combine egg whites and cream of tartar. Beat until foamy.

3. Mix sugar and cornstarch together. Add sugar mixture 1 tablespoon at a time beating until stiff and glossy. Do not under beat. Beat in vanilla extract. Set aside while preparing pie filling.

Pie Filling

1½	cups sugar
⅓	cup cornstarch
2	tablespoons unsweetened cocoa powder
3	cups milk
4	large **egg yolks**[1]
2	tablespoons butter or margarine
3	squares (3-ounces) **unsweetened baking chocolate**, chopped
1	teaspoon vanilla extract
1	(9-inch) pie shell, baked

1. Mix sugar, cornstarch, and cocoa powder together in a large saucepan.

2. Blend milk and egg yolks together. Slowly stir into sugar mixture.

3. Cook over medium heat until mixture thickens and boils; boil and stir 1 minute.

4. Remove from heat; stir in butter and chopped chocolate, mixing until all is melted and mixture is smooth. Mix in vanilla.

5. Immediately pour into baked pie shell. Top with **meringue**[2] while filling is still hot.

6. Place in a 325° oven and bake 5-7 minutes until meringue is golden brown.

7. Remove from oven and cool. Chill thoroughly (2 hours) before cutting into serving pieces. Refrigerate leftovers.

Diva Tips

[1]**Eggs separate** easier when cold. Break egg into a funnel or into your fingers over one bowl. The white will easily slip into the bowl and the yolk will remain in the funnel or your fingers (as long as it is not broken). Transfer white to a separate bowl and yolk to a third bowl. This keeps an accidentally broken yolk from contaminating the whites already separated. Whites with even a small amount of yolk will not beat up to soft peaks. Repeat with remaining eggs over the first bowl.

[2]To keep **meringue** from weeping and shrinking from pie, spread over hot filling bringing meringue all the way to the edges making sure it is sealed with the crust all around.

Rocky Road Pie

Full of nuts and other goodies, this pie is extraordinary!

12 servings

Pie

½ cup (1 stick) butter or margarine, softened

1 cup sugar

¼ teaspoon salt

½ teaspoon almond extract

1 teaspoon vanilla extract

2 large eggs

¾ cup all-purpose flour

½ cup unsweetened cocoa powder

¼ cup flaked coconut

¼ cup semi-sweet chocolate chips

¼ cup dried cherries or cranberries

½ cup nuts, **toasted**[1] and chopped

2 cups mini-**marshmallows**[2]

1. Preheat oven to 350°.
2. Lightly grease a (9-inch) pie pan (or coat with a nonstick cooking spray).
3. Mix butter, sugar, salt, almond and vanilla extract.
4. Add eggs and beat on low speed until all incorporated.
5. Sift together the flour and cocoa powder; slowly stir into egg mixture.
6. Stir in coconut, chocolate chips, dried cherries and nuts.
7. Spread into the bottom of the prepared pie pan; bake 20-25 minutes or until small cracks appear on the top.
8. Place marshmallows over baked pie in a single layer.

Topping

1 cup semi-sweet chocolate chips

½ cup milk

¼ cup (½ stick) butter or margarine, softened

2½ cups powdered sugar, sifted

½ teaspoon vanilla extract

¼ teaspoon almond extract

1 cup nuts, **toasted**[1] and chopped

1. In a medium saucepan over low heat, combine chocolate chips, milk and butter. Stir constantly, until chocolate is melted.
2. Beat in powdered sugar. Stir in vanilla, almond extracts and nuts.
3. Spread over marshmallows.
4. Cool completely. Refrigerate and thoroughly chill pie before cutting into serving pieces.

(Note: Tightly wrap and freeze up to 2 months.)

Diva Tips

[1]**Toasting nuts** adds crispness and intensifies the flavor. Spread in a single layer on a baking sheet or pan. Preheat oven to 350°; place pan in oven and bake 5-10 minutes, or until nuts release their aroma, being careful not to burn. A smaller portion of nuts will toast much quicker than a larger amount. Toast a larger amount than needed and freeze extras up to 1 year in a tightly sealed container. Four ounces of nuts equals about 1 cup.

[2]**Marshmallows** will keep fresh longer if stored in a tightly sealed plastic bag in the freezer.

French Silk Chocolate Chip Cookie Pie

My husband, Jim, usually request this pie for his birthday instead of chocolate cake.

10-12 servings

Pie Crust

1½ cups chocolate chip cookie crumbs [14-18 (2-inch) cookies]

½ cup pecans, toasted and finely chopped

¼ cup butter or margarine, melted

1. Preheat oven to 350°.
2. Combine cookie crumbs, pecans, and melted butter; mix well.
3. Press into the sides and bottom of a buttered (9-inch) pie dish. Bake 10 minutes.
4. Remove from oven and cool completely.

Filling

1 cup sugar

3 large eggs, slightly beaten

3 squares (3-ounces) unsweetened baking chocolate, melted

½ cup (1 stick) butter or margarine, softened

1 cup heavy cream

½ cups pecans, toasted and chopped

additional whipped cream, if desired

1. In a heavy saucepan, mix sugar with eggs. Heat over medium-low heat, stirring constantly, until thick, about 10 minutes.
2. Remove from heat and stir in melted chocolate and softened butter.
3. Cool to room temperature. Refrigerate until mixture is cold.
4. Remove from refrigerator and beat with an electric mixer or wire whisk until light and fluffy.
5. Whip 1 cup heavy cream until soft peaks form.
6. Fold whipped cream into cold whipped chocolate mixture. Spoon into cooled pie crust and smooth.
7. Refrigerate until serving.
8. Top with additional whipped cream, if desired. Sprinkle with remaining toasted nuts.

Butterfinger Pie

8-10 servings

Crust

1½ cups finely **crushed vanilla wafers**[1] (about 36 cookies)

2 tablespoons brown sugar

¼ cup unsalted peanuts, finely chopped

½ cup butter or margarine, melted

1. Preheat oven to 375°.
2. Prepare a (9-inch) pie pan by buttering or coating with a nonstick cooking spray.
3. Combine vanilla wafer crumbs, brown sugar, peanuts and melted butter.
4. Press into the bottom and sides of the pie pan. Bake until golden and set.
5. Remove from oven and cool completely.

Filling

1 package (8-ounces) cream cheese, softened

1 large container (12-ounces) Cool Whip, thawed

2 boxes (8-ounces each) Butterfinger candy bar, mini size, finely crushed

1 (8-ounces) candy bar milk **chocolate, shaved**[2]

1. Beat cream cheese until light and fluffy; fold in Cool Whip.
2. Stir crushed candies (candies should be completely crushed with no big pieces remaining) and shaved chocolate into cream cheese mix.
3. Pile mixture into completely cooled cookie shell.
4. Chill at least 2 hours or overnight.

   (Note: Butterfinger candies come in (8-ounce) boxes unwrapped. If unavailable, substitute one (14-ounce) bag of mini Butterfinger bars.)

Diva Tips

[1]To make **cookie crumbs**, 1) place cookies in a plastic bag (don't close all the way). Smash with a meat pounder or rolling pin. Or 2) place cookies in a food processor or blender and process until fine crumbs.

[2]To **shave chocolate**, rub chocolate bar over a coarse grater or shave with a vegetable peeler.

Chocolate Pecan Pie

A twist on an old southern favorite.

12 servings

Pastry

1	cup all-purpose flour
¼	cup unsweetened cocoa powder
½	cup powdered sugar

pinch salt

6	tablespoons butter or margarine, cold
1	large **egg yolk**[1]
1	tablespoon cold water (plus more if needed)

1. Preheat oven to 350°.

2. Mix flour, cocoa, powdered sugar and salt. Cut in the butter with a pastry blender or rub flour and butter together with fingers until crumbly. Mix in the egg yolk and water.

3. Bring to a ball and knead 1 or 2 times until it holds together.

4. Pat into a disk and refrigerate 1 hour to chill thoroughly. (If dough is still too crumbly add a little ice water 1 teaspoon at a time until dough holds together. Dough should not be too dry or too wet.)

5. Roll out dough and place in a (9-inch) pie pan. Press dough with fingers against the bottom and sides of the pan. Prick bottom with a fork and bake 15 minutes. Remove from oven and cool slightly.

Filling

2	cups pecans, toasted, and divided
6	tablespoons butter or margarine
1	cup brown sugar
3	large eggs
2	tablespoons heavy cream
2	tablespoons all-purpose flour
1	teaspoon vanilla
1	cup semi-sweet chocolate chips
2	tablespoons powdered sugar (optional)

1. Chop 1 cup pecans roughly. Set aside.

2. Cream butter and sugar together.

3. Add eggs one at a time, mixing until incorporated.

4. Stir in cream, vanilla and flour. Mix in 1 cup chopped nuts and chocolate chips.

5. Spoon into the baked crust and smooth the top.

6. Top with circles of pecan halves (1 cup) working from the edge to the center, gently pressing into filling.

7. Bake at 350° 55 minutes. Cover with foil halfway through baking, to prevent over-browning. Allow the pie to cool completely before cutting into serving pieces. When pie is cold dust with powdered sugar if desired.

Sweet Potato Pie

A true Southern traditional dessert at Thanksgiving!

8 servings

2 cups (about 3 medium) **sweet potatoes, baked**[1,2]**, peeled and mashed**

1 cup **sugar**

2 **large eggs, slightly beaten**

¼ cup **butter or margarine, melted**

¼ teaspoon **salt**

1 teaspoon **vanilla extract**

¾ cup **half-and-half or milk**

1 **(9-inch) pie crust, unbaked**

1. Preheat oven to 350°.

2. Mix all ingredients in a large mixing bowl.

3. Pour into pie crust. Bake 50-60 minutes or until a knife inserted halfway between the center and the edge comes out clean.

4. Remove from oven and cool completely on a wire rack before cutting into serving pieces.

Best Apple Pie

8 servings

2   pie crusts (9-inch), unbaked
4   **apples**[1] peeled, cored, and thinly
        sliced (6 cups)
½   cup sugar
¼   cup brown sugar, packed
1   teaspoon cinnamon
¼   teaspoon **nutmeg**[2]
2   tablespoons all-purpose flour
2   tablespoons butter or margarine, cut
        into pieces
     ice cream or whipped cream (optional)

1. Preheat oven to 375°.

2. Place one pie crust in the bottom of a (9-inch) pie pan that has been lightly buttered or coated with a nonstick cooking spray.

3. Combine apples, sugars, cinnamon, nutmeg and flour, tossing to coat apples thoroughly.

4. Pile apple mixture into pie crust, mounding in the center; dot apples with pieces of butter.

5. Cover with remaining pie crust, easing to fit over apples. Pinch the two pie crusts together to seal or press pie crusts together with a fork. Cut 5 small "vents" in the center of the top of the crust to allow steam to escape. (Can be made to this point and refrigerated up to 1 day.)

6. Bake 45 minutes or until filling is bubbly and crust is golden brown.

7. Remove from oven and cool slightly before cutting into serving pieces. Serve with ice cream or whipped cream, if desired.

   (Note: I suggest using 1 McIntosh, 1 Granny Smith, and 2 Golden Delicious apples.)

Diva Tips

[1]One of the best gadgets in my kitchen is an **apple corer/slicer**. In one swift action it removes the core and cuts the apple into 8 equal pieces. It is great for reducing the time for making pies, desserts or apple salads.

[2]Freshly grated **nutmeg** has a superior flavor over ground nutmeg found in a can or jar in the spice section. Whole nutmegs can be located in most spice sections. Use a very fine grater or a small nutmeg grater for best results. Whole nutmegs can be kept indefinitely in a jar in a cool, dark place.

Apple Tarte Innocence

Yummy crust!

8 servings

Crust

- 1¾ cups all-purpose flour
- 1 cup sugar
- ½ teaspoon salt
- ¼ teaspoon baking powder
- ¾ cup (1½ sticks) butter or margarine, cut into 12 pieces
- 4 medium apples, peeled, cored, and thinly sliced
- ¾ teaspoon cinnamon
- ¼ teaspoon nutmeg

1. Preheat oven to 375°.
2. Lightly grease a (9-inch) round cake pan (or coat with a nonstick cooking spray).
3. Combine flour, sugar, salt and baking powder.
4. Using a pastry blender or fingers, rub butter into flour mixture until crumbly.
5. Put flour mixture into the prepared pan and press firmly into the bottom and up the sides.
6. Toss apple slices with cinnamon and nutmeg. Arrange apples over crust.
7. Bake 15 minutes; remove from oven and cool slightly.

Filling

- 3 large **egg yolks**[1]
- ½ cup sugar
- 1 tablespoon all-purpose flour
- ¾ cup heavy cream
- 1 teaspoon vanilla extract

1. While crust is baking, beat egg yolks with sugar, 1 tablespoon flour and cream in a medium saucepan. Cook over medium heat until slightly thickened, stirring constantly.
2. Remove from heat. Stir in vanilla. Pour over apples.
3. Return to oven and bake an additional 20-25 minutes until filling is set.
4. Remove from oven and cool completely before cutting into serving pieces. Store leftovers in the refrigerator.

Diva Tips

[1]**Eggs separate** easier when cold. Break egg into a funnel or into your fingers over one bowl. The white will easily slip into the bowl and the yolk will remain in the funnel or your fingers (as long as it is not broken). Transfer white to a separate bowl and yolk to a third bowl. This keeps an accidentally broken yolk from contaminating the whites already separated. Whites with even a small amount of yolk will not beat up to soft peaks. Repeat with remaining eggs over the first bowl. Freeze leftover egg whites individually in an ice cube tray. When frozen remove from tray and place in a plastic bag. Thaw whites in the refrigerator when a recipe calls for egg whites.

Brownie Hearts

Passion and love in a dish: a decadent treat for your sweetheart.

4 hearts

½ cup (1 stick) butter or margarine
2 squares (2-ounces) unsweetened baking chocolate
1 cup sugar
2 large eggs
1 teaspoon vanilla
¾ cup all-purpose flour
½ teaspoon baking powder
½ teaspoon salt
½ cup heavy cream
2 tablespoons powdered sugar
¼ teaspoon vanilla
   caramel sauce
¾ cup **pecans, toasted**[1] and **coarsely chopped**[2]

1. Preheat oven to 350°.

2. Lightly grease an (8x8-inch) baking pan (or coat with nonstick cooking spray).

3. In a large saucepan, melt the butter and chocolate over low heat.

4. Remove from heat and mix in sugar. Add eggs and vanilla, stirring until well blended. Add flour, baking powder and salt and stir just until mixed.

5. Spread mixture in prepared pan. Bake 20-25 minutes until brownies begin to pull away from the sides of the pan and center is slightly puffed. Do not over bake.

6. Remove from oven and cool completely. When cool, carefully remove entire square of brownie from the pan.

7. Using a (2-inch) cookie cutter, cut out 4 heart shapes, saving scraps in between.

8. Cut scraps into cubes and set aside.

9. Beat cream with powdered sugar and vanilla until soft peaks form.

10. To serve: put brownie heart on a serving dish; drizzle with caramel sauce and nuts. Top with brownie cubes; drizzle with more caramel. Top with more pecans and spoon whipped cream over all.

Diva Tips

[1]**Toasting nuts** adds crispness and intensifies the flavor. Spread in a single layer on a baking sheet or pan. Preheat oven to 350°; place pan in oven and bake 5-10 minutes, or until nuts release their aroma, being careful not to burn. A smaller portion of nuts will toast much quicker than a larger amount. Toast a larger amount than needed and freeze extras up to 1 year in a tightly sealed container. Four ounces of nuts equals about 1 cup.

[2]To **chop nuts**, place ½ to 1 cup nuts in a plastic bag and smash with a meat pounder on a hard surface. Turn bag over and repeat on the other side. Smashing takes a fraction of the time chopping or slicing does.

Desserts

Old Fashioned Rice Pudding

One of my son, Chris' favorite dessert!

6 servings

2 large eggs, lightly beaten
⅔ cup sugar
¼ teaspoon salt
2 cups half-and-half or milk
2 cups **cooked rice**[1]
1 teaspoon vanilla
2 tablespoons butter or margarine, softened

1. Preheat oven to 325°.

2. Lightly butter a (1½ quart) casserole dish.

3. In a large saucepan, mix eggs with sugar and salt.

4. Gradually stir in half-and-half.

5. Mix in rice. Cook over medium heat just until mixture is hot and steaming, stirring constantly.

6. Remove from heat and stir in vanilla and butter.

7. Pour into the prepared dish. Bake uncovered 30 minutes or until pudding is set. Store leftovers in the refrigerator.

Diva Tips

[1]Use leftover rice or to **cook rice**, bring 1⅓ cups of water to a boil. Add ⅔ cup rice. Stir and tightly cover. Lower heat to simmer and cook 14 minutes or until all liquid is absorbed.

Magic Peach Cobbler

This cobbler magically creates its own crust.

12 servings

½ cup (1 stick) butter or margarine
1 cup sugar
1 cup **self-rising flour**[1]
1 cup milk
4 cups fresh **peaches**[2], (4 medium),
    peeled, pit removed and sliced
2 tablespoons sugar
    ice cream, optional

1. Preheat oven to 400°.

2. Coat a (9x13-inch) baking pan with a nonstick cooking spray.

3. Melt butter in the prepared pan.

4. Mix sugar, flour and milk in a bowl. Pour batter into butter.

5. Mix peaches with 2 tablespoons sugar.

6. Distribute peaches, with any accumulated juices, in the center of the batter. Do not stir.

7. Bake 20-30 minutes or until crust is brown.

8. Remove from oven and serve hot with ice cream if desired.

   (Note: substitute 1 quart frozen peaches, thawed. Recipe is also delicious with strawberries, blueberries, raspberries, or blackberries when substituted for fresh peaches.)

Diva Tips

[1]To make **self-rising flour**, add 1 teaspoon baking powder and ¼ teaspoon salt to every cup of all-purpose flour, mixing thoroughly.

[2]A ripe **peach** will be a deep golden color with a strong perfumy aroma. For the fullest flavor, store peaches (and all fruits with a pit) at room temperature.

Chocolate Brownie Trifle

16 servings

1 pan (9x13-inch) baked brownies

¼ cup Kahlúa or other coffee-flavored liqueur (optional)

3 small (3.9-ounces each) packages instant chocolate pudding mix

6 cups (1½ quarts) milk

1 large (12-ounces) container Cool Whip, divided

½ cup pecans, toasted and chopped

1. Crumble brownies; sprinkle with Kahlúa, if using. Set aside.

2. Stir pudding and milk together until thoroughly mixed.

3. Put ⅓ of brownies into the bottom of a trifle bowl or a tall, straight-sided glass bowl.

4. Top with ⅓ of the pudding, spreading to cover brownies.

5. Top pudding with ⅓ of the Cool Whip, spreading to cover pudding.

6. Repeat layers twice more, ending with Cool Whip.

7. Chill 8 hours. When ready to serve, top with chopped pecans.

Black and White Trifle

8 servings

¼ cup (½ stick) butter or margarine, softened

1 package (8-ounces) cream cheese, softened

1¾ cups milk

1 small package (3.4-ounces) instant vanilla pudding mix

1 large (12-ounces) container Cool Whip, divided

¾ pound (½ package) chocolate sandwich cookies (like Oreos), crushed

2 medium bananas, sliced ¼-inch thick

1. Beat butter and cream cheese until light and fluffy.

2. Mix milk with pudding mix. Stir into cream cheese mixture.

3. Fold 2 cups Cool Whip into pudding mixture, reserving the remaining Cool Whip for top garnish.

4. In a tall, straight-sided glass (or trifle) bowl, put ½ of the cream cheese mix, ½ bananas, then ½ of the cookies.

5. Repeat these layers, ending with cookies. Top with additional Cool Whip if desired and a sprinkle of additional crushed cookies. Refrigerate 2 hours before serving.

Strawberry Cheese Pie

Light and luscious.

8 servings

Crust

1½ cups vanilla wafer cookie crumbs (about 50)

1 tablespoon brown sugar

¼ cup (½ stick) butter or margarine, melted

½ cup almonds, toasted and finely chopped

1. Preheat oven to 350°.

2. Lightly butter a (9-inch) pie pan (or coat with a nonstick cooking spray).

3. Mix together cookie crumbs, sugar, butter and almonds. Press into the bottom and up the sides of prepared pan. Bake 8 minutes. Remove from oven and cool completely before adding filling.

Filling

1 package (8-ounces) cream cheese, softened

¾ cup powdered sugar

1 teaspoon vanilla extract

1 teaspoon almond extract

1½ cups heavy cream

3 tablespoons instant vanilla **pudding mix**[1]

2 pints strawberries, halved (try to use same size berries)

¼ cup strawberry jelly

1 cup heavy cream

2 tablespoons powdered sugar

2 tablespoons Amaretto **liqueur**[2] (or substitute 1 teaspoon almond extract)

1. In a medium mixing bowl, beat cream cheese and powdered sugar together until smooth. Mix in vanilla and almond extracts.

2. In another large mixing bowl, beat heavy cream with instant vanilla pudding until stiff peaks form. Mix into cream cheese mixture. Pour into pie crust, smoothing top.

3. Refrigerate 2 hours or until firm.

4. Decorate the top of the pie with strawberry halves, putting berries end-to-end in concentric circles until the surface is covered.

5. Heat strawberry jelly in a saucepan or microwave just until melted. Brush over strawberries to add a shiny glaze. Refrigerate until ready to serve.

6. When ready to serve, beat cream, powdered sugar, and Amaretto until soft peaks form. Spoon onto individual dessert slices.

(Note: Pie can be made the day ahead omitting strawberries. Put strawberries and jelly glaze on pie up to 6 hours before serving.)

Diva Tips

[1]There are 6-7 tablespoons of **pudding mix** in each 3.4 or 3.9 ounce box.

[2]Small bottles (airline serving size-about 3 tablespoons) of **liqueurs** can be purchased at most liquor store.

Payday Pie

If you like the candy bar, you will love this pie.

12 servings

Crust

- ¾ cup all-purpose flour
- ⅓ cup brown sugar
- ¼ teaspoon salt
- ⅛ teaspoon baking soda
- ¼ cup (½ stick) butter or margarine
- ½ teaspoon vanilla extract
- 1 large egg yolk
- ½ cup lightly salted peanuts, finely chopped
- 2 cups miniature marshmallows

1. Preheat oven to 350°.
2. Lightly butter a (9-inch) pie pan (or coat with a nonstick cooking spray).
3. Combine, flour, brown sugar, baking soda, and salt; cut butter in with a pastry blender or rub flour and butter together with fingers until mixture is crumbly.
4. Stir in vanilla and egg yolk; mixture will be crumbly. Add peanuts. Press into the bottom of a prepared pie pan.
5. Bake 12-15 or until golden brown.
6. Remove from oven and place marshmallows evenly over the crust in a single layer.
7. Return to oven and heat an additional 1-2 minutes or until marshmallows puff. Cool while preparing topping.

Filling

- ⅓ cup light corn syrup
- 2 tablespoons butter or margarine
- 1 teaspoon vanilla extract
- 1 cup (½ of a 12-ounce package) peanut butter chips
- 1 cup crispy rice cereal
- 1 cup lightly salted peanuts
- ½ cup (3-ounces) semi-sweet chocolate chips, melted

1. Combine corn syrup, butter, vanilla, and peanut butter chips in a medium saucepan over low heat. Heat until chips are melted and mix is smooth, stirring constantly.
2. Remove from heat and stir in cereal and peanuts.
3. Immediately spoon mixture over marshmallows, carefully spreading to cover completely.
4. Drizzle melted chocolate chips over warm topping in a criss-cross pattern. Refrigerate until firm.

   (Note: Chocolate chips can be melted in a zip top bag. Place sealed bag in hot water until chocolate is melted or carefully melt in the microwave. Snip one end of the bag to drizzle chocolate over pie.)

Key Lime Tease

This pie is a new alternative to key lime pie.

12 servings

Crust

½   cup (1 stick) butter or margarine
1   cup all-purpose flour
½   cup pecans, toasted and finely
      chopped

1. Preheat oven to 325°.

2. Lightly grease a (9-inch) springform
   pan or an (8-inch) square baking pan
   (or coat with a nonstick cooking spray).

3. Cut butter into flour with a pastry
   blender or rub butter and flour
   together with fingers until mixture is
   crumbly (can also use a food
   processor).

4. Mix in finely chopped pecans. Press
   evenly into the bottom of prepared pan.

5. Bake 15 minutes or until golden brown
   and fragrant. Remove from oven and
   cool thoroughly in pan.

Cream Filling

1   package (8-ounces) cream cheese,
      softened
1½ cups powdered sugar
½   teaspoon vanilla extract
½   cup heavy cream

1. Beat cream cheese and powdered
   sugar until creamy. Mix in vanilla
   extract.

2. Beat cream until soft peaks form. Fold
   whipped cream into cream cheese
   mixture.

3. Spread over cooled crust. Refrigerate
   while preparing lime tease.

Lime Tease

1½ cups sugar
7   tablespoons cornstarch
1½ cups water
3   large eggs yolks, lightly beaten
3   tablespoons butter, softened
½   cup lime juice (4-5 limes)
1   teaspoon lime zest[1] (1 lime)

1. In a medium saucepan, stir together
   the sugar and cornstarch.

2. Gradually stir in water and cook over
   medium heat until thick and bubbly.
   Boil and stir 1 minute.

3. Stir ⅓ hot mixture into egg yolks, stirring
   yolks constantly. Add yolk mixture back
   into saucepan with remaining hot
   mixture. Return to boil, stirring
   constantly and cook 1 additional minute.

4. Remove from heat and add butter,
   1 tablespoon at a time until well
   blended.

5. Stir in lime juice and zest.

6. Spread over cream cheese mixture.

Meringue

3   **large egg whites**
¼   **teaspoon cream of tartar**
6   **tablespoons sugar**
1   **teaspoon vanilla**

1. Beat egg whites with the cream of tartar until foamy

2. Add sugar, 1 tablespoon at a time, beating until stiff and glossy. Beat in vanilla.

3. Spread meringue over hot pie filling.

4. Bake at 325° 5-7 minutes or until meringue is golden. Remove from oven and cool to room temperature. Refrigerate 8 hours or until fillings are chilled.

Diva Tips

[1]To **zest** lemon, lime or orange, wash fruit in hot water. Before cutting or juicing, remove zest (the very outermost layer of the fruit-the thin, colored part, avoiding the white pith which is bitter) with the finest part of a grater, or by peeling with a vegetable peeler and finely chopping with a knife or remove zest with a special tool called a zester.

Lemonade Pie

This recipe makes a refreshing summertime dessert!

8 servings

Crust

2 **cups gingersnap cookie crumbs (about 45-1½-inch)**

2 **tablespoons sugar**

⅓ **cup (5⅓ tablespoons) butter or margarine, melted**

1. Lightly butter a (9-inch) pie pan (or coat with a nonstick cooking spray).
2. In a medium bowl, combine cookie crumbs, sugar, and melted butter until well blended.
3. Press mixture firmly against the bottom and sides of the prepared pan. Chill 1 hour.

Filling

1 **package (8-ounces) cream cheese, softened**

1 **can (14-ounces) sweetened condensed milk**

1 **small can (6-ounces) frozen lemonade concentrate, thawed**

2 **tablespoons freshly squeezed lemon juice**

1 **teaspoon lemon zest[1]**

1 **cup heavy cream, whipped (makes 2 cups)**

1. In a large mixer bowl beat cream cheese until creamy on medium speed of an electric mixer.
2. Gradually mix in condensed milk. Blend in lemonade concentrate, lemon juice and lemon zest until smooth.
3. Whip cream until soft peaks form. **Fold[2]** whipped cream into lemon mixture.
4. Spoon into cooled crust. Freeze at least twelve hours. Place in the refrigerator 1 hour before serving to ease in cutting.

   (Note: Can be made ahead and stored tightly covered in the freezer for 6 weeks. To make a lime pie, substitute 1 (6-ounce) can frozen limeade for the lemonade, equal parts lime juice and lime zest for the lemon.)

Diva Tips

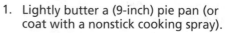

[1]To **zest** lemon, lime or orange, wash fruit in hot water. Before cutting or juicing, remove zest (the very outermost layer of the fruit-the thin, colored part, avoiding the white pith which is bitter) with the finest part of a grater, or by peeling with a vegetable peeler and finely chopping with a knife or with a special tool called a zester.

[2]To **fold** ingredients together, insert rubber spatula in the center of the mix; drag it across the bottom and then up the sides, rotating spatula and bringing some of the bottom of the mix to the top. Keep repeating this movement while turning the bowl to mix from all sides.

Key Lime Cheesecake

24 (2-inch) pieces

Crust

2 cups vanilla sandwich cookie crumbs (about 16 cookies)

4 tablespoons butter or margarine, melted

1. Preheat oven to 350°.

2. Lightly butter a (9x13-inch) baking pan (or coat with a nonstick cooking spray).

3. Combine cookie crumbs and butter. Press mixture firmly in the bottom and halfway up the sides of the prepared pan. Bake 8 minutes. Cool on a wire rack.

Filling

3 packages (8-ounces each) cream cheese, softened

1¼ cups sugar

4 large eggs, separated

1 cup (8-ounces) sour cream

½ cup freshly squeezed lime juice (4-5 limes)

1 teaspoon lime zest[1]

additional whipped cream, optional

1. Beat cream cheese at medium speed of a mixer until fluffy; gradually add sugar, mixing until well blended.

2. Add egg yolks, one at a time, mixing just until yellow disappears.

3. Stir in sour cream, lime juice and lime zest.

4. In another large mixing bowl, beat egg whites until stiff peaks form but mixture is not dry. Fold into creamed mixture.

5. Pour into baked crust. Bake at 350° for 1 hour or until center is just set (center may still jiggle a little when pan is shaken).

6. Turn oven off and partially open door. **Cool in the oven**[2] 15-20 minutes.

7. Remove from oven and cool completely on a wire rack.

8. Cover and chill 8 hours. Cut into serving pieces and top with whipped cream if desired.

(Note: Cheesecake can be made two days in advance and refrigerated or frozen for three months. Thaw in the refrigerator.)

Diva Tips

[1]To **zest** lemon, lime or orange, wash fruit well in hot water. Before cutting or juicing, remove zest (the very outermost layer of the fruit-the thin, colored part, avoiding the white pith which is bitter) with the finest part of a grater, or by peeling with a vegetable peeler and finely chopping with a knife or with a special tool called a zester.

[2]**Cheesecakes** need to cool slowly after baking to prevent cracking.

Almond Cookie Cake

It doesn't matter if this dessert can't decide if it is a cookie or cake, it makes a very rich, delectable dessert!

16 servings

Crust

2⅔ cups all-purpose flour
1⅓ cups sugar
½ teaspoon salt
1⅓ cups butter or margarine, softened

1. Preheat oven to 325°.
2. Generously butter a (9-inch) springform pan or a (9-inch) round cake pan. Place a **wax paper liner**[2] in the bottom of the pan and butter the paper.
3. In a large bowl mix together flour, sugar, salt; stir in butter just until mixture comes together. (Do not over mix or crust will be tough.) Divide into two equal pieces.
4. Press one half evenly into the bottom and slightly up the sides of the prepared pan.
5. Refrigerate remaining dough until ready to use.

Filling

1 roll (7-ounces) or can (8-ounces) almond paste[1]
1 large egg, slightly beaten
½ cup sugar
½ teaspoon almond extract
1 teaspoon vanilla
½ cup almonds, finely chopped and toasted

1. Roll or press almond paste to an (8½-inch) circle and lay over the bottom crust.
2. In a small bowl, mix egg and sugar together until well blended. Stir in almond and vanilla extract and finely chopped almonds.
3. Spread over almond paste to within ½-inch of the sides of the pan.
4. Remove dough from refrigerator and roll between two sheets of waxed paper to a (9-inch) circle. Remove top waxed paper; place dough-side down over almond filling. Press dough into place. Remove remaining waxed paper and gently press edges of pie down: top crust should meet the bottom crust at the sides.
5. Place pan in the oven and bake 60-70 minutes or until top is light golden brown.
6. Cool 30 minutes in the pan.
7. Carefully remove pie from pan (you may need to run a knife around the edges to loosen). Cool completely on a wire rack. For best results, carefully slice pie with a serrated knife in a sawing motion.

[1]**Almond paste** can be found in the baking section of most grocery stores or in specialty shops.

[2]**Waxed paper** (or parchment paper) **liners** for baking pans can be made by placing the desired pan on a sheet of waxed paper and tracing around the outside of the pan. Trim shape with scissors. Cut several at one time (cut multiple layers of waxed paper at the same time) and store in a large manila envelope for use later. Lining pans with paper almost always guarantees recipe does not stick to the bottom of the pan.

Vanilla Sandwich Cookie Crust

1 (9-inch) pie crust

1¾ **cups vanilla sandwich cookie crumbs (about 12 two-inch cookies)**

3 **tablespoons butter or margarine, melted**

¼ **cup pecans, toasted**[1] **and finely chopped (optional)**

1. Preheat oven to 350°.

2. Lightly butter a (9-inch) pie pan (or coat with a nonstick cooking spray).

3. Combine cookie crumbs, butter and pecans until well mixed.

4. Press firmly and evenly in the bottom and up the sides of the prepared pan.

5. Bake 6-8 minutes until golden and set. Remove from oven and cool.

Diva Tips

[1]**Toasting nuts** adds crispness and intensifies the flavor. Spread in a single layer on a baking sheet or pan. Preheat oven to 350°; place pan in oven and bake 5-10 minutes, or until nuts release their aroma, being careful not to burn. A smaller portion of nuts will toast much quicker than a larger amount. Toast a larger amount than needed and freeze extras up to 1 year in a tightly sealed container. Four ounces of nuts equals about 1 cup.

"Nawlens" Bread Pudding

Don't forget the bourbon sauce!

16 servings

Bread Pudding

1 loaf (12-inch) day-old French bread cut into cubes (6-8 cups)
1 cup golden raisins
1 cup pecans, toasted and chopped
4 large eggs
2 cups sugar
½ cup (1 stick) butter or margarine, melted
4 cups (1 quart) half-and-half
2 teaspoons vanilla extract
1 teaspoon cinnamon
½ teaspoon nutmeg

1. Generously butter a (9x13-inch) baking dish (or coat with a nonstick cooking spray).

2. Scatter bread cubes in the prepared pan, filling to the top. Add raisins and pecans.

3. In a large mixing bowl beat eggs and sugar until well blended. Stir in melted butter, half-and-half, cinnamon, nutmeg and vanilla extract.

4. Pour over bread mixture; let sit for 30 minutes to 1 hour (or overnight in the refrigerator) for bread to absorb liquids. It may be necessary to weigh bread mixture down with plastic wrap to keep bread cubes submerged in liquid.

5. Preheat oven to 350°.

6. Put bread pudding pan in a larger roasting pan. (If pudding is cold, let come to room temperature before baking.) Place pans in the oven. Add enough boiling water to the roasting pan (being careful not to spill water into bread pudding) to come about halfway up the pudding pan.

7. Bake 1 hour and 15 minutes or until pudding is set and top is golden. Remove bread pudding pan from water, and cool 30 minutes on a wire rack.

8. Serve warm with bourbon sauce.

Every Kitchen Diva should know where to go:

—be it her best friend's kitchen table

—or to the corner store

—or in her kids' Halloween candy stash for chocolate when her soul needs soothing.

Bourbon Sauce

2 cups

3 egg yolks[1]
⅓ cup sugar
1 cup heavy cream
⅓ cup milk
2 tablespoons butter
¼ cup bourbon
1 teaspoon vanilla extract
⅛ teaspoon salt

1. Beat the egg yolks and sugar in a medium mixing bowl until well blended.

2. Combine cream and milk in a heavy saucepan, and bring to a boil.

3. Remove from heat and gradually add 1 cup of the hot cream to the egg mixture, stirring eggs constantly. Slowly stir the egg mixture back into the rest of the hot cream. Return the pan to medium-low heat and continue cooking until mixture begins to thicken. DO NOT BOIL!

4. Remove from heat and stir in butter 1 tablespoon at a time until it is incorporated.

5. Stir in bourbon, vanilla and salt. Cool slightly before serving over bread pudding.

   (Note: Bourbon Sauce can be made ahead, cooled and refrigerated up to 1 week. To serve, bring to room temperature, or heat slightly and serve with warm bread pudding. Bourbon Sauce is also delicious with pound cake slices topped with fresh fruit.)

Diva Tips

[1]Eggs separate easier when cold. Break egg into a funnel or into your fingers over one bowl. The white will easily slip into the bowl and the yolk will remain in the funnel or your fingers (as long as it is not broken). Transfer white to a separate bowl and yolk to a third bowl. This keeps an accidentally broken yolk from contaminating the whites already separated. Whites with even a small amount of yolk will not beat up to soft peaks. Repeat with remaining eggs over the first bowl. Freeze leftover egg whites individually in an ice cube tray. When frozen remove from tray and place in a plastic bag. Thaw whites in the refrigerator when a recipe calls for egg whites.

Strawberry Grand Tart

A little effort but well worth it!

10 servings

Crust

1 cup all-purpose flour
2 tablespoons sugar
1 teaspoon salt
½ cup (1 stick) butter or margarine

1. Preheat oven to 375°.

2. Mix flour, sugar and salt together in a small bowl. Cut butter in with a pastry cutter or rub butter and flour together with fingers (or use a food processor) until mixture is crumbly. Squeeze together to form a ball. (It may be necessary to add 1 teaspoon cold water to the mixture to bring crust together.)

3. Press into a (10-inch) tart pan with a removable bottom (or into the bottom of a 9-inch square pan). Bake 10 minutes or until golden brown. Remove from oven and cool completely.

Filling

1 cup heavy cream
½ cup sugar
¼ cup (½ stick) butter or margarine
¼ teaspoon vanilla extract
2 pints strawberries
¼ cup red jelly (apple or plum)
1 cup **crème fraîche**[1,2]
2 tablespoons powdered sugar
2 tablespoons **Grand Marnier**[3] (or other orange liqueur)

1. In a small saucepan over low heat, combine the cream, sugar, and butter; cook until sauce is reduced, thickened and a light golden color (about 20 minutes). Cool.

2. Spread cooled filling over the bottom of the tart shell.

3. Cut the stem end off the strawberries (choose berries that are similar in size) and place them flat side down, side-by-side, filling the crust.

4. Heat jelly in a small saucepan or in the microwave until melted. Brush lightly over the strawberries, glazing.

5. Whip cold crème fraîche, powdered sugar, and Grand Marnier until soft peaks form.

6. Pipe whipped crème fraîche in between strawberries, leaving the tops of the berries showing. Refrigerate until ready to serve. Can be made 4 hours in advance.

Diva Tips

¹To make **crème fraîche**, mix ¼ cup warm buttermilk into 1 cup warm cream in a jar. Lightly cover jar and set in a warm place (70°-100°) 24-36 hours, until mixture is thickened. Cover and chill (it will thicken more as it chills to the consistency of soft yogurt). Or it can be found in some grocery stores in the dairy section. Whipped crème fraîche will keep whipped when refrigerated up to a week or several hours at room temperature.

²To make a **crème fraîche** substitute for this recipe, mix 1 cup heavy cream with ½ cup sour cream. Whip until soft peaks form.

³Small bottles (airline serving size— about 3 tablespoons) of **liqueurs** can be purchased at most liquor stores.

Vanilla Wafer Pie Crust

1 (9-inch) pie crust

1½ cups vanilla wafers (about 36 cookies), finely crushed

2   tablespoons brown sugar

½   cup butter or margarine, melted

½   cup nuts, toasted and chopped (optional)

1. Preheat oven to 375°.

2. Lightly butter a (9-inch) pie pan (or coat with a nonstick cooking spray).

3. Combine vanilla wafer crumbs, brown sugar, and melted butter (and optional nuts).

4. Press into the bottom and sides of the pie pan.

5. Bake 6-8 minutes until golden and set. Remove from oven and cool.

Brownie Turtle Cheesecake

This cheesecake is tempting and hard to resist.

16 servings

Crust

1¾ cups **vanilla** sandwich cookie crumbs, (about 12 two-inch cookies)

¼ cup **pecans, toasted**[1] and finely chopped

3 tablespoons butter or margarine, melted

1. Preheat oven to 350°.
2. Lightly grease a (9-inch) springform pan (or coat with a nonstick cooking spray).
3. Combine cookie crumbs, pecans and butter until well mixed.
4. Press firmly into the bottom and 2-inches up the sides of prepared pan. Bake 5-7 minutes just to set. Remove from oven.

Filling

1 package (14-ounces) individually wrapped caramels, unwrapped

⅓ cup heavy cream

2 cups pecans, toasted and coarsely chopped

2 cups crumbled unfrosted brownies

3 packages (8-ounces each) cream cheese, softened

1 cup packed brown sugar

3 large eggs

1 cup (8-ounces) sour cream

2 teaspoons vanilla

1. In a medium saucepan combine caramels and cream. Cook over low heat until caramels melt, stirring often. Mix in 2 cups pecans. Pour over crust.
2. Scatter brownie pieces over caramel.
3. Beat cream cheese in a large mixing bowl until light and fluffy, 2-3 minutes. Gradually add sugar, mixing well. Add eggs, one at a time, mixing until well blended. Stir in sour cream and vanilla.
4. Pour cream cheese mixture over brownies.
5. Bake at 350° 1 hour or until cheesecake is set (cheesecake is done when edges are firm, but center still jiggles a little when pan is shaken).
6. Turn off oven and partially open oven door; **cool**[2] 15-20 minutes.
7. Remove from oven and cool completely on a wire rack. Chill 8 hours.

   (Note: Cheesecake can be made two days in advance and refrigerated or frozen tightly covered for three months. Thaw overnight in the refrigerator.)

Diva Tips

[1]**Toasting nuts** adds crispness and intensifies the flavor. Spread in a single layer on a baking sheet or pan. Preheat oven to 350°; place pan in oven and bake 5-10 minutes, or until nuts release their aroma, being careful not to burn. A smaller portion of nuts will toast much quicker than a larger amount. Toast a larger amount than needed and freeze extras up to 1 year in a tightly sealed container. Four ounces of nuts equals about 1 cup.

[2]Cheesecakes need to **cool** slowly after baking to prevent cracking.

Desserts

Traditional Pie Crust

All ingredients should be very cold when making this crust.

1 (9-inch) pie crust

1¼ cups cake flour (or any low protein flour)

¼ teaspoon salt

⅓ cup shortening

⅓ cup cold butter, cut into pieces

2-3 tablespoons ice water

1. Combine flour and salt in a medium mixing bowl.

2. Cut in shortening and butter with a pastry blender or rub flour, shortening and butter together with your fingers until mixture is crumbly.

3. Add 1 tablespoon of ice water at a time while mixing with a fork.

4. Mix just until dry ingredients are moistened. (Overworking the dough will cause the pie crust to be tough.)

5. Press together and flatten into a disk; chill.

6. Roll pastry to ⅛-inch thickness on a lightly floured surface.

7. Fold dough in half and then into a triangle. Ease dough into a lightly greased (9-inch) pie pan with point of triangle in the center of the pan. Unfold dough; trim off excess pastry along edges. Proceed as recipe directs.

Chocolate Cookie Pie Crust

1 (9-inch) pie crust

1¼ cups chocolate wafer cookie crumbs (about 30 cookies)

2 tablespoons brown sugar

⅓ cup (5⅓ tablespoons) butter or margarine, melted

¼ cup unsalted peanuts, finely chopped (optional)

1. Preheat oven to 375°.

2. Lightly butter a (9-inch) pie pan (or coat with a nonstick cooking spray).

3. Combine chocolate wafer crumbs, brown sugar, (and optional peanuts) and melted butter.

4. Press into the bottom and sides of the prepared pan. Bake 6-8 minutes until set.

5. Remove from oven and cool.

Black Bottom Tiramisu

The best tiramisu you ever tasted and you made it!

12 servings

2   large **egg yolks**[1]
3   tablespoons sugar
¼   cup Marsala wine
2   packages (8-ounces each) cream cheese, softened
¼   cup sour cream
⅔   cup powdered sugar
1   cup cooled espresso or strong coffee, divided
⅓   cup Kahlúa, (or any coffee-flavored liqueur), divided
1   cup heavy whipping cream, whipped
1   cup (6-ounces) semi-sweet chocolate chips, melted and cooled
1   tablespoon sugar
2   packages (7-ounces each) dry, crisp Italian ladyfinger cookies
2   tablespoons cocoa powder, optional

1. Beat egg yolks and sugar together until light and creamy. Stir in Marsala. Cook in a **double boiler**[2] until mixture begins to thicken. Cool.

2. In a large mixing bowl, beat cream cheese, sour cream, powdered sugar, 2 tablespoons espresso and 2 tablespoons Kahlúa 1-2 minutes just until well blended. Beat cream until soft peaks form. Fold into cream cheese mixture.

3. Divide cream cheese mixture in half. Fold cooled melted chocolate into one half of cream cheese mixture until no white streaks remain.

4. Combine remaining espresso, 1 tablespoon sugar and remaining Kahlúa in a shallow dish. Quickly dip one side of enough ladyfingers to completely line the bottom of a (9x13-inch) baking dish (or a 10-inch springform pan) in the espresso mixture. (It is important to dip quickly so cookies do not get too wet and soggy.) Place ladyfingers dry-side down in the bottom of the pan. Trim-to-fit enough remaining ladyfingers to stand around the inside edge of the pan. Brush standing ladyfingers with espresso mixture just to moisten.

5. Pour chocolate-cheese mixture over ladyfingers spreading to cover the bottom of the pan.

6. Cover chocolate layer entirely with another layer of dipped ladyfingers, dipped-side up.

7. Spread remaining (white) cream cheese mixture over ladyfingers, carefully spreading to cover second layer of ladyfingers. (If using a springform pan, set pan on aluminum foil; bring foil up around the edges to catch any leaks.)

8. Cover with plastic wrap and refrigerate 6 hours or overnight. Remove sides of springform pan. Sift cocoa powder over cake before serving if desired.

(Note: I recommend Savordi® cookies.)

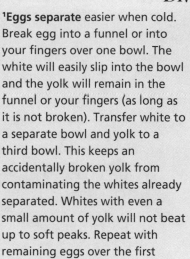

Diva Tips

[1]**Eggs separate** easier when cold. Break egg into a funnel or into your fingers over one bowl. The white will easily slip into the bowl and the yolk will remain in the funnel or your fingers (as long as it is not broken). Transfer white to a separate bowl and yolk to a third bowl. This keeps an accidentally broken yolk from contaminating the whites already separated. Whites with even a small amount of yolk will not beat up to soft peaks. Repeat with remaining eggs over the first bowl. Freeze leftover egg whites individually in an ice cube tray. When frozen remove from tray and place in a plastic bag. Thaw whites in the refrigerator when a recipe calls for egg whites.

[2]If you do not have a **double boiler**, you can easily make one by nestling a smaller saucepan in a larger one or use any heatproof bowl that will sit securely on top of a saucepan without touching the boiling water. The heat of the steam, generated by the boiling water, cooks the food.

Shortbread Cookie Crust

1 (9-inch) pie crust

1½ cups shortbread cookie crumbs (about 28 cookies)

3 tablespoons butter or margarine, melted

1. Preheat oven to 350°.
2. Lightly butter a (9-inch) pie pan (or coat with a nonstick cooking spray).
3. Mix cookie crumbs with butter.
4. Press firmly and evenly in the bottom and up the sides of the prepared pan.
5. Bake 6-8 minutes until golden and set. Remove from oven and cool.

Half-A-Cake

Sometimes less is more!

1 (9-inch) layer

1½ cups all-purpose flour
1 cup sugar
2 teaspoons baking powder[1]
½ teaspoon salt
⅓ cup shortening
⅔ cup milk
1 large egg

1. Preheat oven to 350°.

2. **Grease and flour[2]** a (9-inch) square or round cake pan.

3. Measure all ingredients into a medium bowl. Mix on low speed for 30 seconds, scraping bowl constantly. Beat on high speed for 3 minutes more.

4. Pour into prepared pan. Bake 25-30 minutes or until toothpick inserted into the center comes out clean.

5. Cool in pan 5 minutes. Remove cake from pan and cool completely on wire rack.

6. Frost with your favorite frosting.

Diva Tips

[1]**Baking powder** still active? To test, drop ½ teaspoon into a glass of warm water; if it fizzes it is o.k. to use. Always measure and level off. Never put a wet spoon into the container; it will deactivate the whole can.

[2]To **grease and flour** baking pans, cover fingers with plastic wrap or a plastic sandwich bag and spread about ½ tablespoon butter or vegetable shortening over the inside baking surface of the pan. Spoon in 1 tablespoon flour, shaking pan to evenly distribute flour. Turn pan up side down and remove excess flour by tapping edge of pan on the counter.

Half-A-Spice Cake

Make this cake when you need just a little spice in your life.

1 (9-inch) layer

Cake

1½ cups all-purpose flour
1   cup sugar
2   teaspoons baking powder
½   teaspoon salt
⅓   cup shortening
⅔   cup milk
1   large egg
1   teaspoon cinnamon
½   teaspoon nutmeg[1]
¼   teaspoon cloves
frost with Butterscotch Icing

Butterscotch Icing

⅓   cup butter
⅔   cup brown sugar[2]**, packed**
3   tablespoons milk
1½ cups powdered sugar

1. Preheat oven to 350°.

2. Grease and flour a (9-inch) square or round cake pan.

3. Measure all ingredients into a medium bowl. Mix on low speed for 30 seconds, scraping bowl constantly. Beat on high speed for 3 minutes more. Pour into prepared pan.

4. Bake 25-30 minutes or until toothpick inserted into the center comes out clean.

5. Cool in pan 5 minutes. Remove cake from pan and cool completely on wire rack before frosting.

1. Melt butter in a medium saucepan.

2. Mix in brown sugar. Bring to a boil and stir 2 minutes.

3. Stir in milk. Return to boil stirring constantly. Remove from heat and cool slightly.

4. Gradually stir in powdered sugar and continue beating until spreading consistency.

Diva Tips

[1]Freshly grated **nutmeg** has a superior flavor over ground nutmeg found in a can or jar in the spice section. Whole nutmegs can be located in most spice sections. Use a very fine grater or a small nutmeg grater for best results. Whole nutmegs can be kept indefinitely in a jar in a cool, dark place.

[2]To store **brown sugar**, place opened bag of sugar in another plastic bag. Remove as much air as possible and tightly close. If sugar has hardened, soften by placing in a microwave-safe dish, covering tightly and microwave on high power for about 30 seconds. Generally, light-brown or dark-brown sugar can be interchanged for each other. When measuring, always lightly pack sugar in measuring cup.

Pee Wee Fudge Cake

Just enough chocolate cake for a family dinner.

1 (9-inch) layer

1	**cup all-purpose flour**
1	**teaspoon salt**
1	**teaspoon baking soda**
⅓	**cup shortening**
⅓	**cup sugar**
½	**cup dark corn syrup**
1	**large egg**
1	**teaspoon vanilla extract**
2	**squares (2-ounces) unsweetened baking chocolate[1], melted and cooled**
¾	**cup buttermilk[2]**

1. Preheat oven to 350°.

2. Grease and flour a (9-inch) square or round cake pan.

3. In a small bowl mix together the flour, salt and baking soda. Set aside.

4. In a medium bowl beat together shortening and sugar thoroughly, 2-3 minutes. Add syrup and mix well. Add egg, vanilla and melted chocolate, mixing until creamy. Mix the buttermilk and the flour into creamed mixture just until well blended.

5. Pour into prepared pan.

6. Bake 25-30 minutes or until toothpick inserted in the center comes out clean.

7. Cool in pan 5 minutes. Remove cake from pan and cool completely on wire rack before frosting with your favorite frosting.

Diva Tips

[1]To **melt chocolate**, chop chocolate bars into small pieces. 1) Place uncovered in a microwave-safe dish and microwave on high power (100%); stir every 20 seconds. Chocolate can be removed from oven while still lumpy; the heat of the dish and the chocolate will continue to melt lumps. Be careful not to overheat; chocolate burns at a low temperature. Or 2) put chocolate pieces into the top of a double boiler and place over hot water. Stir occasionally until chocolate is melted. Do not let any water droplets or steam mix with chocolate or it will become a hardened, grainy mass. If this happens, stir in a small amount of melted vegetable shortening, 1 teaspoon at a time, until chocolate returns to a liquid state.

[2]No **buttermilk**? To make a good substitute, stir ¾-tablespoon vinegar into enough milk to measure ¾ cup. Let stand 5 minutes.

Sour Cream Chocolate Cake

This cake is as easy to make as any prepackaged mix: all the ingredients are measured into a bowl, beaten together and baked.

8-10 servings

1 **cup (8-ounces) sour cream**
1 **teaspoon baking soda**
½ **cup (1 stick) butter or margarine, softened**
¼ **cup shortening**
4 **squares (4-ounces) unsweetened chocolate, melted[1] and cooled**
2 **cups sugar**
2 **large eggs**
2 **teaspoons vanilla extract**
2½ **cups all-purpose flour**
¼ **teaspoon salt**
1 **cup boiling water**

1. Preheat oven to 325°.

2. Grease and flour a (10-inch) tube pan, or a (13x9x2-inch) pan, or 3 (8-inch) or 2 (9-inch) cake pans.

3. Measure all ingredients into a large bowl. Mix ½ minute on low speed scraping bottom and sides constantly. Beat 3 minutes on high speed scraping sides occasionally.

4. Pour into prepared pan(s). Bake as directed for pan size or until a toothpick inserted into the center comes out clean.

5. Cool in pan 5 minutes. Remove cake from pan and cool completely on wire rack before frosting. Frost with your favorite frosting.

Bake: (10-inch) tube pan:
1 hour-1 hour and 10 minutes
(13x9x2-inch) pan: 40-45 minutes
(8-inch) cake pans: 30-35 minutes
(9-inch) cake pans: 25-30 minutes

Diva Tips

[1]**To melt chocolate**, chop baking chocolate into small pieces. 1) Place uncovered in a microwave-safe dish and microwave on high power (100%), stirring every 20 seconds. Chocolate can be removed from oven while still lumpy; the heat of the dish and the chocolate will continue to melt lumps. Be careful not to overheat; chocolate burns at a low temperature. Or 2) put chocolate pieces into the top of a double boiler and place over hot water. Stir occasionally until chocolate is melted. (Do not let any water droplets or steam mix with chocolate or it will become a hardened, grainy mass. If this happens, stir in a small amount of melted vegetable shortening, 1 teaspoon at a time, until chocolate returns to a liquid state.)

Chocolate Ecstasy Cake

This cake will inundate your senses and tickle your tongue.

16-20 servings

Cake

2	cups **self-rising flour**[1]
¼	teaspoon baking soda
2	cups sugar
1	cup warm water
¾	cup sour cream
¼	cup shortening
2	large eggs
4	squares (4-ounces) unsweetened baking chocolate, melted
1	teaspoon vanilla extract

Topping

1	can (14-ounces) sweetened condensed milk
1	jar (16-ounces) caramel ice cream topping or hot fudge sauce
1	container (8-ounces) Cool Whip, thawed
1	cup **coconut, toasted**[2]
1	cup pecans, toasted and chopped
1	cup mini-chocolate chips

1. Preheat oven to 350°.

2. Grease and flour a 9x13-inch baking pan (or coat with a nonstick cooking spray).

3. Measure all cake ingredients into a large bowl. Beat with an electric mixer 30 seconds on low speed scraping down sides constantly. Beat on high speed for 3 minutes. Pour into prepared pan.

4. Bake 30-40 minutes or until a toothpick inserted in the center comes out clean.

5. Remove from oven and while cake is hot, poke all over with a meat fork or skewer and drizzle with condensed milk. Cool completely.

6. Pour or carefully spread caramel or fudge topping over cake (may be easier if topping has been warmed).

7. Spread Cool Whip over top of caramel. Sprinkle with coconut, pecans and mini-chocolate chips. Store in refrigerator.

(Note: You may substitute your favorite chocolate cake mix for the cake recipe. After baking cake, proceed with topping as recipe directs.)

Diva Tips

[1]To make **self-rising flour**, add 1 teaspoon baking powder and ¼ teaspoon salt to every cup of flour; mixing thoroughly.

[2]To **toast coconut**, place on a large cookie sheet. Bake at 350° until lightly toasted, about 10-12 minutes, stirring frequently.

Sour Cream Chocolate Pound Cake

Cake just like grandma used to make.

16 servings

1   cup (2 sticks) butter or margarine, softened
2   cups sugar
5   large eggs
1   cup unsweetened cocoa powder
2   teaspoons vanilla extract
1   cup (8-ounces) sour cream
2   teaspoons baking soda
2½ cups all-purpose flour
¼   teaspoon salt
1   cup boiling water

1. Preheat oven to 325°.

2. Grease and flour a (10-inch) tube pan or (12-cup) Bundt pan.

3. Cream the butter and sugar 7-8 minutes in a large mixing bowl with an electric mixer on medium speed until light and fluffy.

4. Add eggs one at a time beating well after each addition.

5. Stir in cocoa (sift if cocoa is lumpy) and vanilla.

6. In a separate bowl, mix the sour cream and baking soda together. Stir into the butter mixture.

7. Stir together the flour and salt. Add to the creamed mixture.

8. Mix in boiling water.

9. Pour into prepared pan. Bake 1 hour and 10 minutes or until a toothpick inserted in the center comes out clean.

10. Cool in pan 5 minutes. Remove cake from pan and cool completely on wire rack before frosting. Frost with your favorite chocolate frosting, if desired.

It's always darkest before dawn, so if you are going to steal your neighbor's newspaper that is the best time to do it.

Seven-Up Pound Cake

I love having this cake in the freezer at all times. It is a delicious breakfast treat (occasionally) with a hot cup of cappuccino. Unexpected guests also think you are brilliant for having such a great dessert available in a matter of minutes. (They don't have to know that it was just hanging out waiting for them.)

16 servings

1   **cup (2 sticks) butter (margarine not recommended), softened**
½   **cup shortening**
3   **cups sugar**
5   **large eggs**
2   **teaspoons vanilla extract**
3   **cups all-purpose flour**
1   **cup 7-Up or any lemon-lime soda (room temperature)**

1. Preheat oven to 325°.

2. Grease and flour a (10-inch) tube or (12-cup) Bundt pan.

3. Cream the butter, shortening and sugar in a large mixing bowl with an electric mixer on medium speed 7-10 minutes until light and fluffy.

4. Add the eggs, one at a time, mixing well after each. Add the vanilla.

5. Stir the flour in slowly until well blended.

6. Gently **fold¹** in 7-Up.

7. Bake 1 hour and 10 minutes or until a toothpick inserted in the center comes out clean.

8. Cool in pan 10 minutes. Remove cake from pan carefully and cool on a wire rack.

Diva Tips

¹To **fold** ingredients together, insert large rubber spatula in the center of the mix; drag it across the bottom and then up the sides, rotating spatula and bringing some of the bottom of the mix to the top. Keep repeating this movement while turning the bowl to mix from all sides.

Carrot Cake

This carrot cake has no pineapple in it. I like that.

8-10 servings

Cake

4 large eggs
2 cups sugar
1½ cups vegetable oil
2¼ cups all-purpose flour
2 teaspoons cinnamon
¼ teaspoon nutmeg[1]
2 teaspoons baking soda
1 teaspoon salt
3 cups finely grated carrots, (about 4 medium)
½ cup pecans, toasted[2] and finely chopped
Cream Cheese Frosting

1. Preheat oven to 350°.
2. Grease and flour 3 (8-inch) cake pans.
3. Combine eggs, sugar and oil. Beat 2 minutes at medium speed.
4. In a separate bowl combine flour, cinnamon, nutmeg, baking soda and salt; mix into egg mixture and beat 1 minute at low speed.
5. Stir in carrots and nuts.
6. Pour into prepared pans. Bake 25-30 minutes or until a toothpick inserted in the center comes out clean (cake will spring back in center when lightly touched).
7. Remove from oven and cool in pans 5 minutes. Remove cake from pans and cool completely on wire rack before frosting. Store in refrigerator.

Cream Cheese Frosting

1 package (8-ounces) cream cheese, softened
½ cup (1 stick) butter or margarine, softened
1 pound (3½ cups) powdered sugar
1 teaspoon vanilla extract

1. Beat cream cheese and butter together until smooth and creamy.
2. Mix in the powdered sugar. Stir in vanilla.

Diva Tips

[1]Freshly grated **nutmeg** has a superior flavor over ground nutmeg found in a can or jar. Whole nutmegs can be located in most spice sections. Use a very fine grater or a small nutmeg grater for best results. Whole nutmegs can be kept indefinitely in a jar in a cool, dark place.

[2]**Toasting nuts** adds crispness and intensifies the flavor. Spread in a single layer on a baking sheet or pan. Preheat oven to 350°; place pan in oven and bake 5-10 minutes, or until nuts release their aroma, being careful not to burn. A smaller portion of nuts will toast much quicker than a larger amount. Toast a larger amount than needed and freeze extras up to 1 year in a tightly sealed container. Four ounces of nuts equals about 1 cup.

Apple Delight

A great cake for a breakfast treat or snack.

16 servings

1	**cup brown sugar**
¾	**cup sugar**
⅔	**cup vegetable oil**
3	**large eggs**
1	**teaspoon vanilla extract**
2	**cups all-purpose flour**
1	**teaspoon baking soda**
1	**teaspoon cinnamon**
4	**medium apples, peeled** and thinly **sliced**[1]
½	**cup pecans** or **walnuts, toasted**[2] and chopped
½	**cup raisins** (optional)

1. Preheat oven to 350°.

2. Lightly grease a (9x13-inch) baking pan (or coat with a nonstick cooking spray).

3. In a large mixing bowl, beat the sugars with the oil until light and creamy, about 5 minutes.

4. Add eggs and vanilla and beat until well blended.

5. Mix in flour, baking soda and cinnamon, stirring until blended.

6. Stir apples in (with a spoon), coating well.

7. Add nuts and raisins.

8. Spread in prepared pan. Bake 45-55 minutes or until golden and a toothpick inserted in the center comes out clean. Cool before cutting.

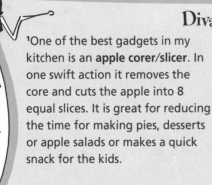

Diva Tips

[1]One of the best gadgets in my kitchen is an **apple corer/slicer**. In one swift action it removes the core and cuts the apple into 8 equal slices. It is great for reducing the time for making pies, desserts or apple salads or makes a quick snack for the kids.

[2]**Toasting nuts** adds crispness and intensifies the flavor. Spread in a single layer on a baking sheet or pan. Preheat oven to 350°; place pan in oven and bake 5-10 minutes, or until nuts release their aroma, being careful not to burn. A smaller portion of nuts will toast much quicker than a larger amount. Toast a larger amount than needed and freeze extras up to 1 year in a tightly sealed container. Four ounces of nuts equals about 1 cup.

Italian Cream Cake

By the name, you would think that this recipe is a big secret handed down from my husband's family, but truthfully, there is nothing Italian about it, except that it is so, so delicious.

12 servings

Cake

- ½ cup (1 stick) butter or margarine, softened
- 2 cups sugar
- ½ cup shortening
- 5 large eggs, separated
- 2 cups all-purpose flour, sifted
- 1 teaspoon salt
- 1 teaspoon baking soda
- 1 cup **buttermilk**[1]
- 2 cups flaked coconut
- 1 cup pecans, toasted and finely chopped
- Cream Cheese Frosting

1. Preheat oven to 350°.
2. Grease 3 (8-inch) round baking pans. Cut and fit **parchment[2] or wax paper** in the bottom of the pans. Grease the parchment paper and flour pans.
3. Cream the butter, sugar, shortening and egg yolks.
4. Sift the flour, salt and baking soda together.
5. Mix the buttermilk and the flour into creamed mixture just until well blended.
6. Beat the egg whites until stiff but not dry and fold into mix.
7. Carefully stir in the coconut and pecans.
8. Bake for 25-35 minutes or until a toothpick inserted in the center comes out clean.
9. Cool in pan 5 minutes. Remove cake from pan and cool completely on wire rack before frosting.

Cream Cheese Frosting

- 1 package (8-ounces) cream cheese, softened
- ½ cup (1 stick) butter or margarine, softened
- 1 pound (3½ cups) powdered sugar
- 1 teaspoon vanilla extract

1. Beat cream cheese and butter until smooth and creamy.
2. Add powdered sugar and mix well. Stir in vanilla.

Diva Tips

[1]No **buttermilk**? To make a good substitute, stir 1-tablespoon vinegar into enough milk to measure 1 cup and let stand for 5 minutes.

[2]**Parchment paper** can be purchased in some grocery stores (check near the wax paper and foil aisle) or specialty shops. Parchment paper (or wax paper) liners for baking pans can be made by placing the desired pan on a sheet of waxed paper and tracing around the outside of the pan; trim shape with scissors. Cut multiple layers of paper at the same time and store in a large manila envelope for use later. Lining pans with paper almost always guarantees a recipe does not stick to the bottom of the pan.

Sweet Potato Cake

My mother, Hazel, usually makes this cake every Christmas. When I was very young, she stored the cake out on the screened porch. Unfortunately, someone forgot and let our pet German Shepherd into the porch. It was the best Christmas, Bruno, ever had! I always think of that half-eaten cake every time I make this recipe.

12-16 servings

Cake

1½ **cups vegetable oil**
2 **cups sugar**
4 **large eggs, separated**
4 **tablespoons hot water**
2½ **cups all-purpose flour**
3 **teaspoons baking powder**
¼ **teaspoon salt**
1 **teaspoon cinnamon**
1 **teaspoon nutmeg**
2½ **cups (2 medium) grated sweet potatoes**
1 **cup nuts, toasted and chopped**
1 **teaspoon vanilla extract**
  Coconut Frosting

1. Preheat oven to 350°.
2. Grease and flour 3 (8-inch) round pans.
3. In a large mixing bowl, beat the oil and sugar on medium speed with an electric mixer until light and creamy, 3-4 minutes.
4. Beat in egg yolks and hot water.
5. In a separate bowl, sift the flour, baking powder, salt, cinnamon, and nutmeg.
6. Stir flour into egg mixture, blending well.
7. Mix in sweet potatoes, nuts and vanilla.
8. Beat egg whites until stiff but not dry. Fold into cake batter.
9. Divide evenly among the prepared pans. Bake 25-35 minutes, or until a wooden toothpick inserted in the center comes out clean.
10. Remove from oven and cool in pans 5 minutes. Remove cake from pan and cool completely on wire rack before frosting.

Coconut Frosting

⅔ **cup (11 tablespoons) butter or margarine**
1 **can (15-ounces) evaporated milk**
1½ **cups sugar**
4 **egg yolks, beaten**
1 **tablespoon vanilla extract**
2 **cups flaked coconut**

1. Melt butter in a heavy saucepan; add milk, sugar, and egg yolks. Bring to a boil and cook over medium heat 12 minutes stirring constantly.
2. Remove from heat and add vanilla and coconut.
3. Stir until frosting is cooled and spreading consistency.

Pumpkin Spice Roll

16 slices

Roll

3 large eggs
1 cup sugar
¾ cup all-purpose flour
1 teaspoon baking powder
½ teaspoon salt
⅔ cup canned pumpkin
1 teaspoon lemon juice
2 teaspoons cinnamon
½ teaspoon ginger
½ teaspoon nutmeg
½ cup nuts, toasted and chopped
¼ cup powdered sugar
　 Cream Cheese Filling

1. Preheat oven to 350°.

2. Line a (15x10x1-inch) pan with **parchment paper¹** or wax paper. Lightly grease paper and sides of pan (or coat with a nonstick cooking spray).

3. Beat eggs on high speed for 5 minutes until light and lemon-colored. Gradually beat in sugar.

4. In separate bowl combine the flour, baking powder and salt. Mix into the egg mixture.

5. Add the pumpkin, lemon juice, cinnamon, ginger and nutmeg, mixing until well blended.

6. Pour batter into prepared pan.

7. Scatter nuts over the top.

8. Bake 20-25 minutes. Sprinkle powdered sugar on a kitchen towel. When done, turn cake upside down onto the towel and remove from pan. Roll up the cake in the towel starting with the short side.

9. Cool completely.

Cream Cheese Filling

1 package (8-ounces) cream cheese, softened
4 tablespoons butter or margarine, softened
1 cup powdered sugar
½ teaspoon vanilla

1. Beat cream cheese and butter until light and creamy. Stir in powdered sugar and vanilla.

2. Spread over cooled cake, putting more at the beginning of the roll and in the middle than at the end.

3. Roll cake back up.

4. Tightly wrap with plastic wrap and chill thoroughly.

5. Slice cake into rounds with a serrated knife.

Diva Tips

¹Parchment paper can be purchased in some grocery stores (check near the wax paper and foil aisle) or specialty shops.

Creamy Coconut Cake

This is the lightest, most delicious coconut cake I have ever made.

18 servings

Cake

½ cup (1 stick) butter or margarine, softened
½ cup shortening
1 cup sugar
4 large eggs, separated
1½ cups cake flour
2 teaspoons baking powder
¼ teaspoon salt
½ cup milk
1 teaspoon vanilla extract
   Creamy Coconut Frosting

1. Preheat oven to 350°.

2. Grease and flour 2 (8-inch) round cake pans.

3. Cream butter and shortening until light and fluffy. Slowly add sugar and beat an additional 2-3 minutes, scraping bowl down. Add egg yolks, one at a time, mixing well to incorporate after each addition.

4. In a separate bowl, mix flour, baking powder and salt.

5. Add ⅓ of the flour and ½ of the buttermilk to the creamed mixture, mixing just until incorporated. Add another ⅓ of the flour and the remaining buttermilk, again mixing until incorporated. Mix in the remaining flour; stir in vanilla.

6. In a separate bowl, beat the egg whites until stiff but not dry. Fold into the batter.

7. Pour into the prepared cake pans. Bake 25-35 minutes or until a toothpick inserted in the center comes out clean.

8. Cool in pan 5 minutes. Remove cake from pan and cool completely on wire rack before frosting.

In the South we experience all the seasons:

  –Almost summer

  –Summer

  –Still summer

  –Christmas

Creamy Coconut Frosting

2 cups sugar
1 pint (16 ounces) sour cream
1 teaspoon vanilla extract
1 package (12-ounces) frozen coconut, thawed
1 container (8-ounces) frozen Cool Whip, thawed

1. Stir sugar, sour cream and vanilla mixing well.
2. Stir coconut into sugar mixture.
3. Gently mix in Cool Whip; chill until stiff.
4. **Split each cake layer in half[1] to make 4 layers.**
5. Spread frosting between layers, on the top and sides. Store in an airtight container in the refrigerator.

Diva Tips

[1]To **split layers** easily, use a serrated knife or slice with unwaxed dental floss using a sawing motion.

Sour Cream Chocolate Frosting

4½ cups

⅓ cup (5⅓ tablespoons) butter or margarine, softened
4 ounces (4 squares) unsweetened baking chocolate, melted and cooled
1 pound (3½ cups) confectioners' sugar, sifted
½ cup sour cream
2 teaspoons vanilla

1. Mix butter and cooled chocolate together until smooth and creamy.
2. Blend in confectioners' sugar.
3. Stir in sour cream and vanilla.
4. Beat until smooth and spreading consistency.
5. Makes enough to frost 1 (13x9-inch) cake, 2 (9-inch) layers, or 3 (8-inch) layers.

Cocoa Fudge Frosting

2 cups

1 small can (5-ounces) evaporated milk
½ cup (1 stick) butter or margarine
½ cup unsweetened cocoa powder
2 cups sugar
2 teaspoons vanilla

1. Mix milk and butter in saucepan. Bring to a boil.

2. Stir together cocoa and sugar. Add to hot milk mixture. Return to a boil stirring constantly. Boil 1 minute. Remove from heat and add vanilla. Cool slightly.

3. Beat by hand or with a mixer until mixture is thick enough to spread (mixture will thicken as it cools). Spread on cake.

Real Fudge Frosting

2 cups

2 ounces (2 squares) unsweetened baking chocolate, broken into pieces
½ cup heavy cream
¼ cup milk
2 cups sugar
¼ teaspoon salt
1 tablespoon dark corn syrup
2 tablespoons butter or margarine
1 teaspoon vanilla

1. In a medium saucepan combine chocolate, cream and milk. Stir over low heat until chocolate melts.

2. Add sugar, salt and syrup, stirring constantly until mixture comes to a boil. Boil 5 minutes. Remove from heat.

3. Add butter and vanilla.

4. Let stand 5 minutes to cool slightly.

5. Beat until frosting is thick enough to spread.

> Light travels faster than sound—
> that is why some people seem
> bright until they open their
> mouth and speak.

Mocha Frosting

3½ cups

1½ cups heavy cream

1½ teaspoons instant espresso powder (or 2 teaspoons instant coffee)

3 cups (18-ounces) semi-sweet chocolate chips

1½ tablespoons Kahlúa (or other coffee flavored liqueur)

1 teaspoon vanilla

1. Heat cream just to boiling. Remove from heat.

2. Add instant espresso and stir to dissolve.

3. Add chocolate chips and let stand until chocolate softens, 1-2 minutes. Stir chocolate until melted and smooth.

4. Stir in Kahlúa and vanilla. Let stand until mixture cools, thickens and is firm enough to spread, stirring occasionally.

Creamy Chocolate Ganache

This frosting is my very favorite. With just a few ingredients and simple directions, this fudge topping has to the best.

2 cups

1 cup heavy cream

2 cups (12-ounce bag) semi-sweet chocolate chips

2 tablespoons butter or margarine

1 tablespoon light syrup

1. Heat cream just until it begins to boil. Remove from heat and add chocolate chips, butter and syrup.

2. Let stand 2 minutes to soften the chocolate. Stir until mixture is smooth.

3. Cool to room temperature about 30 minutes. Whip with mixer or wire whisk until light and fluffy.

    (Note: To use ganache as a glaze: place cake layers or cake cutouts on a wire rack over a baking sheet. Pour warm glaze over cake. Reserve and reuse ganache drippings; refrigerate up to 1 week.)

Butter Cream Frosting

3 cups

½ cup shortening
½ cup (1 stick) butter or margarine,
    softened
1 pound (3½ cups) powdered sugar
2-4 tablespoons milk
1 teaspoon vanilla

1. Beat shortening and butter together
   until light and fluffy.

2. Add sugar 1 cup at a time to the butter
   mixture, mixing well after each
   addition.

3. Mix in milk and vanilla until well
   blended. Add more milk or sugar as
   needed to make good spreading
   consistency.

Chocolate Butter Cream Frosting

Enough frosting and filling for 2 (9 or 8-inch) layers.

½ cup (1 stick) butter or margarine,
    softened
1 pound (3½ cups) powdered sugar
½ cup unsweetened cocoa powder
1 teaspoon vanilla extract
4-6 tablespoons milk

1. Beat butter until light and fluffy.

2. Sift together powdered sugar and
   cocoa powder. Add 1 cup at a time to
   the butter mixture, mixing well after
   each addition.

3. Stir in vanilla and enough milk to make
   spreading consistency.

> Being happy doesn't mean that
> everything is perfect; it just
> means you've decided to see
> beyond his imperfections.

White Chocolate Frosting

Enough for 2 (9 or 8-inch) layers.

¾   **cup sugar, divided**
2   **large eggs**
⅓   **cup milk**
8   **ounces white chocolate¹, chopped**
3   **cups heavy cream²**
1   **teaspoon vanilla extract**

1. Combine ½ cup sugar, eggs and milk in a double boiler over simmering water. Whisk constantly until mixture is very thick about 3-5 minutes.

2. Remove from heat and add chocolate stirring until smooth. Cool to room temperature.

3. Beat cream, vanilla and remaining ¼ cup sugar until firm peaks are formed. **Fold³** into cooled chocolate mixture.

Diva Tips

¹Use a good quality **white chocolate** such as Lindt or Ghiradelli.

²**Cream**, bowl and beaters should be very cold before whipping. If you over whip cream (separating into solids and liquids), gently fold in a few tablespoons of milk or more cream.

³To **fold** ingredients together, insert large rubber spatula in the center of the mix; drag it across the bottom and then up the sides, rotating spatula and bringing some of the bottom of the mix to the top. Keep repeating this movement while turning the bowl to mix from all sides.

Chocolate Chip Pan Cookie

The easiest chocolate chip cookie you will ever make!

A boatload—48 (1½-inch) squares

2¼ cups all-purpose flour
1   teaspoon baking soda
1   teaspoon salt
1   cup (2 sticks) butter or margarine, softened
¾   cup sugar
¾   cup packed brown sugar
2   large eggs
1   teaspoon vanilla extract
2   cups semi-sweet chocolate chips
1½ cups **pecans, toasted¹ and chopped²**

1. Preheat oven to 350°.

2. Lightly grease a (15x10x1-inch) baking pan (like a jelly-roll pan) or 2 (9x13-inch) pans.

3. In a small bowl combine flour, baking soda and salt. Set aside.

4. In a large mixing bowl, cream butter with the sugars, beating until thoroughly mixed. Add eggs and vanilla and beat well. Gradually add flour mixture, stirring just until mixed. Stir in chocolate chips and nuts.

5. Spread into prepared pan(s). Bake (15x10-inch) pan 20 minutes; bake (9x13-inch) pans 15-20 minutes until golden brown. Do not over bake.

6. Remove from oven and cool in pan. Cut into serving pieces when cool.

   (Note: Can be made ahead and frozen tightly wrapped for 6 weeks.)

Diva Tips

¹**Toasting nuts** adds crispness and intensifies the flavor. Spread in a single layer on a baking sheet or pan. Preheat oven to 350°; place pan in oven and bake 5-10 minutes, or until nuts release their aroma, being careful not to burn. A smaller portion of nuts will toast much quicker than a larger amount. Toast a larger amount than needed and freeze extras up to 1 year in a tightly sealed container. Four ounces of nuts equals about 1 cup.

²To **chop nuts**, place ½ to 1 cup nuts in a plastic bag and smash with a meat pounder on a hard surface. Turn bag over and repeat on the other side. Smashing takes a fraction of the time chopping or slicing does.

Praline Bars

32 (2-inch) bars

½ **cup (1 stick) butter or margarine**
2 **cups brown sugar[1], packed**
2 **large eggs**
1½ **cups all-purpose flour**
2 **teaspoons baking powder**
1 **teaspoon salt**
1 **teaspoon vanilla extract**
1½ **cups pecans, toasted[2] and chopped**

1. Preheat oven to 350°.

2. Lightly grease a (9x13-inch) baking pan (or coat with a nonstick cooking spray).

3. In a large saucepan, melt butter over low heat. Remove from heat and stir in brown sugar; cool slightly. Add eggs. Stir in flour, baking powder, and salt. Add vanilla and pecans.

4. Spread in prepared pan. Bake 20-25 minutes or until a light touch leaves a slight impression. Do not over bake.

5. Remove from oven and cut into bars while still warm. Let cool slightly before removing from pan.

Diva Tips

[1]To store **brown sugar**, place opened bag of sugar in another plastic bag. Remove as much air as possible and tightly close. If sugar has hardened, soften by placing in a microwave-safe dish, covering tightly and microwave on high power for about 30 seconds. Generally, light-brown or dark-brown sugar can be interchanged for each other. When measuring, always lightly pack sugar in measuring cup.

[2]**Toasting nuts** adds crispness and intensifies the flavor. Spread in a single layer on a baking sheet or pan. Preheat oven to 350°; place pan in oven and bake 5-10 minutes, or until nuts release their aroma, being careful not to burn. A smaller portion of nuts will toast much quicker than a larger amount. Toast a larger amount than needed and freeze extras up to 1 year in a tightly sealed container. Four ounces of nuts equals about 1 cup.

Nutritious Cookies

You decide the kind of cookies you make with this recipe.

6 dozen

2¼ cups all-purpose **flour**[1], divided
2 cups brown sugar
2 large eggs
1 teaspoon baking soda
1 teaspoon salt
1 cup (1 stick) butter or margarine, softened
2 teaspoons vanilla extract
2 cups quick oatmeal, uncooked
1 cup (6-ounces) semi-sweet chocolate chips
1 cup pecans, toasted and chopped
1 cup peanut butter (optional)
1 cup wheat germ (optional)
1 cup flaked coconut (optional)
1 cup powdered milk (optional)

1. Preheat oven to 350°.

2. Lightly grease a cookie sheet (or coat with a nonstick cooking spray or line with **parchment paper**[2]).

3. In a large mixing bowl, mix half the flour, brown sugar, eggs, baking soda, salt, butter, and vanilla until well blended.

4. Stir in remaining flour, oatmeal, chocolate chips, nuts and 1 optional ingredient.

5. Drop by rounded teaspoons (or use a 1-inch mini ice cream scoop) onto prepared pan.

6. Bake 10 minutes or until golden brown.

7. Remove from oven; cool slightly before removing from pan to cool on a wire rack.

   (Note: Cookies can be prepared ahead and frozen tightly wrapped for 3 months.)

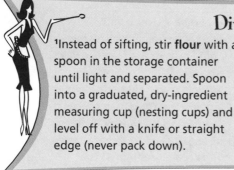

Diva Tips

[1]Instead of sifting, stir **flour** with a spoon in the storage container until light and separated. Spoon into a graduated, dry-ingredient measuring cup (nesting cups) and level off with a knife or straight edge (never pack down).

[2]**Parchment paper** can be purchased in some grocery stores (check near the wax paper and foil aisle) or specialty shops.

Grandma's Oatmeal Cookies

This recipe makes crispy oatmeal cookies!

5 dozen

¾ **cup all-purpose flour**
½ **teaspoon baking soda**
¼ **teaspoon salt**
¼ **teaspoon cinnamon**
¼ **teaspoon nutmeg**
¼ **teaspoon ginger**
½ **cup (1 stick) butter or margarine, softened**
½ **cup sugar**
½ **cup brown sugar**
1 **large egg**
1 **teaspoon vanilla**
1½ **cups quick oatmeal, uncooked**
½ **cup raisins**
½ **cup walnuts, toasted[1] and chopped**
¼ **teaspoon cinnamon (for topping)**
¼ **cup sugar (for topping)**

1. Preheat oven to 350°.

2. Lightly grease a cookie sheet (or coat with a nonstick cooking spray or line with parchment paper).

3. In a small bowl, mix flour, baking soda, salt, cinnamon, nutmeg, and ginger. Set aside.

4. In a large mixing bowl, cream butter and sugars together until light and fluffy. Beat in egg and vanilla.

5. Gradually stir flour into creamed mixture; add oatmeal, raisins and nuts and mix until well blended.

6. Drop rounded teaspoons onto prepared cookie sheet. Flatten slightly with the bottom of a glass buttered and dipped in a mixture of cinnamon and sugar.

7. Bake 8-10 minutes until golden brown.

8. Remove from oven and cool slightly before removing cookies to cool on a wire rack.

   (Note: Cookies can be prepared ahead and frozen tightly wrapped for 3 months.)

Diva Tips

[1]Toasting nuts adds crispness and intensifies the flavor. Spread in a single layer on a baking sheet or pan. Preheat oven to 350°; place pan in oven and bake 5-10 minutes, or until nuts release their aroma, being careful not to burn. A smaller portion of nuts will toast much quicker than a larger amount. Toast a larger amount than needed and freeze extras up to 1 year in a tightly sealed container. Four ounces of nuts equals about 1 cup.

Brownie Decadence

I made this recipe on "Calling All Cooks" on TV's Food Network.

24 squares

Brownies

1 **cup (2 sticks) butter or margarine**

4 **squares (4-ounces) unsweetened baking chocolate**

2 **cups sugar**

4 **large eggs**

2 **teaspoons vanilla**

1½ **cups all-purpose flour**

1 **teaspoon baking powder**

1 **teaspoon salt**

1 **bar (4-ounces) premium white chocolate (such as Lindt® or Ghiradelli®), chopped**

1. Preheat oven to 350°.

2. Lightly grease a (9x13-inch) baking pan (or coat with a nonstick cooking spray).

3. In a large saucepan, melt butter and unsweetened chocolate over low heat.

4. Remove from heat and mix in sugar. Add eggs and vanilla, stirring until well blended.

5. Add flour, baking powder and salt and stir just until mixed.

6. Gently stir in chopped white chocolate.

7. Spread mixture in prepared pan. Bake 25-30 minutes just until brownies begin to pull away from the sides of the pan and center is slightly puffed. Remove from oven and cool completely. While brownies are baking, prepare ganache topping.

Diva Tips

[1]**Toasting nuts** adds crispness and intensifies the flavor. Spread in a single layer on a baking sheet or pan. Preheat oven to 350°; place pan in oven and bake 5-10 minutes, or until nuts release their aroma, being careful not to burn. A smaller portion of nuts will toast much quicker than a larger amount. Toast a larger amount than needed and freeze extras up to 1 year in a tightly sealed container. Four ounces of nuts equals about 1 cup.

[2]To **chop nuts**, place ½ to 1 cup nuts in a plastic bag and smash with a meat pounder on a hard surface. Turn bag over and repeat on the other side. Smashing takes a fraction of the time chopping or slicing does.

Ganache Topping

1 cup heavy cream
2 cups semi-sweet chocolate chips
1½ cups **pecans, toasted[1] and chopped[2]**

1. In a medium saucepan, bring heavy cream just to a boil.

2. Remove from heat and add chocolate chips. Let set for a few minutes to soften chocolate. Stir until mixture is smooth. Set aside, let chocolate mixture cool, and thicken, stirring occasionally, about 30-45 minutes.

3. Spread ganache topping over cooled brownies. Press pecans into topping.

4. When ganache has hardened, cut into 24 squares. Cut squares into 48 triangles if desired. Carefully remove from pan. (Can be tightly covered and frozen up to 3 weeks.)

Minute Chocolate Oatmeal Cookies

These are actually a cross between a cookie and fudge candy!

3 dozen

2½ cups sugar
¼ cup unsweetened cocoa powder
½ cup (1 stick) butter or margarine
½ cup milk
1 teaspoon vanilla extract
½ cup creamy peanut butter
3 cups quick oatmeal, uncooked

1. In a medium saucepan, combine sugar, cocoa, butter and milk. Bring to a boil; boil exactly 1 minute. DON'T OVERCOOK!

2. Remove from heat and stir in vanilla, peanut butter and oatmeal, mixing well.

3. Working quickly, drop by spoonfuls onto waxed paper. Cool completely.

   (Note: Can be made ahead and frozen tightly covered for 3 months.)

Incredible Chocolate Chunk Cookies

A classic! Nobody can make these better than my daughter Lindsey.

4 dozen

1 cup (2 sticks) **butter** or margarine, softened
1 cup **sugar**
1 cup **brown sugar**, packed
2 large **eggs**
1 teaspoon **vanilla** extract
2 cups **all-purpose flour**
2½ cups **oatmeal, blended to a powder**[1]
½ teaspoon **salt**
1 teaspoon **baking powder**
1 teaspoon **baking soda**
1 bar (4-ounces) **chocolate, grated**[2]
2 cups (12-ounces) **chocolate chips**
1½ cups **nuts**, toasted and chopped

1. Preheat oven to 375°.
2. Lightly grease a cookie sheet (or coat with a nonstick cooking spray).
3. Cream butter and sugars. Add eggs and vanilla mixing until well blended.
4. In another large bowl, mix flour, oatmeal, baking powder, and baking soda. Stir into creamed mixture until thoroughly combined.
5. Add grated chocolate, chocolate chips and nuts.
6. Drop from rounded teaspoons (or use a 1-inch mini ice cream scoop) onto prepared pan, spacing 2-inches apart.
7. Bake 10 minutes until golden.
8. Remove from oven and cool slightly before removing to a wire rack to cool completely.

   (Note: Cookies can be made ahead, tightly covered and frozen for 3 months.)

Diva Tips

[1]To make **oatmeal powder**, place oatmeal, in batches, in the container of an electric blender and pulse until oatmeal is pulverized to a powder. Remove oatmeal and repeat until all oatmeal is powdered.

[2]To **grate** or **shave chocolate**, rub chocolate bar over a coarse grater or shave with a vegetable peeler.

Italian Chocolate Spice Cookies

My sister-in-law, Lauren Marchese, makes these chocolate cookies better than anybody !

5 dozen

3¾ cups all-purpose flour

1 cup sugar

½ cup unsweetened cocoa powder

1 teaspoon ground cinnamon

1 teaspoon ground cloves

1 teaspoon ground ginger

1 teaspoon ground allspice

1 teaspoon baking soda

1 teaspoon baking powder

1 cup raisins (optional)

½ cup nuts, toasted and chopped (optional)

½ cup vegetable oil

1 cup milk

1½ cups powdered sugar

3 tablespoons lemon juice

1. Preheat oven to 350°.

2. Lightly grease a cookie sheet (or coat with a nonstick cooking spray).

3. In a large bowl, combine all dry ingredients and sift together four times.

4. Add optional ingredients if desired. Make a well in the center; add oil and milk and mix until dry ingredients are moistened. Dough will be firm.

5. Break off walnut-size pieces and roll between the palms of hands; press lightly onto prepared cookie sheet.

6. Bake 10 minutes until cookies are set. Do not over bake.

7. Remove from oven and transfer cookies to a cooling rack.

8. Mix powdered sugar with lemon juice until smooth (add more juice, if needed, to make a thin glaze).

9. Dip the tops of the cookies into powdered sugar mix. Let icing harden before tightly wrapping and storing.

(Note: Cookies can be made ahead and frozen tightly covered for 3 months.)

Be kind to unkind people; they need it the most.

S'mores Bars

There is nothing similar to its cousin made over a campfire except these treats will keep 'em coming back for s'more!

24 bars

Bar

½   cup (1 stick) butter or margarine
2   squares (2-ounces) unsweetened baking chocolate
1   cup sugar
2   large eggs
1   teaspoon vanilla extract
1   cup all-purpose flour
1   teaspoon baking powder
½   cup pecans, toasted and chopped

1. Preheat oven to 350°.
2. Lightly grease a (9x13-inch) baking pan (or coat with a nonstick cooking spray).
3. In a large saucepan, melt ½ cup butter and 2-squares baking chocolate. Remove from heat.
4. Stir in sugar; add eggs and vanilla blending well.
5. Stir in flour, baking powder and pecans.
6. Spread into prepared pan.

Filling

1   package (8-ounces) cream cheese, softened
½   cup sugar
2   tablespoons all-purpose flour
¼   cup (½ stick) butter or margarine, softened
1   large egg
½   teaspoon vanilla extract
¼   cup pecans, toasted and finely chopped
1   cup (6-ounces) semi-sweet chocolate chips
2   cups mini-**marshmallows**[1]

1. In a small bowl, combine 8-ounce cream cheese, sugar, flour, butter, egg and vanilla, beating until smooth and creamy.
2. Stir in pecans and chocolate chips.
3. Spread evenly over bar mixture. Bake 25-30 minutes or until a toothpick inserted in the center comes out clean.
4. Remove from oven and scatter marshmallows over baked mixture and return to oven an additional 2 minutes until marshmallows are puffed. Remove from oven.

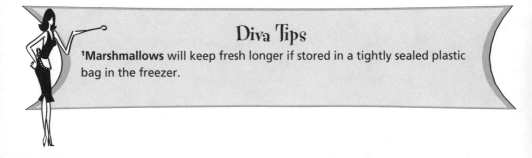

Diva Tips

[1]**Marshmallows** will keep fresh longer if stored in a tightly sealed plastic bag in the freezer.

Frosting

¼ **cup (½ stick) butter or margarine**
2 **squares (2-ounces) baking chocolate**
1 **package (3-ounces) cream cheese, softened**
¼ **cup milk**
1 **pound (about 3½ cups) powdered sugar**
1 **teaspoon vanilla extract**

1. In a large saucepan, melt butter, 2-squares chocolate and 3-ounces cream cheese over low heat. Add milk, stirring to blend well.

2. Remove from heat and stir in powdered sugar and vanilla, beating until smooth.

3. Immediately pour over hot marshmallows and swirl together with the tip of a knife.

4. Cool completely before cutting into bars. Store in the refrigerator.

   (Note: May be frozen tightly covered for 3 months.)

Give others more than they expect and do it cheerfully.

Old Fashioned Tea Cakes

I was 5 years old when I made my first cookie with my grandmother. These are as good and easy today as they were then.

5 dozen

¼ **cup (½ stick) butter or margarine,** **softened**

¼ **cup shortening**

1 **cup sugar**

1 **large egg**

1 **teaspoon vanilla extract**

2¼ **cups all-purpose flour**[1]

1 **teaspoon baking soda**

¼ **teaspoon salt**

3 **tablespoons buttermilk or milk**

⅓ **cup sugar (for topping)**

1. Preheat oven to 400°.

2. Lightly grease a cookie sheet (or coat with a nonstick cooking spray).

3. In a large mixing bowl, cream the butter and shortening together until light and creamy, 4-5 minutes.

4. Add the sugar and continue beating 2 additional minutes.

5. Beat in egg and vanilla until blended well.

6. Combine dry ingredients; add to creamed mixture with the buttermilk, stirring until mixed well. (Stir in an additional ¼ cup of flour if dough seems too sticky.)

7. Cover and chill.

8. Drop by rounded teaspoons (or use 1-inch ice cream scoop) onto prepared sheet.

9. Lightly dampen the bottom of a glass and dip in extra sugar; slightly flatten the cookies.

10. Sprinkle tops with additional ½ teaspoon sugar each.

11. Bake 6-8 minutes or until golden brown.

12. Remove pan from oven and cool slightly; transfer cookies to a cooling rack. Cool pan between batches for best results.

Diva Tips

[1]Instead of sifting, stir **flour** with a spoon in the storage container until light and separated. Spoon into a graduated, dry-ingredient measuring cup (nesting cups) and level off with a knife or straight edge (never pack down).

Diabetic Cookies

My sister, Ilene Slaughter, shared this recipe with me for a sugar-free treat for Alex, Chris and Lindsey when they were young. Check with your nutritionist or physician to make sure this recipe is compatible with your diet.

6 dozen

½   **cup (1 stick) butter or margarine**

1   **square (1-ounce) unsweetened baking chocolate**

¼   **cup milk**

1   **box (8-ounces) chopped dates, ground[1] (or finely chopped)**

1   **box (8-ounces) raisins, ground[1] (or finely chopped)**

½   **cup creamy peanut butter**

3   **cups quick oatmeal, uncooked**

1½ **cups nuts, toasted and chopped**

1   **teaspoon liquid sweetener (saccharin)**

1. Melt butter and chocolate in a large saucepan over low heat. Stir in milk and bring to a gentle boil; cook and stir an additional minute.

2. Remove from heat and stir in remaining ingredients. Cool.

3. Pinch off walnut-size pieces and flatten into patties. Do not bake. Store in the refrigerator or cookies may be frozen.

Diva Tips

[1]To **grind dates** and **raisins**, put batches in the bowl of a food processor or blender and pulse until finely ground. Or use a knife coated with a nonstick cooking spray to finely chop.

Porcupines

These cookies are brown sugar shortbread dipped in chocolate and pecans.

4 dozen

1 **cup (2 sticks) butter or margarine, softened**

¾ **cup packed brown sugar**

2 **teaspoons vanilla extract**

2 **cups all-purpose flour**

2 **cups (12-ounces) chocolate chips, melted[1], (for dipping)**

1½ cups pecans, toasted and finely chopped (for dipping)

1. In a large mixing bowl, cream butter and sugar with an electric mixer on medium speed. Add vanilla and flour, mixing on low speed just until well blended.

2. Refrigerate dough at least 1 hour.

3. Preheat oven to 325°.

4. Shape dough into (1-inch) balls; press into logs (2-inches) long x (1-inch) wide.

5. Place 2-inches apart on ungreased baking sheets.

6. Bake 18 minutes or until cookies spread and are golden brown. Remove from oven and cool slightly; transfer cookies to a cooling rack. Cool pans between batches for best results.

7. When cookies are completely cooled, dip the end of each cookie in the melted chocolate and then in the pecans.

8. Place cookies on waxed paper and refrigerate to set chocolate.

Diva Tips

[1]To **melt chocolate**, 1) place chocolate chips uncovered in a microwave-safe dish and microwave on high power (100%); stir every 20 seconds. Chocolate can be removed from oven while still lumpy; the heat of the dish and the chocolate will continue to melt lumps. Be careful not to overheat. Chocolate burns at a low temperature. Or 2) put chocolate into the top of a double boiler and place over hot water. Stir occasionally until chocolate is melted. (Do not let any water droplets or steam mix with chocolate or it will become a hardened, grainy mass. If this happens, stir in a small amount of warm, melted vegetable shortening, 1 teaspoon at a time, until chocolate returns to a liquid state.

Anisette Toast

This is a crispy, Italian biscotti recipe given to me by my mother-in-law, Rose Destino.

45 toasts

6　large eggs, lightly beaten
1½　cups sugar
1　cup vegetable oil
1　teaspoon anise extract
　　　(or substitute almond extract)
3　cups all-purpose flour
1½　teaspoons baking powder
1　cup sliced **almonds, toasted**[1]

1. Preheat oven to 350°.

2. Lightly grease a (15x10-inch) cookie sheet or a jelly-roll pan (or coat with a nonstick cooking spray).

3. In a large mixing bowl, beat eggs, sugar, oil and anise extract until light, about 3 minutes.

4. Stir in flour and baking powder.

5. Spread dough on prepared baking sheet. Scatter almonds over the dough.

6. Bake 25 minutes or until golden brown. Remove from oven and cool slightly.

7. Cut into (1x3-inch) bars.

8. Place toasts (bars) on an ungreased baking sheet on their cut side.

9. Bake an additional 7 minutes; turn over and bake on the other side another 7 minutes.

10. Transfer cookies to a cooling rack.

(Note: Cookies can be made ahead and frozen tightly covered for 3 months.)

Diva Tips

[1]**Toasting nuts** adds crispness and intensifies the flavor. Spread in a single layer on a baking sheet or pan. Preheat oven to 350°; place pan in oven and bake 5-10 minutes, or until nuts release their aroma, being careful not to burn. A smaller portion of nuts will toast much quicker than a larger amount. Toast a larger amount than needed and freeze extras up to 1 year in a tightly sealed container. Four ounces of nuts equals about 1 cup.

Chocolate Almond Biscotti

2 dozen

4 **squares (4-ounces) unsweetened baking chocolate**
½ **cup (1 stick) butter or margarine**
½ **teaspoon vanilla extract**
4 **large eggs**
1½ **cups sugar**
3 **cups all-purpose flour**
1 **teaspoon baking powder**
1 **cup almonds, toasted**[1] **and chopped**

1. Preheat oven to 350°.
2. Melt chocolate and butter in a medium saucepan over low heat; remove from heat and stir in vanilla extract; cool.
3. Beat eggs at medium speed with an electric mixer until frothy; gradually add sugar, beating until thick and light (about 5 minutes).
4. Add chocolate mixture, stirring to blend well.
5. Add flour and baking powder stirring until blended. Stir in nuts.
6. With floured hands, form dough into a (14-inch) log.
7. Place on a lightly greased baking sheet. Bake 45 minutes.
8. Remove from pan and cool on a wire rack. When cooled cut with a serrated knife crosswise into 24 (½-inch) slices.
9. Place cookies on cut side on an ungreased baking sheet.
10. Bake at 350° 10 minutes.
11. Turn cookies over and bake another 10 minutes.
12. Remove from oven and transfer cookies to a cooling rack.

Diva Tips

[1]**Toasting nuts** adds crispness and intensifies the flavor. Spread in a single layer on a baking sheet or pan. Preheat oven to 350°; place pan in oven and bake 5-10 minutes, or until nuts release their aroma, being careful not to burn. A smaller portion of nuts will toast much quicker than a larger amount. Toast a larger amount than needed and freeze extras up to 1 year in a tightly sealed container. Four ounces of nuts equals about 1 cup.

Pirouette Lace Cookies

These are a delicate-looking, lacy cookie. Great for ladies dessert or tea, but men love them too.

4 dozen

½ **cup (1 stick) butter or margarine**

⅔ **cup brown sugar**

½ **cup light corn syrup**

1¼ **cups all-purpose flour**

1 **cup pecans, toasted[1] and finely chopped**

2 **cups (12-ounces) chocolate chips, melted**

1. Combine butter, sugar and corn syrup in a large, heavy saucepan; bring to a boil stirring constantly.

2. Remove from heat and stir in flour and pecans. Cool.

3. Preheat oven to 350°.

4. Line a baking sheet with **parchment paper[2]**.

5. Shape cooled dough into ¾-inch balls. Place 2-inches apart on prepared baking sheet.

6. Bake 10-11 minutes or until cookies spread and the middle is bubbly.

7. Remove from oven and cool 30 seconds. Working quickly, peel the cookie off baking sheet and roll around the handle of a wooden spoon; remove from handle and place on a wire rack to cool. Repeat with remaining cookies. (If cookies become too hard to roll, return to oven briefly to reheat.)

8. When cookies are cool, dip ends into melted chocolate. Lay on parchment paper to harden. Store at room temperature.

Diva Tips

[1]**Toasting nuts** adds crispness and intensifies the flavor. Spread in a single layer on a baking sheet or pan. Preheat oven to 350°; place pan in oven and bake 5-10 minutes, or until nuts release their aroma, being careful not to burn. A smaller portion of nuts will toast much quicker than a larger amount. Toast a larger amount than needed and freeze extras up to 1 year in a tightly sealed container. Four ounces of nuts equals about 1 cup.

[2]**Parchment paper** can be purchased in some grocery stores (check near the wax paper and foil aisle) or specialty shops.

Pecan Macaroons

More like a candy bar than a cookie.

40 pieces

⅔ cup (½ of a 14-ounce can) sweetened condensed milk

1 teaspoon vanilla extract

3 cups flaked **coconut**[1], toasted

1 cup pecans, toasted and chopped (or substitute toasted almonds)

2 **egg**[2] whites

⅛ teaspoon salt

2 cups (12-ounces) chocolate chips, melted

1. Preheat oven to 350°.

2. Lightly grease a cookie sheet (or coat with a nonstick cooking spray or line with parchment paper).

3. Combine condensed milk and vanilla in a large bowl. Mix in coconut and pecans thoroughly.

4. With an electric mixer, beat egg whites with salt until stiff but not dry.

5. Fold egg whites into coconut mixture.

6. Drop by rounded teaspoons (or use 1-inch mini ice cream scoop) onto prepared pan.

7. Bake until macaroons turn golden around the edges, 12-14 minutes.

8. Cool completely on cookie sheet.

9. When cool, dip cookie bottoms into the melted chocolate and place cookies, chocolate side down on wax paper-lined pans. Refrigerate until chocolate is set, about 15 minutes.

   (Note: Can be prepared 4 days ahead. Store in an airtight container.)

Diva Tips

[1]To toast **coconut**, place on a large cookie sheet. Bake at 350° until lightly toasted, about 12 minutes, stirring frequently.

[2]Add a dash of salt to leftover **egg** yolks and store in the freezer (1 month) or refrigerator (1 day). Use in custards or add to scrambled eggs.

Buckeyes

My daughter, Lindsey, has made this recipe her holiday tradition every Christmas.

7 dozen

1   cup (2 sticks) butter or margarine, softened
1   jar (16-ounces) creamy peanut butter
1½ pounds (5⅔ cups) powdered sugar, sifted
2   cups (12-ounces) chocolate chips
½   cake paraffin wax

1. In a large bowl, mix butter and peanut butter together thoroughly; stir in powdered sugar.

2. Roll into walnut-size balls.

3. Place on a baking sheet lined with wax paper and refrigerate 1 hour.

4. In a medium saucepan, melt chocolate chips and paraffin over low heat, stirring to mix well. Cool slightly.

5. With a toothpick or candy-dipping fork, dip balls into chocolate leaving just a sliver of the top showing to resemble "buckeyes".

6. Refrigerate until chocolate has hardened.

Candied Popcorn and Peanuts

10 cups

10 cups freshly popped-popcorn, unsalted
2   cups raw peanuts
½   cup (1 stick) butter or margarine
1   cup packed brown sugar
¼   cup dark corn syrup
¼   teaspoon **baking soda**[1]
¼   teaspoon salt
¼   teaspoon vanilla extract

1. Combine popcorn and peanuts in a large roasting pan; set aside.

2. Melt butter in a large saucepan; stir in sugar and corn syrup. Bring to a boil; boil 5 minutes, stirring occasionally.

3. Remove from heat and stir in baking soda, salt and vanilla.

4. Pour sugar mixture over popcorn mixture, stirring until evenly coated.

5. Bake at 250° 45 minutes, stirring every 10 minutes.

6. Cool in pan. Store in an airtight container.

Diva Tips

[1]To test **baking soda** for freshness, mix ¼ teaspoon baking soda into ¼ cup vinegar; if it bubbles like crazy, it is fresh. Never use baking soda in cooking after it has been used as a refrigerator freshener.

Pralines

A true southern treat.

1½-2 dozen

2 **cups sugar**
½ **cup brown sugar**
  dash salt
2 **tablespoons light corn syrup**
1 **small can (5-ounces or ⅔ cup)**
  evaporated milk
½ **cup (1 stick) butter**
½ **teaspoon baking soda**
2 **teaspoons vanilla**
2 **cups pecan halves, toasted¹**

1. Combine the first 6 ingredients in a large, heavy saucepan. Cook over medium heat, stirring until sugar dissolves.

2. Cover and cook 2-3 minutes to wash down sugar crystals from sides of the pan.

3. Remove cover and cook to softball stage (235°) (or until a softball is formed when a little bit of mixture is dropped into cold water).

4. Remove from heat and stir in baking soda. Beat with a wooden spoon, just until mixture begins to thicken.

5. Stir in vanilla and pecans.

6. Working rapidly, drop by tablespoonfuls onto buttered wax paper; let stand until firm.

Diva Tips

¹Toasting nuts adds crispness and intensifies the flavor. Spread in a single layer on a baking sheet or pan. Preheat oven to 350°; place pan in oven and bake 5-10 minutes, or until nuts release their aroma, being careful not to burn. A smaller portion of nuts will toast much quicker than a larger amount. Toast a larger amount than needed and freeze extras up to 1 year in a tightly sealed container. Four ounces of nuts equals about 1 cup.

Diva's
Party Planning

Create a Mood

Kitchen Divas seduce their guests with all their senses: the smell of great food wafting through the air; cold or hot beverages caressing their fingers; the visual of a beautiful table simply set like a beautiful painting; soft lights and music filling the background; and plates filled with appetizing food.

Don't wait until you have better furniture, better dishes or a clean house to entertain guests. Your menu doesn't really matter either: hot dogs and hamburgers from the grill or Chinese take-out can be just as fun and inviting as the most elegant dinner. Entertaining does not have to be frenzied, but should be warm, thoughtful and caring.

Create an Atmosphere

Lower the lights, burn some candles, play music to correspond to the theme of the evening and decorate your table. You don't have to rely of a florist to landscape your table. Look around your house, in your cupboards, on your bookshelves and in your backyard to create interest in your table. By using your imagination and personality with items at your fingertips, you can create such curiosity that your food becomes secondary. Each dinner party becomes an opening for your own art gallery. Some ideas I frequently utilize:

- Upside down wine glasses can become candleholders. Fill the bowls of the glasses with sparkly package stuffing and top with votive candles.

- Scrunch and layer brightly colored tablecloths in the middle of the table for a creative table runner. Or drape tables with quilts, rugs (squeaky clean), or yardage of cloth purchased at a fabric store. Or line the table with butcher paper and provide crayons at each place setting.

- Intermingle various candleholders of all shapes and sizes with chatkes borrowed from your coffee table, cupboards or bookshelves.

- Create different heights in the center of your table by placing cans or small boxes under the tablecloth. Put a small statue or a childhood toy as a focal point on the highest spot. Surround with small pots of fresh, colorful flowers or greenery (these flowers can be planted in the yard later).

- A cake stand becomes host for your own still life: surround a perfect pineapple with shiny red apples, filling in the spaces with greenery collected from your backyard or with woody herbs.

- Glass blocks from a home help center can become ice sculptures. Stand blocks on edge at an angle and let shiny apples, grapes, or any fruit spill over onto the tablecloth.

- Fill a pretty bowl with lemons, limes, or a combination of the two. Add interest with baby artichokes (or any baby vegetables, keeping all the vegetables about the same size). Set the bowl on an overturned silver tray or lace doily.

- Arrange flowers in a pretty pitcher, watering can, teapot, or tea kettle and tie a ribbon round the handle.

- Pull colorful or patterned tissue paper up around a flower vase and secure around the neck with a pretty ribbon for a festive holder for flowers or greenery either purchased or cut from your yard. Or fill with balloons tied to sticks.

- Fill a clear bowl one-third with marbles, rocks, or clear stones, scattering some over the table. Fill with water and float candles mixed with slices of fresh fruit (lemons, limes, star fruit, etc.) or small flowers and set on a ruffled pillow sham. Or float a small candle in a dish at each place setting.

- Alternate tea light candles with small flowers and leaves on a tiered dessert stand.

- Place a small vase of flowers inside a much larger clear vase. Fill the bottom of the large vase with marbles, feathers, leaves or anything you can imagine. Set the vases on a coordinating scarf, square of fabric, or a mirror square with some of the filling spilling onto the table.

- Colorful fall leaves from your yard (pressed flat with a warm iron) surround a small pumpkin for a beautiful autumn decoration.

- Alternating white tree ornaments with white candles on a white tablecloth creates a monochromatic scheme for a Christmas table decoration.

Don't forget to draw attention to your platters and serving dishes.

5-star restaurants recognize the value of decorating plates by making mediocre food look like it belongs on the cover of a magazine. Beautiful presentation is easy to accomplish by simply distracting the eye to something colorful or interesting. Artists use "tension" to create interest to keep the eye moving across the piece by adding something that seems odd or out of place.

1. Don't crowd and be deliberate when arranging food. Leave small vegetables whole and place at an angle.

2. Add an interesting garnish (always edible) to the plate or serving dish:

    -arrange a leaf of flowering kale under the main course

    -decorate with edible flowers (see list on page 330) and leaves

    -make strawberry flowers (cut the pointed end in 6 pieces down to the green cap; carefully spread open).

    -make a tomato rose by removing the peel in one continuous thin strip and then re-rolling the strip; place on a piece of kale. Surround the "rose" with the small leaves from the center of a celery bunch.

Decorate platters of food in the same manner:

- make a celery "flower": cut all the celery stalks off the root end. Rinse the root in between the cut stalks and trim off the bottom. Set on a bed of kale, or any greenery.

- make a flower vignette: melt white dipping chocolate in a small freezer bag. Snip the corner and squeeze a mound of chocolate in the center of a 5x5-inch square of wax paper. Cut edible flowers (see list on page 330) off their stems and secure in the chocolate. Stick leaves under the flowers. Refrigerate until chocolate is firm. Vignettes can be stored in a sealed plastic bag in the refrigerator up to 2 days.

- use baby vegetables (artichokes, bok choy, pattypan squash, etc.) perched in the corner of a serving tray.

Arrangement of food on a plate requires an attitude seeing food as more than nourishment.

Drinks are far more exciting and taste better when you experiment with a variety of unusual glasses.

1. Serve drinks with a sprig of fresh mint (if taste appropriate) or a long curl of citrus zest.
2. Instead of the usual thin sliver of lemon or lime, place a chunk of fruit in the bottom of the glass (rub the rim with the fruit first).
3. Hang a strawberry, a piece of melon or any fruit on the rim.
4. Lightly wet the rim of the glass and dip in sugar or a combination of spices.
5. Float edible flowers (see list on page 330) in pitchers of drinks.

Who says food belongs exclusively in the dining room? Create a mood in different rooms of the house:

1. Dine with picnic food on a blanket thrown on the floor. Chase away the winter blues by serving your picnic in front of the fireplace.
2. Why just enjoy breakfast-in-bed? A simple, late night supper can be just as fun and relaxing.
3. Host a piano recital in the living room and serve finger foods.
4. Dine al fresco. Set up a card table in your garden.

Create a style that is distinctly your own. Scan art books and home décor magazines for inspiration. Think out of the box, mix odd shapes and unexpected combinations, and throw away your inhibitions. Just give 'em something to talk about!

Treat your family as guests from time to time.

1. Use your best china, silverware and crystal. Dress up and eat in the dining room. By example children can practice manners and dinner conversation will create lasting memories.
2. Relax and have fun in the kitchen. Always encourage yours and other children, no matter how big or small, to help out in the kitchen. Your rewards will be many because of the valuable time spent together: many of life's lessons are learned in the kitchen.
3. Surprisingly, conversations open up and communicating becomes a breeze. Pleasures of cooking becomes more than treating yourself to a great meal. Start your own or continue with family traditions.
4. Take your spouse on a date in the kitchen. Pamper him or her with a romantic homemade dinner. Let them watch you prepare your special recipes while sipping a glass of wine. Dress in your best clothes, decorate the table, lower the lights and light some candles. Sparks will fly and you'll both feel 16 again!

For easier menu planning for the family, assign a dinner theme to each night of the week:

Italian night; Quick and Easy Dinners; Mexican; Pizza and a Movie; Make it Yourself (everyone makes anything they like for himself); or Family night (everyone takes a turn planning a menu and cooking). Post the schedule on the fridge for the next week along with a grocery list. Everyone in the family should also be assigned a job every night: preparation, clean up, dishwasher, table set up, sweeping, etc. Jobs can be rotated daily or weekly. Make a list and expect it to happen. By working together in the kitchen, minds, bodies, as well as souls will be thoroughly nourished.

Diva's Party Planning Timetable Tips

4 weeks ahead

1. Make an alphabetized guest list with addresses and phone numbers for easy reference for RSVP's and thank you's (also alleviates extra work for the next party)
2. Send invitations
3. Plan the menu; make photo copies of recipes to be used and store in a notebook for easy reference (copies keep the originals clean; can be taken grocery shopping; and all recipes are together at your fingertips when preparations begin.)
4. Reserve bartender, servers, and/or clean up help; agree on a fee to be paid and number of hours to work
5. Reserve any rentals that may be needed (dishes, tablecloths, serving dishes, extra tables, etc.)
6. Make a schedule of dish preparations

1-2 weeks ahead

1. Print and frame a menu or print a place card with the name and description of each dish that will be served (guests will not have to guess what food they are eating; also aids guests with food allergies)
2. Purchase drinks and paper goods
3. Plan table decorations and order centerpieces; purchase candles
4. Prepare and freeze make-ahead recipes
5. Make a complete grocery list and buy nonperishables (also list any foods that will be used to decorate serving platters for a beautiful presentation)
6. Make a list of serving dishes or equipment that will be needed for each recipe
7. Make note of any special equipment needed

1-3 days ahead

1. Clean the house
2. Ready serving dishes, trays and utensils and label (matching menu items to serving dishes)
3. Prepare make-ahead recipes and refrigerate according to recipe directions
4. Set up bar/beverage area
5. Pick out music and set aside
6. Pick up centerpieces
7. Buy perishables from grocery list
8. Clean and press table linens
9. Decorate and set the table
10. Ready your attire for the evening
11. Review the dishes to be served so nothing is forgotten
12. Purchase ice (if enough freezer storage space is available)

Party Day

1. Make last-minute recipes
2. Set food on serving dishes and trays
3. Get ready; relax and greet your guests! Enjoy your party!
   YOU CAN NEVER BE TOO ORGANIZED!!!

Diva's Fast Cocktail Party Tips

- 8-10 bites per person for 2-3 hour cocktail party

- Supplement with pâtés, nuts, spreads or cheeses

- Balance colors, textures, temperatures and complexity of dishes served; always include at least a couple vegetarian dishes

- Serve bite-size individual desserts

- Provide at least 3 paper napkins per guest to accommodate for appetizers, drinks and dessert

- Provide 2 forks, 2 plates and 2 glasses per guest

Diva's Fast Dinner Party Tips

- Limit appetizers to 2-3 bites per guest

- Meat, Poultry, Fish per person:
    - 4-6 ounces boneless (uncooked weight)
    - 6-8 ounces bone-in (uncooked weight)

- Vegetables or Fruit per person:
    - ½ cup cooked
    - or ¼ pound uncooked

- Pasta or Rice per person:
    - ½ cup for a side dish
    - 1 cup as a main dish

- Tossed Salad per person:
    - 1-1½ cups (1-2 ounces)

- Always make 2-3 servings extra to accommodate hearty appetites or unexpected guests

Diva's Well-Stocked Basic Bar

Tools

Corkscrew
Bottle opener
Cocktail shaker
Strainer
Stirrer
Knife
Ice Bucket
Shot Glass
Electric Blender

Liquor

Bourbon
Whiskey
Scotch
Vodka
Gin
Rum
Tequila
Red Wine
White Wine
Beer

Liqueur

Triple Sec
Kahlúa (or other coffee-flavored liqueur)
Amaretto (almond flavor)
Frangelico (hazelnut flavor)
Sweet and Dry Vermouth
Irish Cream

Mixers

Lemon-lime Soda
Cola
Ginger Ale

Tonic Water
Club Soda
Orange Juice
Bloody Mary Mix
Margarita Mix
Bottled Water
Cream
Coffee
Garnishes
Lemons
Limes
Olives
Cocktail Onions
Celery Stalks
Cherries

Extras

Salt
Sugar
Pepper
Bitters
Worcestershire Sauce
Tabasco Sauce
Whipped Cream

Glasses

Wine Glasses
Old Fashion (Short)
High Ball (Tall)
Martini
Champagne
Shot Glasses
Coffee Cups

Diva's Fast Bar Tips

Of course there are many variables that will affect the amount of beverages that you will serve at your next get-together such as the occasion for celebration, how much your guests typically drink, or the length of the party. There are no hard and fast rules only guidelines:

- Plan for 1-1½ drinks per person per hour

- Buy 1-2 pounds of ice per person (amount depends on the temperature outside)

- Provide an interesting selection of non-alcoholic drinks for your guests (for designated drivers and nondrinkers)

- Always have bottled water available

Diva's Fast Bar Facts

- A 750 ml bottle of wine (3 cups) yields 4-5 servings

- A 750 ml bottle of liquor yields 17 (1½ ounce) shots

- One liter bottle of liquor yields 22 (1½ ounce) shots

- A gallon of punch yields 20-24 servings

- One liter of soda or drink mix fills 6-7 (12 ounce) glasses (with ice and a shot of liquor)

- 5 pounds of ice fills 20 (12 ounce) glasses

Diva's Sample Bar for a Party of 10
(adjust to any number of guests):

- Assorted bottles of liquor

- Four (750 ml) bottles of white wine

- Two (750 ml) bottles of red wine

- 12 cans or bottles of beer

- 2 liters of lemon-lime soda

- 2 liters of cola

- 1 liter ginger ale

- 2 liters tonic water

- 2 liters club soda

- 2 quarts orange juice

- 1 quart Bloody Mary mix

- garnishes (lemons, limes, cherries, olives)

- 15-20 pounds ice

- Twelve (16-ounce) bottles of water

Diva's Coffee Bar

Set up a coffee bar at your next party and let your guests make their own flavored coffees.

- Offer regular and/or decaf (rent a big urn for a large party, if necessary)
- Sugar Cubes (less messy than spoonable sugar)
- Sugar Substitute
- Creamer (cream, milk or flavored creamers from the dairy case)
- Cinnamon Sticks (for stirring) or cinnamon sugar in a shaker
- Chocolate Shavings
- Whipped Cream
- Flavorings (choose all or any)
    - Kahlúa (or any coffee-flavored liqueur)
    - Grand Marnier (or any orange-flavored liqueur)
    - Frangelico (hazelnut flavor)
    - Brandy
    - Irish Whiskey
- Cups or Mugs
- Spoons

Diva's Fast Coffee Tips

- Start with a very clean pot
- For the best flavor use freshly ground beans and fresh cold water (1½-2 tablespoons per ¾ cup water)
- Brew just before serving; heat destroys the flavor of coffee if left on the burner too long
- Never reheat; coffee will become very bitter

Wine Over-Simplified

Wine Fast Facts

White	Compares to:	Red
Riesling	skim milk (light body)	Pinot Noir
Sauvignon Blanc Pinot Grigio	whole milk (medium body)	Merlot
Chardonnay	cream (full body)	Cabernet Sauvignon Shiraz (Syrah)

Serve Wines at the Proper Temperature

	White		Red	
(full-bodied)	Chardonnay	50°-55°	Cabernet/Shiraz	65°-70°
(medium bodied)	Sauvignon	45°-50°	Merlot	60°-65°
(light body)	Riesling	below 45°	Pinot Noir	55°-60°
	Sparkling (Champagne)	below 45°		
	Sweet	below 45°		

Wine and Food Pairing Fast Tips

Wine should compliment the food and not over power it, and the food should not over power the wine as well. Here are some guidelines to follow, but let your taste be your guide. For fun, keep a wine journal and note the wines you enjoy with the food served.

1. Hearty foods (beef, pasta, cheese) need a more full-bodied wine.

2. Lighter foods (grilled chicken or fish) need a medium-bodied wine.

3. Foods with a touch of sweetness should be served with a light-bodied wine. (If the food is sweeter than the wine, the wine may taste dry and tannic.)

4. Spicy, smoked or heavily seasoned foods, should be paired with light, fruity wines.

5. Serve chocolate with Cabernet or Port.

6. Serve desserts with Champagne or Riesling.

A Diva's Well-Stocked Kitchen

2-3 wooden spoons

Wire whisk

Rubber spatula (preferably heat resistant)

Instant-read meat thermometer

Grater

Meat pounder

Rolling pin

Paring knife, serrated knife,
Chef's knife (large)

Measuring spoons

Measuring cups (nesting)

Glass measuring cup

Tongs

Kitchen scissors

Metal spatula

Vegetable peeler

Zester

Mesh strainer

Slotted spoon

Timer

Jelly-roll pan (can use as a cookie sheet)

8-inch square pan

Tube or Bundt pan

9-inch springform pan

Two (9-inch) cake pans

Wire cooling racks

One (8-inch) skillet

One (10-inch) skillet (preferably nonstick)

1-quart, 2-quart and 3-quart saucepans

1 spaghetti pot (can substitute for a
stockpot with insert removed)

Electric mixer (preferably on a stand)

Blender

Food processor (optional, but nice to have)

Parchment paper

Plastic wrap

1 and 2 gallon zip top plastic bags

Aluminum foil

Baking bags

Diva's Pantry Staples to Have on Hand

Condiments: Worcestershire sauce; white wine Worcestershire sauce; Dale's steak seasoning; Tabasco sauce; Dijon mustard; browning and seasoning sauce (like Kitchen Bouquet); lobster base; Italian salad dressing

Vinegars: apple cider vinegar; Champagne vinegar (or other white wine vinegar); rice wine vinegar; balsamic vinegar; red wine vinegar; raspberry vinegar

Oils: extra virgin olive oil; canola vegetable oil; nonstick cooking spray; chili oil, dark sesame oil; almond oil (or any nut oil)

Canned Goods: sweetened condensed milk; chicken broth; beef broth; diced tomatoes

Extras: garlic; shallots; ginger; onions; sweet onions

Salt Fast Facts

1. **Sea Salt** - Has a milder flavor with irregular grains with some subtle nuances.

2. **Kosher Salt** - Free of additives; half as salty as table salt (measure 1½ times more Kosher salt to equal the taste of table salt.)

3. **Table Salt** - Is ground and refined rock salt. Has the harshest flavor.

4. **Coarse Salt** - Has large grains. Primarily used for topping pretzels and bread loaves.

Soup Terms Over-Simplified

1. **Soup** - Vegetables and meat cooked in water, stock or broth.

2. **Stock** - Made by simmering bones or shellfish in water.

3. **Broth** - Made by simmering meat and/or vegetables in water.

4. **Bisque** - Thick, pureed soup (usually with shrimp or other shellfish) with added cream or tomatoes.

5. **Chowder** - Simple, thick stews made with potatoes.

6. **Stew** - Thickened soup.

7. **Consommé** - A clear, strong broth made by slowly simmering meat and bones in water for a long time and then strained.

8. **Bouillon** - A clear, highly seasoned broth made by simmering meat in water and strained, or by dissolving bouillon cubes or instant granules in hot water.

Flour Fast Tips

Professional bakers might bristle at my simplification of such a complex matter, but for the home cook, these tips should be acceptable.

For simplicity, I have divided flours into two categories: soft wheat (low protein) and winter wheat (high protein).

Soft wheat flours include:

White Lily

Martha White

All brands of cake flours

Gold Medal self-rising

Pillsbury self-rising

Use soft wheat flour to bake anything using leavening (baking powder or baking soda) for a light texture:

cakes

cookies

pie crusts

quick sweet breads (tea breads)

muffins

pancakes

waffles

biscuits

dumplings

dredging or dusting meats

thickening of sauces and gravies

Winter wheat flours include:

unbleached Gold Medal

unbleached Pillsbury

Robin Hood

King Arthur

All brands of bread flours

Use winter wheat flours for recipes using yeast for a sturdy texture:

breads

pizza dough

rolls

sticky buns

popovers (doesn't require yeast but needs a strong dough for rising)

The national brands, Gold Medal and Pillsbury, fit right in between these two categories and are good for baking cakes and cookies, but are too low in protein to make excellent yeast breads.

List of Edible Flowers

Carnations

Chive blossoms

Chrysanthemum Daisies

Day Lilies

Dianthus

Hibiscus

Lavender

Marigolds

Nasturtiums

Pansies

Rose of Sharon

Roses

Snapdragon

Squash or Pumpkin blossoms

Sunflowers

Tulips

Violets

List of Non-poisonous Leaves

Camilla Leaves

Gardenia Leaves

Grape Leaves

Ivy Leaves

Lemon Leaves

Lime (Kiffir) Leaves

Rose Leaves

Edible Flower Fast Facts

1. Edible flowers and leaves to be used for garnishing, in salads, or food preparations can be purchased in some produce departments of grocery stores, specialty stores or farmer's markets. Flowers and leaves from a florist are often sprayed with toxic pesticides. Flowers for consumption should be organically grown.

2. Be sure to proper identify flowers you are choosing as edible, whether home grown or purchased.

3. Pick edible flowers as soon as they open and just before they will be served. Remove the pistils and stamens.

4. Inspect for insects. Gently rinse and store in dampened paper towels up to 1 day in the refrigerator.

Which Apple to Use...

This chart is a general guideline for the best usage. Individual preferences may vary. Experiment with different varieties.

VARIETY	EATEN FRESH	PIES	SALADS	BAKED	SAUCE	FREEZING	COMMENTS
Braeburn	•	•	•	•	•		stores well; hard
Cortland	••	•	(•••)	•	•	•	slow to brown; fragile; crisp
Crispin (Mutsu)	••	•	•	••	••	••	crisp; sweet
Empire	••	•	••	••	•	•	does not store well; mealy; crisp
Fuji	•••	•	••		••		not recommended for cooking; crisp
Gala	•••	•	••				very sweet; crisp
Gingergold	••		(•••)				slow to brown; crisp
Golden Delicious	•••	••	••	•	••	•	stores well; crisp
Granny Smith	•	(•••)	•		•		best for pies; hard
Ida Red	•	••	•	••	••	•	great for cooking; stores well; crisp
Jonagold	••	•	••	••	••	•	great for cooking; fry in butter
Jonathan	•	•	•	•	••		does not store well; can get mealy; crisp
McIntosh	••	•	•		(•••)		best for sauce; cooks down quickly
Northern Spy		•••		•	•		hard; slightly tart
Pippin	•	••	•	•	••		hard; slightly tart
Red Delicious	••		••				stores well; sweet; crisp
Rome	•	••	••	(•••)		•	does not store well; can get mealy; tart
Staymen/Winesap	•	••	•	••	•		slightly tart; crisp

••• Excellent   •• Very Good   • Good   (no dot) Not Recommended   (circled) Best for category

Apple Fast Facts

1. A fresh apple should be firm, feel solid and heavy for its size, not soft and lightweight. It should be smooth-skinned and well colored for its variety. Avoid apples with bruises, soft spots or wrinkled skin.

2. Store apples in a sealed plastic bag at 32°-35° F (in the coldest part of the refrigerator).

3. 50% of the apples grown in the United States are eaten fresh.

4. The favorite varieties in the United States are Red Delicious, Golden Delicious, and Granny Smith accounting for 65% of varieties grown.

CHEESE VARIETY	MELTS	CRUMBLES	CUBES	FINELY GRATES	SHREDS	SLICES	SPREADS	CHARACTERISTICS
AMERICAN	X		X		X	X		Smooth & mild
ASIAGO	X		X	X				Semi-hard; pungent
BEL PAESE							X	Creamy; slightly tart; fruity
BLUE	X	X					X	Gets stronger as it ages
BRIE	X						X	Creamy; slightly salty
CAMEMBERT	X						X	Creamy; similar to Brie but milder
CHEDDAR	X		X		X	X		Taste ranges from mild to sharp
CHESHIRE	X	X						Pleasant salt flavor; used in Welsh Rarebit
COLBY	X		X		X	X		Mild
EDAM	X		X			X		Light and buttery
FETA	X	X					X	Salty, sharp and pungent
FONTINA	X		X			X	X	Buttery flavor
GOAT CHEESE		X						Flavor ranges from mild to tart; distinctive taste
GORGONZOLA		X						Mild blue flavor
GOUDA	X		X			X		Nutlike, buttery flavor
GRUYÈRE	X		X		X	X		Nutty, fruitlike flavor
HAVARTI	X		X			X		Mild; slightly tangy
JARLSBERG			X		X	X		Nutty flavor, improves with age
MARSCAPONE	X						X	Stronger than cream cheese used in desserts
MONTEREY JACK	X		X		X	X		Smooth and mild
MOZZARELLA	X		X		X	X		Elastic with a mild flavor
MUENSTER	X		X		X	X		Strong taste; penetrating odor
PARMESAN	X		X	X				Stores indefinitely
PORT SALUT	X		X			X		Mild and smooth
PROVOLONE	X		X		X	X		Mild to sharp with a slight smoky flavor
ROMANO	X			X				Hard and sharp tasting
ROQUEFORT		X						Sharp, piquant Blue flavor
SWISS	X		X			X		Nutty with a sweet aftertaste

Cheese Fast Facts

1. Cheese is the most flavorful at room temperature. Remove from the refrigerator at least 1 hour before serving.

2. Cheese needs to "breathe". Store cheese wrapped in waxed paper. Place in a loosely sealed plastic bag in the refrigerator between 34°-40°.

3. Fresh mozzarella can be frozen. Defrost in the refrigerator prior to use.

4. Hard, aged cheese (used for finely grating like Parmesan) can be stored whole for long periods of time in the refrigerator.

5. If a firm cheese has spots of mold, simply cut away 1-inch around the moldy areas. Moldy soft cheeses (Bel Paese, Brie, Camembert, Mascarpone, and cream cheese) should be discarded.

6. Serve 3-4 ounces per person on a cheese platter.

7. Gruyère and Jarlsberg belong with Swiss in the same family of cheeses.

8. Gorgonzola, Roquefort, and Stilton all belong with Blue in the same family of cheeses.

Which Pear to Use...

This chart is a general guideline for the best usage. Individual preferences may vary. Experiment with different varieties.

VARIETY	AVAILABILITY	EATEN FRESH	SALADS	COOKING	CANNING	COMMENTS
Asian	limited	●●	(●●●)			Called apple-pear; crisp
Red Barlett	Aug-Dec	●●		●●	●●●	Bright red when ripe; sweet, aromatic, juicy
Yellow Barlett	Aug-Dec	●●		●●	●●●	Bright yellow when ripe; most popular in U.S.
Bosc	Sept-Apr	●		(●●●)	●●●	Retains shape when cooked; brown skin
Comice	Sept-Mar	(●●●)	(●●●)			Not recommended for cooking; sweetest, juiciest; large and soft; excellent with cheese
Green D'Anjou	Year Round	●●	●●		●	Sweet, crisp, juicy; no color change when ripe
Red D'Anjou	Oct-May	●●	●●		●	Sweet juicy; ripens to maroon-red
Seckel	Aug-Feb	(●●●)	●●		●●	Tiny; ultra-sweet flavor

●●● Excellent   ●● Very Good   ● Good   (no dot) Not Recommended   (circled) Best for category

Pear Fast Facts

1. Let stand a few days at room temperature to ripen, increase in sweetness and juice content. Don't rely on color changes for ripeness; some change color (turning from green to a yellow blush or deeper red color) and others do not.

2. Ripened pears will yield to gentle pressure at the stem end.

3. Store ripened pears in a sealed plastic bag at 32°-35° F (in the coldest part of the refrigerator).

Diva's Party Planning

Index

Cookies and Bars *(see Desserts)*

Corn

Crêpes

D

Desserts

Cakes

Candy

Cheesecakes

Cookies and Bars

Index

O

Oranges

P

Pasta

Peaches

Pears

Peas *(see Beans and Peas)*

Pies *(see Desserts)*

Pineapple

Pork

Bacon
Chops
Ham

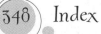

TO ORDER COPIES OF THIS BOOK:

Mail to:

Confessions of a Kitchen Diva
Claudine Destino
P.O. Box 769122
Roswell, Georgia 30076

Please send me _____ books @ $21.95 = _____

Georgia residents add $1.05 sales tax for each book _____

Add $3.00 for gift wrap for each book _____

Include $3.00 for postage and handling for the 1st book _____

and $1.00 for each additional book _____
(if shipped to the same address)

TOTAL: _____

(Make check or money order payable to Claudine Destino)

Ordered by: *(Please print)*

Name _____

Address _____

_____

City _____ State _____ Zip _____

Ship to: *(if different)*

Name _____

Address _____

_____

City _____ State _____ Zip _____

REORDER ADDITIONAL COPIES

TO ORDER COPIES OF THIS BOOK:

Mail to:

Confessions of a Kitchen Diva
Claudine Destino
P.O. Box 769122
Roswell, Georgia 30076

Please send me _____ books @ $21.95 = _____

Georgia residents add $1.05 sales tax for each book _____

Add $3.00 for gift wrap for each book _____

Include $3.00 for postage and handling for the 1st book _____

and $1.00 for each additional book _____
(if shipped to the same address)

TOTAL: _____

(Make check or money order payable to Claudine Destino)

Ordered by: *(Please print)*

Name _____

Address _____

_____

City _____ State _____ Zip _____

Ship to: *(if different)*

Name _____

Address _____

_____

City _____ State _____ Zip _____

REORDER ADDITIONAL COPIES